Chiefdoms and Other
Archaeological Delusions

Issues in Eastern Woodlands Archaeology
Editors: Thomas E. Emerson and Timothy R. Pauketat

Issues in Eastern Woodlands Archaeology emphasizes new research results and innovative theoretical approaches to the archaeology of the pre-Columbian native and early colonial inhabitants of North America east of the Mississippi River Valley. The editors are especially seeking contributors who are interested in addressing/questioning such concepts as historical process, agency, traditions, political economy, materiality, ethnicity, and landscapes through the medium of Eastern Woodlands archaeology. Such contributions may take as their focus a specific theoretical or regional case study but should cast it in broader comparative or historical terms. We seek to both challenge and inform the targeted graduate student and professional audience. Proposals currently under consideration include topics such as indigenous warfare, Archaic complexity, Iroquoia, and cultures in contact.

Books in the series:
Chiefdoms and Other Archaeological Delusions, by Timothy R. Pauketat (2007)

Chiefdoms and Other Archaeological Delusions

Timothy R. Pauketat

ALTAMIRA
PRESS

A Division of
ROWMAN & LITTLEFIELD PUBLISHERS, INC.
Lanham • New York • Toronto • Plymouth, UK

ALTAMIRA PRESS
A division of Rowman & Littlefield Publishers, Inc.
A wholly owned subsidiary of The Rowman & Littlefield Publishing Group, Inc.
4501 Forbes Boulevard, Suite 200, Lanham, MD 20706
www.altamirapress.com

Estover Road, Plymouth PL6 7PY, United Kingdom

British Library Cataloguing in Publication Information Available

Library of Congress Cataloging-in-Publication Data

Pauketat, Timothy R.
  Chiefdoms and other archaeological delusions / Timothy R. Pauketat.
    p. cm. — (Issues in eastern Woodlands archaeology)
  Includes bibliographical references and index.
  ISBN-13: 978-0-7591-0828-8 (cloth : alk. paper)
  ISBN-10: 0-7591-0828-5 (cloth : alk. paper)
  ISBN-13: 978-0-7591-0829-5 (pbk. : alk. paper)
  ISBN-10: 0-7591-0829-3 (pbk. : alk. paper)
  1. Mississippian culture—East (U.S.) 2. Indians of North America—East (U.S.)
—Politics and government. 3. Chiefdoms—East (U.S.) —History. 4. East (U.S.)
—Antiquities. I. Title.
  E99.M6815P385 2007
  977'.01—dc22
                            2006101558

Printed in the United States of America

∞™ The paper used in this publication meets the minimum requirements of American
National Standard for Information Sciences—Permanence of Paper for Printed Library
Materials, ANSI/NISO Z39.48-1992.

In memory of my father, Bobby Pauketat

CONTENTS

FIGURES

ACKNOWLEDGMENTS

First, I want to acknowledge Susan Alt, who saw me through the conceptualization, writing, and production of this book. Tom Emerson provided the initial encouragement, helped out by Mitch Allen, who was then at AltaMira. However, the book would have remained unwritten except for an Ethel-Jane Westfeldt Bunting Fellowship at the School of American Research in Santa Fe in 2005. Thank you, SAR! I am most grateful to SAR President James Brooks and then-interim president George Gumerman, both of whom enabled me to spend a summer on this book, joined by my compatriots Susan Bruning, Steven LeBlanc, Marit Munson, Everett Pikyavit, Bob Preucel, and Alan Swedland. Thanks also to the wonderful SAR staff, especially Catherine Cocks, Laura Holt, Nancy Owen Lewis, Leslie Shipman, and the late Judith Scasserra.

I am grateful to those associated with AltaMira Press for seeing this book through to completion: Sarah Walker, Jehanne Schweitzer, Jack Meinhardt, and Chrisona Schmidt. I am even more appreciative to David Anderson for amicably tolerating my use of our mutual near-death experience for this book and for his good-humored and patient corrections of my exaggerations and memory lapses. He looked down the barrel of that Arkansan's loaded shotgun and got us safely out of there. I can't imagine most of us doing the same with such poise, and so he wins, deservedly, the award for best leading man in an archaeological drama. I am equally grateful to Greg Wilson, Kit Wesler, Mark Rees, John Clark, and Tom Emerson for their comments on and criticisms of earlier versions of this

ACKNOWLEDGMENTS

book. Ditto to Steve Lekson for his helpful thoughts on improving the text for AltaMira, and thanks to Terry Norris for his permission to use his original field photos. Of course, I am responsible for any errors of fact, mischaracterizations of intent, slipshod summaries of data, or other shortcomings.

INTRODUCTION

In the 1960s, Americanist archaeology was recast as a generalizing, scientific field of inquiry, where laws of cultural development were thought within reach of an anthropological archaeology. Shortly after the dawn of this so-called New Archaeology, a prominent rogue anthropologist—a "cultural materialist"—was asked to comment on the studies of these new, ostensibly more scientific archaeologists (Binford and Binford 1968). Marvin Harris read their papers and dispensed sage advice. Avoid, he warned, the "sophisticated delusions" of sociocultural anthropology (Harris 1968:360). At the time, he specifically meant the kinship systems—long a staple among his nonarchaeologist colleagues—that some archaeologists were seeking among the remains of North America's southwestern pueblos and northeastern longhouse villages. Kinship *systems* were the constructs of ethnologists, he pointed out, not native peoples. The ways people traced their kin ties and ancestry didn't amount to a system. Presumably anyone who thought they did was, well, delusional.

Here's why: consider that this particular assertion—kinship was systemic—involves a huge leap of faith based on the observations of a few anthropologists. Why make that leap? Why believe that the observations of a few anthropologists at a few places can be extrapolated to the rest of the world? And why assume that the *written words* of the anthropologist are superior to the hard evidence of the archaeologist? Wouldn't the material evidence of archaeologists stand up better in a court of law than the shallow interpretations of historians and ethnologists? Enough archaeologists believe that the answer to this question is yes to make one wonder.

1

Why have so many archaeologists before and after Harris borrowed the delusional constructs of their nonarchaeologist colleagues to explain the ancient past?

The answer is that archaeology has an inferiority complex. This is the reason, I suspect, why E. A. Hoebel thought archaeology was "doomed always to be the lesser part of anthropology" (cited by Willey and Sabloff 1993:152) and why some archaeologists insisted that there is no archaeological theory, only anthropological theory (Flannery 1982). Archaeologists, according to such logic, are forced to borrow the theoretical constructs of ethnologists or others, making the former the consumers and the latter the providers of theory.

It's a view that survives to this day because, for the Hoebels out there, archaeology's Cinderella status seems deserved. Surely, the logic goes, the observations of historians, with their written texts, or ethnographers, with their rich firsthand observations of living people, are superior to the miscellaneous bits of refuse in abandoned villages dug up by context-impoverished archaeologists. But this wasn't the logic of Marvin Harris. And neither is it the logic of certain contemporary archaeologists.

Today we might say that the reality of the past—the reality of history—is not so far removed from the evidence of that history—the potsherds, charred plant foods, bones—that archaeologists routinely recover. That is, the reality of the past was *what people did* and *how people experienced* social life. As it turns out, such a doing and experiencing of life almost always has a material and spatial dimension (Joyce 2005; Meskell 2004; Meskell and Preucel 2004; Pauketat 2001b; Tilley 2004). Archaeologists have direct access to this dimensionality through artifacts, spaces, and places. In fact, it is precisely this dimensionality of people's cultural practices and social experiences that newer theories in archaeology aim to understand. From the point of view of these theories (of practice, agency, memory, or landscape), archaeologists track the continuous *culture making* of people through the histories, trajectories, or genealogies of things, spaces, and bodies. Thus in some theoretical circles, archaeologists now claim explanatory priority with respect to the cultural processes that reside not in the mind alone but at the interface of the human body and external world.

For people like me, that's comforting. We archaeologists are the detectives of the past. We can explain the past in a way that few others can and, at our best, the way everyone should. A growing number of us are developing the new theories by attempting to piece together particular scholarly puzzles in specific research areas. Such archaeological theorizing is not commonplace everywhere. For instance, it is rare in the practice of eastern North American archaeology (but see Cobb 2005; Cobb and King 2005; Sassaman 2004, 2005; Pauketat 2001a, 2003a,b). Perhaps that's understandable. We have all endured a lot of theorizing over the past thirty years. Some of it good, some of it not so good. Either way, we live in a world of theoretical plurality and disparate archaeologies, a world where even contradictory theoretical positions or interest groups seem able to coexist within both particular regions and specific research domains. Some of these positions and groups, as it turns out, survive by clinging to one or another sophisticated delusion that, ultimately, originated outside of archaeology.

One such delusion, a whopper in fact, is encapsulated by the idea of the chiefdom. First defined in northern South America and Africa by ethnologists, the chiefdom concept was perfected in Polynesia (Goldman 1970; Kirchoff 1955; Sahlins 1958, 1972). Over the years, those who have made use of the concept of chiefdom have shifted from ethnology to archaeology. In addition, the definitional basis for the notion of the chiefdom has shifted, as has the location of the stereotypical chiefdom. Today, with archaeology taking the lead, eastern North Americanists are the frontrunners in chiefdom studies (Carneiro 1998b:182). When people think of chiefdoms, they might think of *The Savannah River Chiefdoms* (Anderson 1994), *The James River Chiefdoms* (Gallivan 2003), *The Cahokia Chiefdom* (Milner 1998), *The Chattahoochee Chiefdoms* (Blitz and Lorenz 2006), *Timucuan Chiefdoms of Spanish Florida* (Worth 1998), *Ancient Chiefdoms of the Tombigbee* (Blitz 1993), *Archaeology of the Moundville Chiefdom* (Knight and Steponaitis 1998), *Etowah: The Political History of a Chiefdom Capital* (King 2003), *Coosa: The Rise and Fall of a Southeastern Mississippian Chiefdom* (Smith 2003), *Lamar Archaeology: Mississippian Chiefdoms in the Deep South* (Williams and Shapiro 1990), or *Caborn-Welborn: Constructing a New Society after the Angel Chiefdom Collapse* (Pollack 2004). The frontrunner status, however, belies an archaeological irony. In sticking to their chiefdoms, Mississippian archaeologists are "drifting away from the ethnological mainstream, both in theory and in vocabulary" using concepts that now stand as obstacles to understanding what really happened in the ancient world (Moore 1994:141).

This book is an attempt to explain why we find ourselves in this situation, why it matters, and what we need to do about it. With this book, I aim to reexamine Midwestern and southern chiefdoms in both comparative and historical terms. Why? I am dissatisfied with recent attempts to remedy the conceptual problems associated with the study of what are imperfectly called ancient complex societies or civilizations.

Various researchers in some parts of the world have already remedied the conceptual problems associated with the chiefdom and other sophisticated delusions, or so they believe (but see Chapman 2003). One reviewer of a recent book by Norman Yoffee, who questions "neoevolutionary" models, asks, "Does anyone still really believe this?" (Mathews 2005:255). Despite the reviewer's disbelief, the answer is a resounding yes. Despite a host of critiques over the past thirty years, such recent attempts seem unable to dissociate a theoretical understanding of the development of inequality, identity, hegemony, and government, among other things, from the unfortunate—and sometimes unstated—metaphor of social evolution. Even Yoffee (2005) does not abandon social evolutionary models. But he does question models that see "the rise of states as a series of 'punctuated' ... changes" where "all social institutions—politics, economy, social organization, belief system—were linked" and changed "at the same time, at the same pace, and in the same direction" (Yoffee 2005:22).

Evolutionary theory is fine for biology, but, in the archaeology of complexity, its conceptual clutter is counterproductive. Social evolutionary thought, I argue, emasculates an archaeology of complexity in general. A comparative and historical reconsideration of eastern North America, I think, makes this case. And given an accelerating rate of archaeological site destruction in many places, and the disheartening complicity of some pseudoarchaeologists in that destruction, that case and this book seem urgent.

This book seeks to convey that urgency. In so doing, it probably bares my impatience with archaeological models that retain social evolutionary underpinnings. These, I worry, numb us to a very real crisis in archaeology. But not wanting to offend, I borrow a technique from Kent Flannery (1976, 1982). Alongside living and breathing archaeologists of today, I draw heavily on three composite caricatures of contemporary archaeologists that I've known over the years: the Southern Pragmatist, Dr. Science, and the Uncertain Graduate Student (UGS). In addition, I'll introduce a fourth, a shady character who's sold his archaeological soul to corporate interests. None of the four represent actual individuals. Rather, they are contrived characters and their dialogue is fictitious. They embody the best and worst of contemporary archaeology and, similar to Flannery's allegorical figures, we find in them the human characteristics all too common to archaeologists: honesty, generosity, pomposity, stupidity, and deceit.

Sometimes right and other times wrong, the four characters exemplify the potential for each one of us to shape an understanding of the past and thus affect how we proceed into our collective future. That is the underlying message in this book. However, to appreciate it, we need to begin with a reality check outside a small town in the middle of the Mid-South and the so-called Mississippian heartland. Then chapter 1 sets up the characters and the problems at hand. Chapters 2 and 3 explain the problems in greater detail, with reference to the history of anthropology, the practice of archaeology in the eastern United States, and the evidence of complexity before the Mississippian period. UGS, Dr. Science, and the Pragmatist voice their concerns and opinions here, to help ground some rather abstract theoretical points. In chapters 4 and 5, we'll examine Mississippian archaeology generally and the better-known Mississippian places and regional histories specifically. UGS sleeps for most of those chapters, but we'll wake her up for chapter 6 to cap off the discussion of Mississippian places with the King Kong of eastern North America: Cahokia. Following that, we'll compare the eastern phenomena to the American Southwest, early Mesoamerica, and ancient Mesopotamia (chapter 7) before returning again to our characters and their struggles (chapter 8).

CHAPTER ONE

PRINCIPLES AND PRINCIPALS

One feels a little foolish in proclaiming a scientific law.

—Marshall Sahlins and Elman Service, 1960

What goes around comes around.

—American Indian proverb

Late that midsummer afternoon, three redneck white men in a pickup were escorting our two vehicles—a rented station wagon and a beat-up Ford Bronco—out along a dirt road that paralleled the L'Anguille River in northeast Arkansas. We drove past the site where two of our crew members had been working but were now missing. At that moment, we could only guess what had happened to them. David Anderson, our driver and project director, would later find them hiding among the cypress trees down by the river, afraid for their lives.

The putrid carcass of a large, hairy dog was rapidly liquefying in the Arkansas heat as we turned onto the state highway. The redneck escort had left, Dave reassured Preston and me, sitting in the backseat. A short while later, alone with Pat Garrow, the owner of our contract archaeology firm, Dave would begin to shake uncontrollably, realizing how close we—and particularly he—had come to death.

Graduate students at the University of Michigan, Preston Miracle and I hadn't expected anything of this sort working on a survey and testing project outside Marianna, Arkansas. Perhaps no one had. It was 1987.

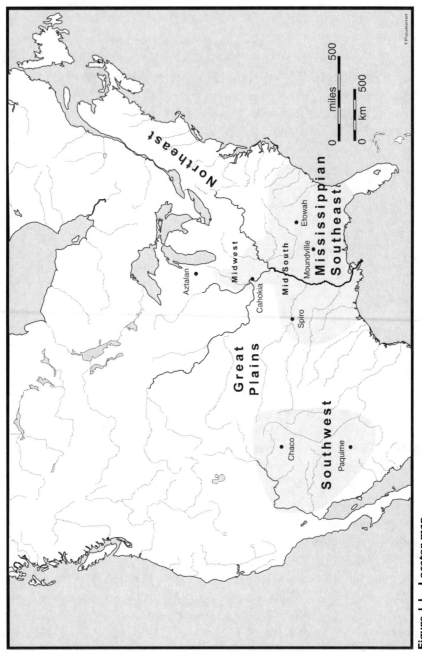

Figure 1.1 Locator map

We were naive. Then again, the L'Anguille survey was a model project, a credit to its director, himself a senior Michigan graduate student and veteran archaeologist. We had found and recorded 222 archaeological sites and conducted controlled surface collections and test excavations on 47 of them (Anderson 1999a; Anderson et al. 1989).

But we were a world away from the University of Michigan. Cottonmouths, aggressive poisonous water snakes known for their unusual ability to strike repeatedly, swam through the waters we occasionally waded. Segregation was still in effect in certain places of business, and we sometimes worked in fields alongside poor black sharecroppers who lived in clusters of single-room shacks—some without electricity. The nice ranch-style homes of the wealthy white landowners who granted us permission to conduct our research provided a sharp contrast. And then there were the letters, *JU*, spray painted into the town name on the railroad overpass: "M a r i^{JU}a n n a." Eventually we would learn—at gunpoint—that one of the three white men in the pickup, whose elderly mother had given us permission to do research on her property, thought that I had lied to her in order to gain access. Later, a rumor circulated that marijuana plants were hidden within certain agricultural fields in the vicinity. We hadn't noticed.

In any event, permission in hand, we thought our work was going rather well. We had found a number of small Mississippian sites along this stretch of river bottomland. Dave had split us into teams to excavate one-meter-square units at the various small sites in the field. Five of us worked together on a couple of nearby sites. One team of two was farther down the dirt road. Another team of two had been left beyond the bend up the dirt road a mile away and out of sight.

From that very direction, the rest of us spotted the billowing dust trail of a vehicle headed toward us at top speed. We stood together on the dirt road and watched, speculating about what was happening. Thinking the pickup would slow down, we waited in the road. It did not, and at the last moment all five of us leaped from the dirt road as the truck skidded toward us. The truck's doors flew open before the dust could settle and three men encircled us before we knew what was happening. The driver, smallest and oldest of the three, racked a pump-action shotgun as he exited the truck and demanded to know, in language as redundant as it was foul, "what the f—k" we "f—kers" were doing in his "f—king field." The other two men positioned themselves around our group, each grasping an ax handle. I stood in the middle, wondering why the three men were surrounding us.

When David Anderson stepped forward to explain, the gunman leveled the black steel barrel at his belt line and ordered us to leave. The gunman's eyes bulged and his face reddened with anger as Dave attempted to explain to him that, no, we weren't trespassing. Shaking with rage and spewing expletives, he tightened his finger on the trigger of the shotgun just inches from Anderson's gut. The gist, in paraphrased form: Get the f—k out of here, *now*, or you're dead. Pat Garrow, Dave's boss (who had arrived the previous day to see how the project was going) was tugging at his field director's arm. "Let's go, Dave . . . Let's go, Dave . . ."

But who were these guys? For an indeterminable period of seconds or minutes, Dave—project map in hand—stood his ground, attempting to straighten out what was clearly a big misunderstanding. *We did have permission*, and so he sought to reason with the gunman—boiling mad—who was ready to discharge his weapon into Dave's abdomen.

And if David Anderson was shot, who'd be next? Such a thing runs through one's panicked mind, as do nutty contingency plans. Through whispers, Preston and I had planned to sidle off to our left under the pretense of retrieving our field equipment. From there we could dive into the woods or maybe into the green, slimy waters of the L'Anguille. I could have outswum a swarm of cottonmouths that day, but I wouldn't get the opportunity. The gunman waved us back with the shotgun and a few choice words.

That summer day comes back to me now and again, as I imagine it does to all nine of us who were there (Akridge and Davis 1993; Anderson 1993). It was a close encounter with the dark forces responsible for erasing the pre-Columbian history of vast stretches of the Mississippi alluvial valley. Today these forces are as powerful as ever, although they tend to be less obvious if more insidious than those along the L'Anguille.

In the 1980s, this region—at one time thought to be the heartland of Mississippian culture—was undergoing a dramatic social, economic, and physical transformation. Corporate landowners were leveling the valley floor and converting vast stretches of land, entire rural counties, into rice fields. Machines scraped away the hills and ridges, and the perfectly flat fields were flooded by tapping deep, ancient aquifers. Tenants like those wielding the shotgun and ax handles rented the property and grew the crops. And while we lived through the encounter, few archaeological sites survive the process. In fact, the remains of entire Mississippian polities—their settlements including towns surrounded by farmsteads or hamlets—were expunged from the face of the earth.

This was the same land that Hernando de Soto had traversed in A.D. 1541 after he "discovered" the Mississippi River, devastating the indigenous populations as he went. Near present-day Memphis, the chroniclers of that expedition described powerful caciques whose people and principal towns sometimes shared a name: Quizqui, Aquixo, Quiguate, Casquí, or Pacaha. The Spaniards referred to their political territories as provinces. Later some would cautiously refer to them as kingdoms (Phillips et al. 1951:441). Today, most people label them "chiefdoms." Whatever they are called, we must ask ourselves if it matters that, of the many hundreds of such entities that once dotted eastern North America, some continue to be erased by the forces of globalization.

In actuality, the question is highly theoretical and should prompt us to ponder: Did the people of each province contribute in some way to the larger history of North America? Did they change the history of other people? And what if they did, and our one means of accessing this knowledge—the group's archaeological remains—were wiped from the face of the earth?

The Education of an Uncertain Graduate Student

Such questions have occurred to our first character, the early-twenty-first-century version of Kent Flannery's (1976) "Skeptical Graduate Student." But times have changed. *Her* professor *was* a Skeptical Graduate Student, a sort of smart-ass know-it-all who questioned his teachers and believed in truth, justice, and the archaeological way. She, on the other hand, is not so sure of herself, at least not enough to be skeptical of received wisdom. She's young—in her twenties—and a little uncertain of what she really believes or why she's doing archaeology. It's not that she is uninterested in archaeology. Quite the opposite. She is interested in everything everywhere, which is another way of saying that she lacks focus, even as she approaches her doctoral research. Graduate school was a logical step for her, but she remains uncertain about her core beliefs. We'll call her our Uncertain Graduate Student (UGS).

I met UGS a few years ago at a meeting of the Southeastern Archaeo-logical Conference (SEAC) in Knoxville, Lexington, Baton Rouge or some midsize southern city—they blur together in my memory. I chatted with her about the paper she'd presented, her first. SEAC is a good place to present your first paper. It's an annual affair that embodies the odd mix of genteel scholarship and rowdy partying that defines southern American archaeology. The high point is always the dance. Into his nineties, the great-godfather and elder statesman of eastern North American archae-ology, James B. Griffin, would still cut a rug at SEAC. David Anderson would bring his camcorder to record it all for posterity.

UGS's first paper was a sort of promotional statement about her planned dissertation research at the Obion site in western Tennessee (Garland 1992). She needed to hone her thoughts about what she could and couldn't know in order to land the funding that would support the field research leading to her hoped-for Ph.D. dissertation. Her professor, himself a product of academia in the early 1980s, already knew what UGS could and couldn't possibly dis-cover. He'd told her so repeatedly and in no uncertain terms over the course of his two favorite graduate seminars: "Chiefdoms and States" and "Archaeo-logical Theories: Dumb and Dumber." He's a smart fellow committed to understanding social evolution, but he doesn't suffer fools lightly. He has no patience for "speculative scenarios," as he calls them, that are untestable. To UGS, it seems that he's worked all over the world: Peru, Belize, New Mexico (well, who hasn't?), and both the Midwest and South (ditto). His scholarly pedigree is impressive, his friends influential. Dr. Science, UGS calls him. What he knows, he knows he knows. What he doesn't, isn't knowable.

Late one cold February evening we find UGS alone in the basement of the anthropology building of a major state university somewhere in the Midwest, struggling to compose the opening lines of a grant proposal. After a couple of hours, UGS settles on an introduction. "Chiefdoms are middle-range societies," she begins, "that developed in various parts of the world before ancient states in response to the growing resource-distribution inequities inherent to noncentralized societies. In southern North America, the prehistoric 'Mississippian' chiefdoms that evolved around A.D. 1000 were characterized by one or more ceremonial centers, 'towns with mounds,' where hereditary chiefs presided over important ritual events and maintained loyal followings through their kin obligations and controls over esoteric knowledge."

She likes the scientific sound of it so far: big words and abstract concepts. She cites a few prominent studies by people-who-might-review-the-proposal and continues with some specifics: "The proposed research at the Obion site in western Tennessee will build on previous suggestions that the rise and fall of chiefdoms were caused by several factors—environmental change, trade, and warfare—that at first permitted and later undercut a tenuous social balance maintained by society's elites. Ancient Obion society, it is proposed, represents a complete 'cycle' of a single chiefdom that will help us comprehend the causal factors behind social evolution generally." There, UGS smiles, that's good! Dr. Science will approve. Now, she ponders, how will I prove it?

We'll leave UGS here for the moment, contemplating the tricky issue of scientific proof, and return to our first order of business: chiefdoms. What are they? Why do archaeologists study them? Why should average taxpaying citizens care, especially about one in western Tennessee eight or nine centuries ago?

The answers to such questions are never simple. In fact, I must beg the indulgence of the reader; in the process of providing answers, I will be changing the questions. Infuriating, I know. But it's an academic thing, and I figure archaeologists have earned the right, what with those long years of graduate school followed by annual income averages on a par with high school janitors. Besides, the problem of chiefdoms is far too important to be left to the Dr. Sciences out there. Their analytical approaches to this critical step in world historical development have gone awry.

There is a whole host of misused concepts pertaining to the way archaeologists approach what many still gloss as "complex societies" in North America, Mexico, Europe, the Andes, Southeast Asia, sub-Saharan Africa, the Near East, and the Far East. The most misused concept is chiefdom or, if you prefer, middle-range society or prestate polity which, it is argued, comes in simple, complex, communal, corporate, network, apical, and constituent variants. Sometimes it seems that we should simply throw out the words along with their conceptual baggage and start anew. But history doesn't work like that. People have tried that before, but the words remain. Obviously we have to use words that have some conceptual baggage attached to them.

However, it is time to return chiefdom to a purely *descriptive* usage. Use it if you like, as loosely as you like, or use another word as you prefer. Ditto for "state" (Yoffee 2005). In fact, I will advocate an alternate approach to chiefdoms and states. We desperately need to retire the evolutionary emphasis on these societies with their so-called political structures or institutions that, once evolved, are said to have taken on a life of their own. Evolutionary approaches require us to produce a definition of that structure or institution first, and such a priori definitions are part of the reason we're in the fix we're in. Frankly, nothing ever fits the definitional ideal. So, I'm advocating a way around the definitional impasses and evolutionary dead ends. I'm pointing to a back door to understanding complexity.

The Back Door to Complexity

There are some who already come and go by the back door. They're friends of mine, good people. But others, I have no doubt, will not like my backdoor approach. As you will see, it violates the fundamental tenets of their social evolutionary thought. It undercuts several important scholarly works on chiefdoms and states. And it allows us to consider alternate forms of central places—besides "ceremonial centers" or "towns with mounds"—and to consider different ways of conceptualizing polities, confederacies, states, or other transregional political–cultural phenomena. Entering through the back door, we can rethink the historical causes and consequences of such places, polities, peoples, and processes.

We could identify my backdoor approach as the *historical-processsual approach* and oppose it to the standard evolutionary approaches to political administrations with their a priori (front door) categories (Pauketat 2001b, 2003a,b). The latter is quite common today—although often disguised—because people want to believe that the roots of change within a society lie in its form of government and its political institutions. Recently Norman Yoffee (2005) distinguished older "neoevolutionary" approaches from modified social evolutionary ones. Of course, the old neoevolutionary approach, which amounted to little more than pigeon-holing societies into evolutionary stages, has been sidestepped and questioned since the 1970s. The most successfully modified evolutionary approaches have stressed the transformational potential of political administrations. These either consider the information processing constraints and historical contingencies of governmental administrations or inject a dose of history and agency into their models (Blanton et al. 1996; Feinman 1995; Flannery 1972, 1999b; Johnson 1982; Upham 1990; Wright 1984). For a number of reasons, the argument goes, administrations could be rapidly transformed (along with the society that was built up around it).

But problems with social evolutionism remain. Big problems. In some areas of the world—especially the American Midwest and South—there is only one way around the problems: we must abandon social evolutionary thinking altogether. A pragmatic southern friend of mine puts it succinctly: "It's time to kick in the front door of evolutionary theory."

The historical approach I'm advocating doesn't dismiss the importance of administrative information processing nor the idea that there may be tensions and contradictions within governments that constrain historical possibilities. However, like its 1980s precursors, the backdoor approach does reject the idea that administrative evolution determines the look and shape of ancient societies (McGuire 1992; Paynter and McGuire 1991). And it deemphasizes the rules of governance and the politicking of governors, the latter being a contemporary obsession in the archaeology of "chiefdoms" in eastern North America—an obsession whose time has passed.

In short, the historical approach emphasizes understanding that governance and governors can only be explained with reference to histories of who did what, where, and how in the past. This is not to say that we should be content with locating the official, elite histories of administrators, written in the day books of task masters or carved on the stelae of ancient cities. No. The historical approach I have in mind is concerned with the unofficial, illiterate, or *unwritten* histories as much as the official texts. And it is concerned with such things as a means of understanding the big picture—North America's "big history" and its "large-scale processes" (Lekson and Peregrine 2004; Peregrine and Lekson 2006). It is pre-Columbian North America's big history and not its so-called chiefdoms, I assert, that we should be explaining. Our units of cross-cultural comparison should also be the historical trajectories or genealogies of change of various world civilizations, not the attributes, institutions, or functions of societies. Only in this way will we achieve a greater understanding of who we are and how we came to be part of our present-day globalizing world.

What was eastern North America's big history? There were anomalous transregional confederacies, foreign contacts, migrations, religious

15

cults, a founding city, the dissimulation of central governance, militariza-tion, provincialization, and the truncation of all by an army of Spaniards and a subsequent flood of colonists. For present purposes, this big his-tory—along with my advocacy of an alternate historical mode of analy-sis—won't be based on grand theoretical statements. This isn't a theory book. It's an informed and opinionated empirical review of some of the best-known Mississippian peoples and places of the eastern United States. And that review carries a series of lessons.

The lessons become clear when we compare Mississippian phe-nomena with pre-Mississippian archaeological complexes in the eastern woodlands (e.g., Poverty Point and Hopewell) and with select Old and New World "complex societies." But my analytical spotlight is squarely on the Mississippian. It is here that the issues of chiefdoms and other archaeological delusions come into sharp focus. It is here that we can see the inadequacies of the accepted approach to understanding. It is here that we must take a stand against the dark forces working against us. And it is here that new questions will come to the fore, making knowable that which seemed unknowable just a few years ago.

Ultimately I want to help UGS write that proposal. Not just so that it gets funded. The old canned chiefdom approaches that I aim to decon-struct remain fundable. But I want UGS to write that proposal so that it drives her to seek significant new insights from among the variable and alternative histories currently being erased from the landscape by those who would keep us ignorant of how different things could be. It will take some serious rethinking and labor-intensive work by UGS and others like her. It will take some nerve to stand up and argue for what's right. And it will take many more model archaeological surveys, like David Anderson's L'Anguille project, along with considerably more (and more extensive) ex-cavations. But that's what archaeologists were placed on this earth to do!

Chiefdoms, States, and Civilizations

Fulfilling that earthly mission involves understanding the develop-ment of civilization, including these things lumped under the rubrics of chiefdoms, states, and civilizations. By chiefdom, people usually mean a political or governmental unit that transcends local autonomy (Marcus and Feinman 1998:4; Curet 2003). Some deemphasize the unit as the subject of our interest and accentuate the transcendence of local autonomy, a phenomenon that was, according to Robert Carneiro, "a critical step in political development—probably the most important one ever taken" (Carneiro 1981:37). Somehow, from uncentralized, kin-based egalitarian societies emerged regional polities "with institutional governance and some social stratification organizing . . . population[s] of a few thousand to tens of thousands of people" (Earle 1997:17). The various cultural identities of the people involved became unified under the banner of a godlike person or chief. And when this happened, people crossed a threshold. They made "a qualitative step. Everything that followed, including the rise of states and empires, was, in a sense, merely quantitative" (Carneiro 1981:38).

In comparison, a state is a more complex regional formation of people where governance transcends kinship and chiefly cults by infiltrating daily practices. What people do everyday, in a state society, references and affirms the state. In the words of Morton Fried (1967:229), the state is not merely equated with "an administrative bureaucracy, or even a government." But this definition of the state also moves it out of the realm of a concrete thing and into the realm of a cultural experience or, one might say, a "cultural hegemony" (Gramsci 1971; see chapter 6). Such a move varies from the influential definition of Henry Wright and Gregory Johnson (1975), who saw the state as an internally specialized bureaucracy, and allows for a Carneiro-esque sense that state making was ongoing within what he would call chiefdoms rather than constituting a qualitative break with prestate polities (Sahlins 1985).

That definition also spills over into what we might label "civilization," by which some mean "the cultural sphere associated with . . . political or governmental unit[s]" (Marcus and Feinman 1998:4). Some people justifiably dislike the word "civilization" since it implies a demeaning ethnocentric bias that simultaneously labels "uncivilized" people as "primitive." Their dislike is noted, and appreciated. But for present purposes, I need a word, and "civilization" is awaiting reclamation from the ethnocentrism and racism of an earlier anthropology. Civilization as I use it isn't a qualitative transformation, a dawning of high culture in some ancient world (cf. Baines and Yoffee 2000). And it isn't an advanced type of social system (contra Blanton et al. 1999:4). It didn't just happen once on each island or continental land mass. No. *Civilization is an ongoing historical process, not an evolutionary phenomenon.* These days, the names have been changed to protect the guilty. We speak of globalization instead of civilization, corporations instead of elite rulers, and consumers instead of commoners.

But by studying how civilizations developed in the past, we can find the answers to why people today give up their local autonomy to "the Leviathan," as he was known to Thomas Hobbes, or, for those who prefer George Orwell, why they sacrifice their agency to Big Brother. We can gain perspective on the causes and consequences of social life now and in the past—hardly an insignificant achievement. People have sought such perspective since, perhaps, the time of the earliest so-called chiefdoms.

Historical Overview

At certain times and in certain places, people began to ask questions about other people because this knowledge helped explain their own history and identity. Sometimes it also helped control those other people. In the Western world, the questions behind chiefdoms are nearly the same ones asked by a host of enlightened thinkers, philosophers, and revolutionaries: Rousseau, Montesquieu, Vico, Hobbes, Marx, and their earlier Greek and Roman precursors such as Aristotle, Thucydides, and Tacitus. The questions posed by these thinkers seem to stem from the experience of people in centralized societies (Helms 1992). They are the questions of civilization, for civilization, and by civilization: Why do people form governments and commonwealths? What is the root cause of population growth and warfare? When is production organized above the family and what are the long-term historical effects?

Heady stuff. Requires somebody with great pretensions to explaining world history. Because Marx and Engels are dead, the task generally falls to anthropologists (who more pretentious than they?). Looking around the world in the 1950s, American and British anthropologists thought they could identify a series of relatively small-scale societies ordered according to some basic principles of governance and economy. They thought these principles might help understand world-historical development generally—the beginnings of social stratification, a division of labor, standing armies, and so on.

At the most basic level, these societies were governed by hereditary leaders who, unlike those of more transient societies, held actual political offices believed legitimate by most members of that society. Size mattered, but there was some elbow room (Carneiro 1967, 1972). One society might be quite small, perhaps a series of allied villages and a few hundred people. Another might be quite large, as in a territorial polity with a series of local chiefs subordinate to a paramount who held sway over tens of thousands. The legitimacy of chiefly leadership, in all cases, was key. People acknowledged it and bowed to it, as attested by their support. That support may have been perceived to be voluntary, obligatory, or symbolic but it was always, in the final analysis, economic. Voilà! Chiefdoms (Oberg 1955; Service 1962; Southall 1956; Steward and Faron 1959)!

Not all anthropologists agreed (no surprise there). Not everyone liked the word "chiefdom." From the beginning, anthropologists recognized the many variants of primitive or Stone Age political organizations, some having elaborate types and subtypes, in their attempts to deduce the reasons for the differences (Firth 1965; Sahlins 1972). In Africa, according to one generous classification scheme, there were despotic, regal, incorporative, and aristocratic polities ("kingdoms") and federations, all stirred around by invasions, migrations, the slave trade, and other sorts of colonial encounters (Vansina 1962). Elsewhere, say in Southeast Asia, chiefdoms seemed to occupy the fringes of civilization, gleaning what they could from traders hailing from the great civilizations of China and Southeast Asia. Likewise, the micos, caddís, weroances, caciques or cacicas, xinesís, and sun kings encountered by the early European powers around the Caribbean, Central America, and northern South America seemed possibly related or marginal to the well-known Latin American states and empires. By contrast, in the islands of Polynesia, the chiefdoms of the historic period seemed more pristine and homogeneous, although several scales were still identified (Sahlins 1958). This variability meant that some anthropologists, especially those standing in the shadow of Franz Boas, disdained categorization. At the same time, some recognized that "great oligarchical republican confederacies" had arisen in North America under certain conditions that "transcended the bounds of locality, language, and culture" (Vincent 1990:176). These, Vincent notes, were "larger than state forms of political organization." Where did they fit in the classificatory schemes?

For some anthropologists in the 1950s and early 1960s, the point of categorizing diversity into chiefdoms and states was to figure out the commonalities of what they called the process of cultural evolution (Stocking 1982). These were the "neoevolutionary" anthropologists, the twentieth-century heirs to earlier nineteenth-century intellectual giants such as Lewis Henry Morgan, Herbert Spencer, and Edward B. Tylor. Like their earlier counterparts, the neoevolutionary anthropologists were committed to the idea of large-scale regularities—things that can be explained through laws of science. Maybe they have to do with inevitability of inequality rooted in how noncapitalist societies distributed marriage partners and wealth (Firth 1965; Leach 1965). Maybe they have to do with how societies "captured energy" or adapted to outside pressure (Sahlins and Service 1960). Maybe they have to do with the inherent tendency of *Homo sapiens* to seek dominion over others (Carneiro 1970). All sought to explain change with reference to principles that impart long-term regularities.

Passing the Torch

Understanding the evolution of human societies soon became the raison d'être of American archaeology. It was now the 1960s, after all, when the whole point of archaeology was the search for laws of human behavior. Most of the "new archaeologists" of the day affirmed a progressive view of human cultural development. If more complex organizations could outcompete simpler ones, then the whole history of humankind should be one of a progression of bands to tribes to chiefdoms to states. This was encoded as scientific law and named the *Law of Cultural Dominance.* Lawgivers Marshall Sahlins and Elman Service (1960:75) decreed "that cultural system which more effectively exploits the energy resources of a given environment will tend to spread in that environment at the expense of less effective systems." Early archaeological efforts aimed to prove the law valid. These were judged successful simply if they managed to identify whether or not some society was organized at the tribe, chiefdom, or state level (Sanders and Price 1968; Gibson 1974; Peebles and Kus 1977; Renfrew 1973). Apparently, once you knew that, all else would be, in the words of Sherlock Holmes, "elementary."

Of course, in all the searching for the correlates of bands-tribes-chiefdoms-states, the causal power of culture—those historically contingent ways of doing and being that defined one's identities and motivated one's practices—was deemphasized. Instead, through the 1970s and beyond, rational decision-maker models were promoted and systems theory seemed to offer the best hope for dealing with complex causal relationships, like those we've all experienced in governmental bureaucracies (Flannery 1972). Moreover, it occurred to archaeologists that the sort of adaptational models that the earlier anthropologists had been interested in were much more suited to a subdiscipline with the ability to actually measure the energy expenditures, caloric intakes, and adjustments in human behavior of various societies over long periods of time. Archaeology, not cultural anthropology, was that subdiscipline (Yoffee 2005).

The passing of the subdisciplinary torch was no more evident than in the graduate seminars at the University of Michigan in the 1960s and early 1970s. The Department of Anthropology's roster of professors included Leslie White, Eric Wolf, Elman Service, and Marshall Sahlins, the latter having been classmates at Columbia University in the 1950s (Vincent 1990). In the early 1970s, after James Griffin stacked with New Archaeologists the Museum of Anthropology, which was located across campus from the department, the full power of the force dealing with early civilizations now included Henry Wright, Jeff Parsons, Kent Flannery, Richard Ford, and Karl Hutterer. Their archaeology graduate students tooled up in both the department and the museum in courses such as Sahlins's seminar on Hawaiian state formation in 1970.

Among the students in that seminar were several who would go on to produce the new "classics" in the chiefdom–state literature: Elizabeth Brumfiel, Timothy Earle, and Susan Kus. Brumfiel's concerns for Aztec settlement and economy spun into studies of prestige goods, political factions, gender, and human agency (Brumfiel 1997, 2000; Brumfiel and Earle 1987). Earle would single-handedly redefine chiefdoms and an archaeological approach to political economy in his dissertation and a series of papers and books (Earle 1987, 1997). Kus would coauthor an influential paper with Christopher Peebles, then teaching at Michigan (Peebles and Kus 1977), her subsequent research moving along the cutting edge of phenomenological theorizing (Kus 1979, 1983, 1989; Kus and Raharigaona 2001). They all embodied the new wave of Michiganism, and in their wake a host of dissertations on related topics were produced under the guidance of the museum professors.[1]

So, archaeologists read up on the range of variability of the societies that the anthropologists—or the later archaeologists—would call chiefdoms. Typically, they all started with the summaries by Elman Service (1962) and Morton Fried (1967) that laid out idealized societal types using ethnographic summaries from around the world. For Service (1962:134), chiefdoms were *"redistributional societies* with a permanent central agency of coordination." This squared more or less with Fried's (1967) notion of "rank society," although Fried gave definitional priority to the central organizing principle, that agency of coordination, the office of chief, a hereditary position filled by someone from a high-ranking kin group. Service tended toward explaining chiefdoms in economic terms, Fried in political terms (although not sufficiently political for Carneiro [1998b:20]).

The difference between Service's and Fried's definitions is our first inkling of an important bifurcation in neoevolutionary approaches. For the former, societal integration and management seemed key to understanding chiefdoms. This has since been glossed as the managerial, integrationist, adaptationist, or "bottom-up" school (Brumfiel and Earle 1987; Chapman 2003; Earle 1987; Haas 1982). Chiefdoms as social systems emerged and disintegrated owing to the overall configuration of the population with respect to the health and happiness of its members. In contrast, Fried's definition led the way for the so-called conflict, top-down, or political approach to chiefdoms. The social systemic qualities of societies were deemphasized in the political approach, which is seen as more open-ended, subject to political machinations, and—in the hands of some—less evolutionary and more historical (Brumfiel and Earle 1987; Carneiro 1981; Earle 1997). Things might not always happen for the good of the society in ways that could have been anticipated by a cost-benefit analysis.

Indeed, the initial wave of Michigan's chiefdom studies seemed to affirm such a political view. Timothy Earle (1977, 1978), Vincas Steponaitis (1978), Mary Helms (1979), and Christopher Peebles and Susan Kus (1977) found little evidence for Servician redistribution (Carneiro 1981; Taylor 1975). This is not to say that redistribution is unknown in the ethnographies and ethnohistories on which such generalizations were based (Halstead and O'Shea 1982; Steponaitis 1978:420). It's just that a characteristic of some society can't be used to explain the genesis of that society (as Service argued). That would constitute an inappropriate *teleology* (not that this has stopped some from using "risk management" rather than redistribution as both cause and consequence of chiefdoms; I'll touch on that later).

The political approach constituted a reformation of neoevolutionary theorizing, but not its abandonment (Chapman 2003). Such reformation, however, seemed to complicate things. More types and more subtypes. Additional ways of divvying up the chiefdoms construct seemed necessary based on additional testing of ethnological models against archaeological data. First among these was the recognition of two sorts of chiefdoms: simple and complex (Cordy 1981; Earle 1987; Steponaitis 1978; Wright 1984). Simple chiefdoms were those "characterized by only one level of superordinate political offices" (Steponaitis 1978:420). In such societies, chiefs were only part-time specialists and were not spared the drudgery of daily food production activities. Their political hold on the rest of society was tenuous, and so most surplus that might have been appropriated for "public" (read: chiefly) use was usually redistributed back to those from whom it had originated. Or at least that was the idea. Most members of society probably rationalized this sort of redistribution as reciprocity, thereby minimizing the inequality inherent to such a government by chiefs (Sahlins 1972). Of course, the reality was still that reciprocity of this sort was centralized, not generalized, no matter how altruistic the chiefly motivations might seem.

Contrast this with the situation in complex chiefdoms (Steponaitis 1978; Wright 1984). These polities were more populous with larger territories owing, it was thought, to their administrative complexity (why not vice versa?). With two or three hierarchical layers of officeholders, the regional economy was organized in ways that permitted redirection of surplus for the greater glory of the central administration. More warriors could have been fielded to eliminate rivals; more labor could have been directed toward central projects; more subsidies might be given to expert craftspeople; and the elites would have realized more freedom (from tradition-minded underlings) to expand their interests beyond the boundaries of their local domain. The interests of such elites might have been well served by the control of knowledge about the natural and supernatural world out there (Helms 1992).

The effects? A "well-developed class structure" with nobles who were "not required to engage in production" (Steponaitis 1978:420). The upper echelons of society had "funds of power" at their disposal that were less subject to the ideology of redistribution (Wolf 1982). Here too were the beginnings of international politics and transregional civilization (Friedman and Rowlands 1978). Following Service's (1962) suggestion, later analysts imagined how chiefdoms, particularly the complex variety, were inherently expansionistic, inspiring others to emulate them if not also installing their own in the paramount offices of newly organized regimes (Renfrew 1987; Wright 1984).

Secondary Developments

Here seems to be the reason why Fried (1967, 1978) identified "pristine" polities versus "secondary" varieties. In the 1970s and 1980s, lacking today's archaeologies of colonization, creolization, identity, and historical process, archaeologists thought that secondary chiefdoms were anomalies that shortcut the evolutionary process. The New Archaeology viewed these as historical developments, not evolutionary ones. As such, they were like so much background noise in the system, the flotsam and jetsam of cultural process, of at best marginal interest (but contrast Price 1978).

This was a big mistake that had lasting consequences for the study of chiefdoms. Beginning in the 1980s, archaeologists should have known better. On the heels of Immanuel Wallerstein's (1974) world systems theory, some realized that world history and cultural evolution are, for all intents and purposes, one and the same (Wolf 1982). From such a global–historical perspective, it became difficult to imagine anything "pristine" such that its dynamic of change was entirely internal. There weren't even any untainted hunter-gatherers (Sassaman 2004). How could there have been sedentary peoples unaffected by cultural contacts with others?

The idea would not die among Mississippianists, even as they managed to reconcile the search for the pristine with the goals of world systems–inspired archaeology. They did this, perhaps unknown even to most of them, by asserting that the entire Mississippian Southeast was a pristine development isolated from the rest of the world. Even today, most agree with Bruce Smith's (1990:1) view of the whole: "contrary to still popular diffusionist 'south-of-the-border story' scenarios, the Mississippian emergence of AD 750–1050 was an independent pristine process of social transformation, uninfluenced by Mesoamerican state-level societies" (a view recently echoed by Brown 2005b:113).

Mississippian researchers in the 1980s latched onto the general idea of interrelated social formations, at least in one way. They had been trained to ignore Mesoamerica by a generation of researchers who had themselves openly flaunted the idea (Griffin 1966; Phillips et al. 1951; Williams and Brain 1983). Besides, some of the supposed Mesoamerican traits—particularly pyramidal mounds—have been proven to be of great antiquity in North America (chapter 3). However, the idea of interrelated social formations was advanced via a subsidiary construct: the prestige goods economy (Brown et al. 1990; Cobb 1993; King and Freer 1995; Pauketat 1992; Peregrine 1992; Welch 1991). Prestige goods were meaningful, moveable objects that circulated in social transactions as coupons of a sort, used for debt payments at births, puberty rites, marriages, funerals, and the like (Douglas 1967). Eric Wolf, in his early 1980s world systems garb, along with other political economists and "structural Marxists" in the 1970s, realized that long-term political–economic changes need not have been caused by outside forces and, furthermore, were inherent to the transregional prestige goods economy (Friedman and Rowlands 1978; Wolf 1982). Here, then, was a long-term historical dynamic that seemed to help explain the spread of chiefdoms (Mississippian and otherwise) without muddying the water with Mesoamerican imaginings.

But given that transregional dynamic, the whole idea of society as a system should have been cast into doubt. Was it reasonable to view any society as some sort of internally self-regulating "system" with a host of political, economic, religious, and jural subsystems? Probably not. And what exactly was "society" anyway—merely an elaborate enlightenment idea that mirrored Western nation-states (Wolf 1982)? If not, where did one society end and another begin in the internationalizing world of ancient prestige goods exchanges and interdigitated political economies (Rowlands 1987)? In fact, few ancient polities ever arose in isolation. Usually they emerged as groups or networks of "peer polities" (Renfrew 1987). Apparently there was more to the evolution of society than either evolution or society.

So, beginning in the 1980s, dissenters again questioned the standard evolutionary perspectives. Those interested in social evolution needed to modify their position. Maybe history—even as caused by human agents—was an important factor in cultural evolution after all (Blanton et al. 1993; Haas 2001; Feinman 1995; Flannery 1999b; Marcus and Flannery 1996). Maybe, as Julian Steward (1955) had once thought, there were multiple pathways to complexity (Upham 1990). Multiple routes could be due to a variety of internal and external factors that pushed and pulled the developmental trajectories of societies depending on historical circumstances. Much of the American Southwest, for instance, is comprised of peoples living in pueblos of a few families to more than 2,000 people. But few would label these chiefdoms. Perhaps inequality and polity didn't develop in lockstep, as per Service's redistributional societies, and should be "decoupled" in our own models, as Randall McGuire (1983) and others have said.

There was quite a lot of diversity even within the so-called chiefdom category (Feinman and Neitzel 1984). Perhaps, as many of the classic ethnological studies had intimated, chiefdoms didn't evolve in a progressive fashion from noncentralized societies to simple chiefdoms, to complex chiefdoms, to states (Yoffee 1993, 2005). Perhaps there were other formations that needed different names (Neitzel 1999; Yoffee et al. 1999). Maybe chiefdoms were devolutionary remnants of collapsed states in some portions of the world, not unlike so many petty kingdoms of medieval Europe after the fall of Rome (Friedman 1982; Muller 1997:59–60). Or maybe these nonstate societies oscillated or "cycled" between more-or-less hierarchical poles (Anderson 1994; Wright 1984).

Indeed, according to David Anderson (1994:1–2), "fluctuation in administrative or decision-making levels" was an "inherent aspect of chiefdoms" that sometimes led, "over time, to pronounced changes in chiefly authority structures." Conceding that point allowed the gist of social evolutionism, generally, and the guts of the chiefdom, specifically, to live on. As for Dave's position, I blame our mutual near-death experience near Marianna, Arkansas, when we realized that things can change quickly, depending on who does what, where, and to whom.

Strategery

It is the particular causes of Anderson's "pronounced changes in chiefly authority structures" that our young proposal writer, still in her basement office, thinks she can locate at the Obion site. It is getting late and she needs to eat supper, but she has just found an exhaustive listing of possible candidate causes in Anderson's tome *The Savannah River Chiefdoms: Political Change in the Late Prehistoric Southeast* (1994). UGS studies it carefully, impressed by its encyclopedic quality.

Word has it that the general editor of the University of Alabama Press, Judith Knight, nearly did a back flip upon seeing the original length of the *Savannah River* manuscript, a University of Michigan Ph.D. dissertation (some 800 pages). So Dave cropped it to 459 book pages. But thankfully for UGS, Anderson cites everything ever written on chiefdoms. And so, to hone her proposal's methodology, UGS focuses on his sixteen possible reasons why chiefdoms might cycle (Anderson 1994:figure 3). According to Anderson, there were primary factors such as "regional physiographic structure, climate, and resource structure" that affect "agriculture/subsistence production, tribute mobilization/surplus appropriation, and storage technology, which in turn shape developments within prestige goods exchange and intrapolity and interpolity alliance and information flow networks" which are somehow loosely related to population change, population movement, ritual institutional support, the strength of elite authority structures, the nature of chiefly succession, and the degree of elite factionalism (Anderson 1994:49–50).

UGS wonders which of these she may find at Obion. Fortunately, all of these causal mechanisms, opines Anderson, are related to an underlying factor. "Competition for prestige and power between rival elites, it is argued, is what initiates and drives cycling in chiefdom societies" (Anderson 1994:50). Apparently, along with "warfare . . . increased information processing demands, and subsistence uncertainty," this same initiating-and-driving cause helps explain the formation of chiefdoms (Anderson 1994:13). Hmm, prestige and power . . . UGS thinks of her major professor. Of course! How typical, she reflects. As always, some guys want to dominate (Maschner 1996; Clark and Blake 1994; Earle 1997). Things get out of hand and there you are, cycling through a complex relationship you never saw coming. David Anderson makes intuitive sense.

Over a late-night falafel at the corner deli, UGS hits on the correlates of chiefdom cycling that she knows can be found digging in Tennessee. If I can find some signs of warfare, a burned house or two, or (as she tightens her grip on the falafel and silently mouths) "broken arrowheads outside the palisade wall," then I will have affirmed the tenuous hold that Obion elites had on their chiefdom. Or better, she thinks, her grip now squeezing tahini sauce out one end, what if I could find prestige goods and surplus stores inside the walls that correlate with the climax of Obion? If they were reduced in quantities before mound building ended, then that would be proof that elite rivalry led to the downfall of the polity! If not? Well, she prefers not to think about the if-nots.

Within the week, she e-mails a copy of her first dissertation proposal draft to Dr. Science. In it, she proposes that a Mississippian polity arose along the Obion River in the eleventh century A.D. to offset the risks associated with corn agriculture. Naturally, logically. The people needed management, and a chiefly authority structure evolved to meet the need. She suspects that Obion might have been a complex chiefdom but can't risk saying it, in part because she's been warned by Dr. Science to avoid what Jon Muller (1997) calls exaggerationalist inferences. So she settles for a "simple chiefdom" label.

She proposes excavations along the site's palisade wall in an area of known domestic occupation that also fronts a small earthen pyramid. The relative dating of domestic features—houses and storage pits—in regard to the mound and palisade wall should allow her to gauge public investment in and protection of the central complex through time, an indirect measure of the "strength of the chiefly authority structure." The kinds of exotic and craft goods in that refuse, relative to the dietary remains and storage spaces, would provide a measure of whether changes in the site's external alliance structure weakened the administration, causing the population to lose faith and do what Sahlins (1972) said: "vote with their feet." She thinks she would dig a series of units in the general vicinity of the remains. Then she waits to hear from Dr. Science.

A week passes, and an e-mail arrives from the professor telling her to come in the following morning to discuss her proposal. On arriving, UGS sees a stack of books and journals on the professor's desk. "I enjoyed your proposal," he begins, "and I think it has excellent potential. However . . ." UGS knows what he'll say next: "I have concerns that you stick to what is testable—for instance the environmental risks that clearly must have underwritten every Mississippian economy. Otherwise, you seem to wander perilously close to speculative scenarios about human agency and ideology."

Shamed, UGS concedes that she found some of the writings in Marcia-Anne Dobres and John Robb's (2000) mysteriously green *Agency in Archaeology* volume compelling. She even admits that she skimmed through the radical *Companion to Social Archaeology* (Meskell and Pruecel 2004). But she assures Dr. Science that she will rein herself in. Dr. Science is pleased and offers her some conciliatory redirection. "Why not consider the Obion polity as a heterarchy, a rituality, or perhaps—in the terms of dual-processual theory—a corporate chiefdom?" he asks (Blanton et al. 1996; Crumley 1995a; Yoffee 2005). "They all involve thinking about the other axes of variation besides hierarchy that might help explain why Mississippian chiefdoms followed the developmental trajectories that they did." He thinks for a second and then continues. "You wouldn't want to exaggerate the importance of hierarchy and politics." Any mention of hierarchy and politics, to Dr. Science, usually seems an exaggeration. He turns to peer out his fourth floor window overlooking the quad. "I've pulled a few things off the bookshelf that you need to incorporate into your proposal."

While reading some of this material earlier, UGS had contemplated the original paper on dual-processualism by Richard Blanton, Gary Feinman, Stephen Kowalewski, and Peter Peregrine (1996), and the various amendments, commentaries, and applications by Feinman (1995, 2000, 2001), Mills (2000), Trubitt (2000), and others. Doubting the basic simple–complex hierarchical chiefdom model, these researchers picked up a line of thought first proposed in militaristic terms by Steward and Faron (1959), in social terms by Renfrew (1973), and in economic terms by D'Altroy and Earle (1985). Although the terminology varied, the idea was that the social relations within any given centralized polity might be more or less "theocratic" and "group-oriented," expressed economically as the bottom-up mobilization of staple goods in support of the political administration. At the opposite end of the spectrum were militaristic or aggrandizing elites concerned with their own power base, through direct controls of wealth to the exclusion of their kinfolk and allies (Beck 2003; Earle 1997; Pauketat 1994). To Blanton and colleagues (1996), the former group-oriented relations translated into corporate strategies while the latter, aggrandizing mode they termed network-based strategies.

The imagination of our Uncertain Graduate Student is stirred. Maybe Obion's elites founded their chiefdom through corporate strategies. Sure, she muses, that's it. After all, according to Elizabeth Garland (1992), Obion's early Mississippian platform mound was pretty impressive, meaning that considerable labor went into it. Certainly other early political behemoths seem to have started out this way (Blanton et al. 1996; Cherry 1978; Collins and Chalfant 1993; Earle 1997:179; Holley 1999:37; Paynter and McGuire 1991; Joyce 2004; Pauketat 2000a; Trigger 1990). Take

Teotihuacán, for example, or Wal-Mart even (but probably not the Wal-Mart at Teotihuacán). But then, perhaps, the Obion elites would have shifted from corporate strategies to network-based strategies in order to maximize their fund of power while minimizing the costs of collaboration with other Obionites. That in turn might have made the lower echelons of society unhappy, perhaps weakening the authority structures and leading to the end of the Obion chiefly cycle. Yes! At least it sounds like science.

All UGS needs to do then is find evidence of early corporate projects (mound building) and later elite aggrandizement (more prestige goods) and she will have proven the model. She runs the idea past Dr. Science, who approves, as long as she considers the corporate strategies in terms of collective risk minimization. She concedes the sense of it, proud that she has navigated through the literature and around her major professor, successfully tying together multiple strands of theory with solid test implications for her Mississippian case. She submits the grant proposal to the National Science Foundation, and three months later, she hears the news. The reviewers love it. NSF has fully funded her.

Note

1. I received my Ph.D. from the University of Michigan under the direction of Henry Wright in 1991. Of the other archaeologists cited by name in the text of this book, the following were trained at the University of Michigan: David Anderson, Alex Barker, Richard Blanton, Elizabeth Brumfiel, Christopher Carr, John Clark, Timothy Earle, Geoff Emberling, Mary Helms, Susan Kus, Paul Minnis, Susan Pollock, John Robb, Martha Rolingson, Bruce Smith, Monica Smith, Vincas Steponaitis, Michael Whalen, and W. H. Wills.

A CRISIS IN MISSISSIPPIAN ARCHAEOLOGY

An object at rest tends to stay at rest unless acted upon by an equal and opposite force.

—Sir Isaac Newton

Two salient characteristics of the chiefdom literature she reviewed continue to weigh on the mind of our Uncertain Graduate Student as she travels through Tennessee in a truck that looks like the one the Clampetts drove to Be-ver-ly (Hills, that is; you know the rest). One was generic and pervasive in the chiefdom literature. From Timothy Earle's *How Chiefs Come to Power* (1997) to my own humble *The Ascent of Chiefs* (1994), it seems that there were "too many chiefs" (Yoffee 1993). Or at least *there was too much agency allotted to chiefs* in our constructs. Anything that changed in an ancient chiefdom seemed explicable owing to some chiefly strategy.

Perhaps this elite-centric modeling makes sense: you can't have chiefdoms without chiefs, right? But something is still out of whack, UGS thinks. Chiefs. Mostly men. Aggrandizing or collaborating. But always instigating, acting, plotting, strategizing. Who made them lords?

The other salient characteristic relates to the first, she thinks, but seems especially pronounced in Mississippian research. *The very idea of chiefdoms cancels out the variability that most people say existed within chiefdom-level or middle-range societies.* Indeed, archaeologists assume with little to no proof that all the political institutions and administrations of these societies were alike. As inclusive catchall constructs, chiefdoms have caught all sorts of hell from critics, who railed for years against them or any societal type for this very reason (Chapman 2003; Crumley 1987; Kristiansen 1991; Patterson and Gailey 1987; Plog and Upham 1983; Upham 1987, 1990; Yoffee 1993).

UGS knows that. But she is unsure how to avoid it. Most archaeologists, while paying lip service to variation, effectively ignore it when push comes to shove. Indeed, *she* had in her own grant proposal! But hey, she thinks, you've got to start somewhere, right? "When separated from undesirable connotations," we are told, catchalls such as chiefdoms and states "serve the all-important purpose of facilitating comparisons" (King 2003:4; Wright 1984:43). It's just too bad we don't practice what we preach, UGS muses. Undesirable connotations abound.

And so resigned, UGS exits the interstate, now heading into Memphis on a two-day detour to attend the annual Mid-South Archaeological Conference held in early June every year. A small version of SEAC, the Mid-South meeting is her chance to rub elbows with a few hard-core Mississippianists, some contract archaeologists (who do most of the work in the Mid-South), a few members of the Chickasaw, Choctaw, or Quapaw nations, and an older generation whose experiences and interpretations still define the range of what is and is not acceptable in Mississippian archaeology.

It is just before dinnertime, and archaeologists are gathering inside the small hotel bar to shoot the breeze and gather for a meal. UGS sidles up to the bar and orders a cold beer. It has been a hot, sticky drive. That first beer leads to a second and then a third. A beady-eyed character sits in the bar's shadowy corner, running those beady eyes over her in a lecherous gaze. Then he smiles, raising his beer and nodding. She turns away and thankfully notices an acquaintance sitting in the full light farther down the bar. He is a well-known government archaeologist from a mid-southern state—we'll call him our Southern Pragmatist. He is gesticulating to the bartender.

UGS met the Southern Pragmatist as a field school student a few years back and recognizes this aging veteran as a well-seasoned, hardworking archaeologist. His career has been filled with more Mississippian archaeology than the best wet dream of academia's brightest star. Consequently he doesn't take academic types too seriously. Besides, he is as much the intellectual as they, albeit an earthier sort. Ordinarily UGS would be too intimidated to introduce herself, but she needs to schmooze, an important activity at conferences. And the beers have anesthetized her Midwestern nerves.

So UGS walks over to greet him. The Pragmatist seems to recognize her as he turns in her direction with a gin and tonic from the bartender. They exchange pleasantries and she explains how she's always wanted to talk to him about, well, archaeology. She describes her graduate experience and her NSF-funded plans for Obion. She drops the name of Dr. Science, whom the Southern Pragmatist knows well. He listens patiently, up to the mention of her dual-processual model. At that, the Southern Pragmatist frowns.

"You know," he says, "I think it's great what you're doing, but you might want to rethink how you conceptualize the Mississippian. I know that some words sound trendy," he continues, "and Dr. Science approves, but they're the same old evolutionary crap previously spewed by my own generation, mostly by would-be academic types."

A would-be academic type herself, UGS is taken aback and falls into a familiar Dr. Science methodological comment. "Well, whatever you think of the jargon, Obion was clearly some sort of polity that rose and fell," she said, "so that surely it's important to test models of the axes of variation that might help explain why. In the end," she concludes, "I guess our tests of such models will prove us right or wrong, right?"

The Pragmatist smiles. "Wrong," he deadpans, waving his gin and tonic. "It's not that easy. You aren't letting your testing procedure do much more than tell you what you already think you know. You're aiming your sights far too low. You'll need to dig a hell of a lot more than you think, just so you *can* think. And if you do that," he advises, "you'll realize just how silly the corporate network model is."

UGS, who begins her excavations in two days, thinks he is being a little harsh. Maybe it's the gin and tonic. So she tries reasoning with him, like a good scientist. "Well, we always need to dig more. But, you know, I've got to stick to what a single person can prove. And besides, isn't the goal ultimately to explain why chiefdoms rose and fell, blinking off and on—as David Anderson says—like so many Christmas tree lights?" She figures invoking Anderson is a good thing. Everybody likes Dave.

"Hell little lady," the Southern Pragmatist rejoins, "I've defined several 'cycling chiefdoms' myself!" He tips the gin and tonic back again before continuing with an ice cube in his mouth. "And I've speculated about the mechanisms. But I'm not really sure that this constitutes 'testing' a model. I'm thinking we're all just reifying our models." He spits the cube back into the glass.

In response, UGS asserts that models are necessary, perhaps unavoidable, to conduct any archaeological research.

"I know that's what Dr. Science tells you," he says, "but it's not my point anyway." His glassy eyes focus. "We can't afford any more models that make it easy to ignore the archaeology of entire regions! There's too much being destroyed out there for our models to be complicit in the destruction!" And with that the Pragmatist hit the nail on the head. It's the real problem, the looming crisis in Mississippian archaeology. "Hell," he segues, "there's now a whole industry of private corporate archaeologists out there working for the very developers who are busily destroying the past!"

UGS nods in acknowledgment. She's heard about this. Even Dr. Science laments the current state of affairs. The housing boom and growing consumer culture that began in the 1990s has led to runaway commercial development in many metropolitan areas. And of course American Indians built some of their most impressive centers in these same places: St. Louis, Missouri; Nashville, Tennessee; Chillicothe, Ohio; Evansville, Indiana. Bulldozers and land levelers are flattening the open woodlands and farmlands of recent memory to make way for shopping malls, superstores, and housing projects. There are so many developments that some profit-minded pseudo-archaeologists—some of the most despicable and poorly trained people to ever pick up a shovel—have made lucrative businesses out of servicing corporations that want nothing more than to get the archaeological remains out of their way.

"Do we need another shopping mall?" protests the Pragmatist. He goes on and on about a character he playfully calls Darth Evader. If there is a way to dodge a law or avoid finding anything of historical significance, Darth Evader knows it. He was never a very good archaeologist, the Pragmatist explains, so maybe it's understandable that he turned to the dark side. He is out to make a buck, and the corporations have bought and paid for him. "He's written off more archaeological sites than I've thought to dig!" exclaims the Pragmatist. "This guy could waltz into the middle of Cahokia," he insisted, "and if the money was right, he'd argue that there wasn't anything worth excavating there."

The two laugh, but UGS knows that the Pragmatist is deadly serious.

"Hell," he says, "it's infuriating. Pretty soon it'll be too late to know much more than we know now. Your generation is going to face a true archaeological crisis." And when UGS asks what can be done, he instructs, "Well, the first thing is to shit-can those silly models and pay attention to finding out what really happened in the past."

UGS doesn't get it. What makes rejecting archaeological models the place to start? The Pragmatist elaborates as best he can, explaining that the models in question are constraining and that newer theories—he isn't sure what to call them but they "deal with cultural landscapes, practice, agency, and some such stuff"—at least encourage us to look for who did what where in the past.

"Well, I guess," says UGS. But remembering Dr. Science's warning, she adds, "But can you ever really know much about specific individuals or historic events before written records? It doesn't seem like common sense. I think I need to stick to what is testable."

The Southern Pragmatist hears the influence of Dr. Science but marvels at how it has come to this, the young upstart across the table being more conservative and "processualist" in her attitudes than he, a worn-out government archaeologist (Hodder 1986; Meskell and Preucel 2004). Where are the idealistic youngsters and the skeptical graduate students who pushed the envelope of theory (Flannery 1976)? He finishes off his gin and tonic and smiles. "Hey," he says, "whose common sense are you referring to, yours or Dr. Science's?"

That's about as harsh as criticism gets in the South. And UGS takes it well. "I guess it still seems to me that a lot of good theory is being applied to Mississippian case studies," she says, "and it builds on the *solid research* of previous researchers like it should. I mean, take the recent pieces on corporate-network strategies" (King 2003; Trubitt 2000). "It's been proven" (she likes that word and repeats it) "*proven* that each underwent a transformation from corporate to network strategies through time! That explains their political development," she boldly asserts. "I'm thinking that Obion's leaders pursued corporate strategies initially and then switched to network-based tactics."

The Pragmatist looks at his empty glass and exhales as he orders another gin and tonic. After the brief pause, he asks slowly, "What were there, a few elite families running around Obion? How many other people were there? And what were all these other people doing while those leaders strategized? I mean, to think that a few elite strategies not only encompassed the thoughts and actions of all Mississippians, but that they were also somehow perfectly realized and put into effect without ever being resisted, thwarted, changed, or forgotten seems a stretch to me. You're not old enough to remember, but even Stalin and Khrushchev didn't have that kind of ability." The bartender hands the Pragmatist his next gin and tonic.

UGS is unsure what to say next. "Look, I understand what you're saying." Of course she does, after sitting through innumerable anthropology courses and viewing at least a couple of PBS television shows about the former Soviet Union. She continues, "But archaeologists *have* qualified their political models in order to recognize that chiefs did negotiate with followers" (Beck 2003; Earle 1997; Pauketat 1994). "Besides, how would you get at this archaeologically? Don't we have to focus on looking for what we know we can find? Don't we have to look at the facts?"

The Southern Pragmatist sits back in his chair, reminding himself that this young academic may be worth saving. So he reassures UGS. "Look, I don't mean to offend you, really. But think about what you're saying: 'If we don't think we can find it with our present methods, then it's not important?' Are you sure you mean that? Because it seems backward to me. That is, theorizing should lead us to, not away from, new questions. Otherwise it's not science at all. It's religion. And it plays right into the hands of my shadowy friend over there." He motions with his gin and tonic in the general direction of the beady-eyed character in the corner. It is Darth Evader.

Imagining Institutions

Despite never reaching resolution, the predinner conversation between UGS and the Pragmatist confronted, if obliquely, the *two salient theoretical problems with chiefdoms* gnawing at UGS. First, there really is a problem of exaggerating the importance of political administrations as if they were the sole source of social change. Second, people treat Mississippian chiefdoms like cookie-cutter copies of each other. There are serious and problematic implications associated with both.

The first salient problem seems to stem from the common belief that certain human beings naturally seek power and control, which somehow led in the past to chiefs whose lifelong goals involved seeking power and control. The instability of that chiefly government means that it would likely collapse within the span of a couple centuries only to reemerge somewhere else owing to the tendency of would-be chiefs to seek power and control.

As cited repeatedly by archaeologists around the world, the cycling model supposedly explains vast sweeps of human history. But is it even an *explanation* at all? That is, when that which is to be explained (the "explanandum") is the same as that which is used to explain (the "explanans"), this is usually called a *tautology*, as UGS recognizes. She has taken a philosophy course and, though a little irked by the Pragmatist, she can see that most chiefdom (and some state) models rely on notions of political structure that tend toward tautologies. That, or they are simply coarse *descriptions* of an archaeological pattern. Yes, people seem to have coalesced around administrative centers that later disintegrated. People may have recoalesced subsequently in the same region or elsewhere. This is the pattern. UGS now wonders, Is it also the process?

Let's give UGS some time to work through her thoughts. Were I to answer as the Pragmatist, the answer would be no. The macroscale pattern of political change is not the process. The Pragmatist's way of thinking follows the lead of Eric Wolf and the other political economists and neo-Marxists critical of the post-Enlightenment notion that societies were organic systems. If we reject that notion, then it becomes difficult to maintain the lengthy causal scenarios that we see in the Mississippian chiefdom literature and in the various modified social evolutionary explanations. One causal mechanism leads to another, bringing about either the rise or the fall of some political administration (Anderson 1994; Milner 1998; Pauketat 1992; Welch 1991).

The voices of dissent heard in the 1980s advanced some interesting theoretical arguments that promised to turn things around (Kristiansen 1991; McGuire 1983; Shanks and Tilley 1987; Upham 1990). Some of these lines of argumentation have continued into the present. Some have morphed into other interesting questions about human agency, memory, personhood, cultural landscapes, heterarchy, and object biographies (Ashmore 2004; Brumfiel 1992, 1995; Heckenberger 2005; Joyce 2004, 2005; Meskell 2004; Van Dyke and Alcock 2003). But the general upswelling of dissent was drowned out by the cacophony of localized debates over complexity and by confusion over alternative theoretical movements of the 1980s and 1990s. Postmodernism threw all of us off balance.

The debates over Chaco Canyon and Cahokia are prime examples but not isolated ones (see chapters 6–7). They are replicated elsewhere in the Southwest, Mesoamerica, and Mesopotamia, if not in most regions where significant archaeological research is under way (chapter 7). People with different epistemological underpinnings and theoretical agendas argue past one another *supposedly* using the same data (Pauketat 2004:68). One side, called exaggerationalist or hyperbolic, includes most people who espouse mother culture scenarios. The other is sometimes termed minimalist and is usually based on a general belief in the idea that societies evolve from within.[1]

This labeling and debating can strain one's desire to engage in high-level theorizing. And so appeals are made to common sense (e.g., Yoffee's Rule). Claims are made that the simplest explanations are the best (e.g., Occam's Razor). And there are assertions that some cultural relationships are inherently more testable than others (e.g., Hawkes's ladder; Hodder 2004:21). But all such appeals, claims, assertions, or counterarguments are also founded on theoretical assumptions that are as complex and as problematic as any (Alt 2005). What's the difference between the opposing positions, Rules, or Razors? The answer is hidden by scientific ideologies. Certain arguments have come to be accepted as common sense, for no other reason than that's what most people assume based on their preconceptions. It's not that one or another argument is more or less testable. Rather, some arguments only *seem* more easily verifiable because few others argue the point.

In the Mississippian Southeast, such scientific ideologies (think of them as little paradigms) were derived from what had been, for Dr. Science and others of his generation, cutting-edge chiefdom theory: political structure—the various "institutions" (organizations with their own cultural norms or rules of behavior)—is an adaptive mechanism that, within certain environmental parameters, causes societies to change in one way or another. If some still find it reasonable, it's because there aren't many good alternatives. Newer models haven't progressed much beyond the old distinctions made between the managerial and the political theories of social evolution.

Consider the latest dual-processual approaches, the recent apical-constitutive model (Beck 2003), or even Charles Stanish's (2003) "materialist and agency approach to modeling cultural evolution." Basically all draw on the old managerial–political distinction, while collapsing the two modes as if they were phases of one political–institutional process. A polity's leaders could enact corporate strategies for a while, thoughtfully managing the interests of its people, before switching to tactics that benefit a few politicos, or vice versa. Verifiable it would seem, or so UGS hoped. But in the end, such bipolar scenarios retain the old social evolutionary logic of change, placing causal emphasis on either rational decision making or principles of administration. So, the question inevitably slips into tautology. Political institutions evolved, it seems, and then took on a life of their own. The larger histories of how they formed and how different interest groups negotiated for power are moot. In a disturbing archaeological inversion of ethnological accounts of chiefdoms, people are epiphenomenal to the evolving political structure.

But what exactly are political institutions? How might they determine the shape of society like some great, unseen hand? And where are they? Do archaeologists dig up institutions? These are questions that I once posed to Dr. Science with regard to Mississippians. He was unimpressed by the theoretical intent of the questions. He answered by rote as if he was lecturing his seminar. "The most reasonable interpretation of Mississippian societies follows V. James Knight's (1986) recognition that the communal, ancestor-temple institution is reflected in the Mississippian platform mound and charnel house complex, while the institution of the warrior chief is indicated by Southeastern ceremonial complex iconography. These institutions," he concluded, "appear to have evolved as components of the Mississippian adaptation to the floodplains of the southern Midwest and Southeast during the Medieval Warm Period of the tenth through thirteenth centuries A.D."

"Ah," I said, and walked off. No reason to think that I could engage this guy in an interesting two-way conversation. But later I thought about his lecture. Dr. Science actually seemed to concede—unintentionally, like all evolutionists—that archaeologists can't find the institutions themselves. Institutions have material correlates, they'd say, but are themselves immaterial (Pauketat 2003a). And yet such archaeologists want to believe that institutions, once evolved, are permanent and irreducible such that they determine subsequent social evolutionary developments.

Take, for example, the political institutions that supposedly evolved out of chiefdoms to form the state—variously defined as a bureaucratic system of government or an all-encompassing hegemonic society. Kent Flannery (1999a:15) believes that the buildings, tombs, and hierarchical arrays of settlements "reflect the social, political, and religious institutions of the archaic state" as defined by "anthropology and political science" (not by archaeology). If the state emerged someplace in the past, then archaeologists will find palaces, royal burials, and a four-tiered hierarchy of sites (from the capital city on down to ordinary residential sites) within the bounds of the state.

Now, contrast that with the view of Norman Yoffee (2005:228), who has concluded that the "central myth about the study of the earliest states . . . is that there was something that could be called *the* archaic state, and that all of the earliest states were simply variations on this model." For a more radical view, contrast the view of sociologist Philip Abrams (1988), who speaks of the state in general as an illusion. "The state" he says, "is not an object" (Abrams 1988:76). It is an "ideological project" that "conceals real history . . . behind an a-historical mask of legitimating illusion" (Abrams 1988:76–77).

For Abrams, the state does not have an institutional reality except that people believe that it does. It is not a set of institutions at all (contra Flannery 1999a) but an aggregate of practices and representations of people orchestrated to continuously regenerate the perception of those institutions. In the same vein, I have argued that, technically, the state is always in a state of becoming. State institutions "never existed outside their continuous reproduction through practice. It does not matter that people in the past might have been cognizant of some structures [or institutions]. . . . These things, by themselves, did not constrain practices" (Pauketat 2003b:44). People—*acting as if these things mattered*—constrained practices.

None of this is to say that, in many times and places, political institutions weren't "real" in some sense. But they were realities, and not our own impositions, if and *only if* people in those times and places *embodied* the institutions, *lived* the institutions, or *acted* as if they were real. The embodiment or the action—the practicing of the institutions—was reality, not the institutions themselves, which would have ceased to exist without the practices. These days, I find such (phenomeno-) logic comforting. Things could change for the better if we wanted them to. Look at the so-called institutions of the former Soviet Union. They ceased to exist in the span of months in 1991 because people simply stopped living them.

Or take the Mississippian chiefdom, please. Based on a series of historic accounts from across the sixteenth- through eighteen-century Southeast, V. James Knight (1986) reasonably concluded that there was a suite of political–religious practices involving the curation of ancestors' bones in special charnel houses, or temples, atop platform mounds. Hernando de Soto's men described the contents and significance of such buildings from South Carolina west to Arkansas (where they watched one war party defile the temple of an enemy's town). And at most Mississippian towns, there seems to have been at least one earthen pyramid topped by a temple (Holley 1999; see chapter 4). Knight also observed that temples and temple mounds were at the heart of "a threefold system of inferred cult institutions . . .with a chiefly cult of nobility contraposed against a communal earth/fertility cult . . . [and with] a third priestly type of cult institution . . . in a mediatory structural role" (Knight 1986:681).

Borrowing an idea from Reinhard Bernbeck (n.d.), one might say that political–religious practices are the central "anchoring" practices that continuously produced Mississippian chiefdoms. But rather than using Knight's insights as a starting point for research into the locally divergent histories of the temples and mounds of Mississippianization, Dr. Science concludes that, without exception, mounds were the material correlates of specific institutions. Accordingly, each mound had a discrete function that, in typical teleological fashion, he believes is the explanation for why the mound was constructed in the first place. "History shmistory," he told UGS. "Archaeology is a science."

But we should give Mississippian temple and mound histories some additional thought. How far back can we project the temple-related institutions? Were Mississippian temple practices politicized versions of pre-Mississippian ones? And how many of the people somehow affiliated with a temple had the same understanding of what the temple and mound represented? Whose bones were kept in a particular temple? Whose were excluded? Who labored on a particular pyramid, when, and why? Did they do it to build an impressive platform for a specific functional reason? Or is there another way of thinking about construction?

Elsewhere I have argued that "no Mississippian platforms and few other central features were constructed as one-time labor projects. All appear, at present, to have been incremental constructions, with the early 'stages' of some . . . mounds being no more than sheer mantles of silt or sand laid down to ritually sterilize the area. From this, we may infer that the central point of mound construction was not simply to construct an imposing tumulus" (Pauketat 2000b:120).

Taking that statement a step further, Susan Alt and I later proposed "appearances are deceptive . . . [and we cannot] assume that all flat-topped pyramid mounds—even within just one region or during just one phase— meant the same thing or functioned in the same ways" (Pauketat and Alt 2003:163). Both the meanings and the proposed functions of any mound might well have been contested through time at some central place. After all, pyramids were "features of living landscapes, observed by all, recollected differently by many, [and] liable to be co-opted" by communities, factions, or specific individuals (Pauketat and Alt 2003:171).

The variability of mound meaning and function would have been exacerbated by gaps and hiatuses between mound constructions at specific places or between regions. In the end, many different people continuously built mound meanings and functions, including those in attendance at huge certain public ceremonies and those with varying memories of what mounds meant. At Cahokia, at least, this was happening before pan-eastern Mississippian patterns had been established (see chapter 4). The mound builders probably came from many different backgrounds, with at least as many different understandings of what earthen construction meant. So the mounds were not simply *reflections* of political institutions as they were. Mounds and mound building were the institutions *coming into being*.

When did such institutions cease becoming? Never. Institutions are always under construction, literally and figuratively. Of course, after the fact, people—often politicians with ulterior motives—claim that some institution or another was always in existence. But their political narratives are always based on their political interests at the time. Who knows what the original practices meant. For instance, possibly the outcome of their pyramid building was a far cry from their original motivations for building with earth. We don't know. And we won't know until we stop pretending that the process is somehow devoid of people, or until we actually examine the materiality of mound building as a process in which people also built institutions. In short, we need to examine how the cultural power of these ordinary mound builders caused the ascent of chiefs, not the other way around.

"Who made them lords?" indeed.

It's Déjà Vu All Over Again

This second salient problem—that Mississippian societies were cookie-cutter copies of each other—was noticed decades ago by Bruce Smith (1978). He observed "there has been a tendency over the last 10 years to think of a single static model of Mississippian settlement patterning [and to] focus upon the overall uniformity of Mississippian settlement patterns" (Smith 1978: 479). And while this may have been justified to some extent, it nonetheless "diverted attention from the related research question of variation in Mississippian settlement patterning." That was nearly thirty years ago. Today the problem is worse than either Bruce Smith originally stated or that UGS yet understands and lies hidden by concepts that (1) artificially synchronize our chronologies and (2) collapse organizational variability into "the Mississippian chiefdom."

Chronologies first. If we assume that Mississippian chiefdoms were cookie-cutter copies of each other, that they all "arrived at generally comparable chiefdom levels of organization, seemingly by roughly similar developmental pathways" (Smith 1990:1), then we needn't look for historical linkages between regions and peoples, and thus we needn't refine our chronologies. Many assume (fallaciously) that the generic evolutionary causes of Mississippianism lie in an "Emergent Mississippian" period, around A.D. 700–1050 (smacked down by Fortier and McElrath 2002; Muller 1997).

This assumption leads to the second hidden trap: we fail to seek and find organizational variability. Any meager, coarse-grained data can be fit into the latest political–economic model, which translates into self-fulfilling research designs that do not allow the collection of sufficient data to even *identify* variability. Such research merely reifies an old sophisticated delusion. Thus Mississippian chiefdom models are *not* being "separated from undesirable connotations" and are *not* "facilitating comparisons" (King 2003:4).

Some researchers do not wish to find variability and intentionally seek not to refine their chronologies. Take Dr. Science. He rationalizes this avoidance by adapting "Yoffee's Rule." Weary of claims that this or that polity in the ancient world was or was not similar to a Mesopotamian state, Norman Yoffee (1993:69; 2005:41) cleverly declares, "If you can argue whether a society is a state or isn't, then it isn't." Dr. Science takes this rule one step further, converting it into a minimalist law: "If you can argue whether some Mississippian case was significantly different from the rest, then it wasn't."[2]

Of course, if you think about it, a broad adaptation of Yoffee's Rule almost got Preston, Pat, Dave, me, and the others shot outside of Marianna, Arkansas: if we had to argue about our permission to be digging in that sorghum field, then we didn't have it (even though we did). What Dr. Science didn't (and probably never will) consider in his commonsense adaptation of Yoffee's Rule was that by this standard, there can never be a new idea. There can be no change in social or scientific attitudes. Conservative arguments, as arguments, ensure the maintenance of the status quo. There can be no scientific paradigm shifts (Einstein would have been lucky to publish a single journal article). Women would have never been given the vote (too many men would have heatedly argued the point). American Indians or African American slaves would have never been allowed to claim the status of human beings (a majority of Europeans clearly argued otherwise in the sixteenth century). And since archaeologists love to argue, Yoffee's Rule and its potential corollaries would ensure that not a single new or controversial theory would ever again be considered in archaeology. The common sense of the powerbrokers in archaeology who set the agenda would reign forever (in the spirit of Yoffee and Sherratt 1993).

Such a commonsense and conservative rule is consistent with the minimalist approach Dr. Science takes to research. He actually does not believe in theorizing at a high level. He hasn't read much social theory and doesn't think people should bother with Rousseau, Foucault, Merleau-Ponty, or Marx, never mind Judith Butler. Instead, he believes that their big, speculative ideas are outside the realm of his brand of science. He doesn't recognize a central role for storytelling in archaeology or that "having a story in mind is necessary to help us think while we dig" (Hodder 1999:55). Instead, as Dr. Science understands it, research involves testing single, simple (he would say elegant) hypotheses one by one, and he seems to think that small-scale excavations are sufficient to test all of his hypotheses. And given *his* hypotheses, he's probably right.

The approach truly irks the Southern Pragmatist. Recently, for instance, Dr. Science hypothesized that he'd find houses at a tenth-century settlement in southeast Missouri, proving whether it was a residential site or a vacant ceremonial center. "Sure enough," the Pragmatist later relayed to me, "one test square, one house located, one hypothesis affirmed!" (Well, not quite, since Dr. Science would say we'd have to find a second house to actually affirm that there were *houses* at the site. But that's for next year.) "If that's science," concluded the Southern Pragmatist, "then Dr. Science is Albert Einstein." And Dr. Science might agree. He likes to act as an omniscient arbiter of archaeological research. He's personally shot down several recent research proposals, including one by the Southern Pragmatist. "The proposal fails in its inductive approach to the past," he wrote in his review of the Pragmatist's proposal, "as evidenced by the breadth of his proposed excavations to recover evidence indirectly related to his hypothetical scenario. He's seeking to collect too much data."

The Building Blocks of Minimalism

It's sad, really. Dr. Science trains his students to believe that a modicum of data is sufficient for all testable hypotheses. And he's not alone. There's a whole culture of archaeological delusion, and it acts as a security blanket. Larger issues, historical details, and social theory scare some people. Uniformity, changelessness, homogeneity are things Dr. Science can wrap his brain around. And he wants people to behave as he does. He truly likes what, perhaps appropriately, might be called the "building block" approach to explanation. Originating in the behaviorism of the New Archaeology, the building block approach remains deeply embedded within archaeological theories of Mississippian and chiefdoms (Flannery 1976; Muller 1997; O'Brien 2001).

The approach is simple and the people who are imagined to populate the past are rational. It recognizes households and communities as static and uniform organizational units, building blocks with typical forms from which societies were constructed. The household (note the singular form, as in "the Mississippian household") is said to have been a "largely autonomous" unit that made most economic decisions (Muller 1997:280). Above that is the community, an organic organization "scaled up from the household" (Muller 1997:192). The community too, it is claimed, was self-sufficient (Milner 1998:74). Finally, there is the society, presumably composed of several communities together. Fortunately, with all the autonomy and self-sufficiency already claimed from below, there wasn't much left for the society to do. Thus the Mississippian household is a microcosm of society (Muller 1997:279).

For this reason, it's difficult for building block advocates to imagine that households—perceiving risks or inappropriate economic demands from above—would tolerate much suprahousehold administration. Household economics and politics, apparently, mix about as well as oil and water. Consequently building block advocates say that if households didn't like the management, they'd vote with their feet and move to a better land (Sahlins 1972). Accordingly neither communal relationships nor the ideas of household and community could be politicized (Pauketat 1994, 2000a). The "communal realm, or the domestic economy" existed "outside the political realm" (Pauketat 2000a:17). People presumably wouldn't tolerate the usurpation of their microeconomic rights. Thus nothing too complex could have ever existed, right?

For such researchers, there is only one answer (yes), which is key in helping us understand the ways that Occam's Razor and Yoffee's Rule have stifled interpretations and led to vituperative debates among Mississippianists. To cut to the chase, certain researchers, based in a building block mind-set, *can't imagine* a historical situation in which autonomous producers, without some insurmountable external pressure, would let themselves be duped into a large-scale political entity. Consequently these researchers reason, quite logically, that no polity too complex or society too populous could have existed in the past, period. They cannot understand how a population, say Cahokia's, could have grown larger than the carrying capacity of the immediate environs. To do so would be illogical or not reasonable (Milner 1998:75, 123).

And so it is not surprising that, as noted by Norman Yoffee, Suzanne Fish, and George Milner (1999:267), southeastern archaeologists are "to a man, downsizers." Try to imagine a range of political possibilities, small to big, simple to complex, or local to far-flung, and these downsizers regularly come down on the side of the bare minimum. James Stoltman (1991), grappling with the obvious effects of Cahokia in a northern frontier zone (from Wisconsin to Iowa and Minnesota), wonders if such minimalism isn't counterproductive. Jon Muller (1997:386), turning the tables, calls such a reaction the "exaggerationalist" view. The truth of the matter is, as so amply demonstrated over the past twenty years, debatable.

What with the legacy of the old mound builder myth and the lingering effects of racism against American Indians in the contemporary world, a position that understates American Indian achievements seems unwise (Kehoe 1998; Pauketat 2004). It also seems to run contrary to the scientific position, which seeks the most appropriate explanation *relative to some explicit theoretical vantage point* (Alt 2005). As a result, I remain happily uncertain that minimalist arguments can be sustained over the long run in the face of both good theorizing and adequate archaeological information. The weaknesses of minimalism are evident in a contradiction inherent to a building block approach.

That contradiction stems from a point on which everyone seems to agree: Mississippian chiefdoms embody considerable variation at the same time that both concepts—Mississippian and chiefdom—imply in-group similarities. George Milner and Sissel Schroeder (1999:96) recognize the problems caused by the "imposition of altogether too restrictive and static cultural categories on archaeological materials." Yet at the same time they believe that

> variation in the best known Mississippian societies, from the smallest to the largest, can be accommodated by simple models consisting of similarly constituted units. . . . It is not at all clear that even the largest Mississippian societies that encompassed several mound centers, such as the Cahokia sociopolitical system, were anything other than bigger versions of their smaller counterparts. (Milner and Schroeder 1999:96)

Well, if it isn't clear that size matters, how do we clarify it? Let's begin by clarifying that what we *shouldn't* do is ignore it. In this case, ignorance is hidden in a graph, one that many Mississippianists and I have used in the past: a common diagram showing simple chiefdoms, consisting of settlements arrayed around single centers, becoming complex chiefdoms when each simple grouping is attached to one overarching paramount center (see figure 2.1). The structure of the component simple chiefdoms is left unaltered, even as the structure of the entire complex entity is simply a large version of the lower-order structure (Anderson 1994; Emerson 1997a; Milner 1998; Welch 1991; compare Pauketat 1994:figure 2.4). Complex chiefdoms are simply larger versions of petty chiefdoms, with no qualitative difference and no long-term historical effects. When the top block is knocked off, a complex chiefdom becomes a series of simple chiefdoms again.

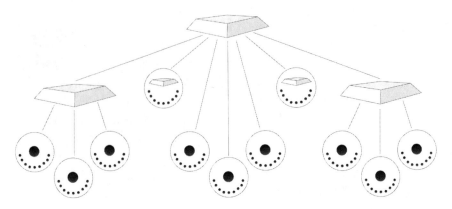

Figure 2.1. Building block diagram of chiefdom settlement hierarchy (after Milner 1998:figure 1.5)

Apparently this applies to the most complex of chiefdoms as well as to the smallest local polities described in historic accounts (LaVere 1998; Hann 1988; Muller 1997; Worth 1998) to the true archaeological behemoth in the American Bottom, centered at Cahokia (Pauketat 2004). It ignores the so-called paramount chiefdoms identified in the written accounts of sixteenth-century Spaniards (Anderson 1996; Smith 2003). These were seemingly comparable to what has elsewhere been called a "chiefdom confederacy" (Gibson 1995). Apparently they can be ignored because they are archaeologically invisible, or so it is said. And so in the building block approach, size doesn't matter. History doesn't matter. And organizational variation, presumably a function of both size and history, is noted but then ignored.

Dr. Science might say that all models are simplifications of reality. Originally, building block models helped tie the neoevolutionary models to the realities of regional data, facilitating comparisons between regions (Flannery 1976). Not a bad thing. However, in today's archaeology, building block models are egregious oversimplifications. The contradiction embodied in various attempts to accommodate Mississippian archaeological remains with simple models is, I think, becoming increasingly evident with greater accumulations of archaeological data in some regions (see chapters 4–6).

Then again, one sure way to continue to delude ourselves is to shut our eyes to the variability around us. It's comforting, perhaps. If we already know the answers and our simple models encapsulate the processes of chiefdom coalescence and fragmentation, why worry about digging more than a few test holes? Why worry about the land leveling of the central Mississippi valley? Affirming preconceptions means you needn't worry about looking down the barrel of an angry farmer's shotgun.

But those sorts of questions and data sets are woefully insufficient to answer the big questions—the origins of war, transition to agriculture, or emergence of civilization sorts of questions. I don't know about Dr. Science, but finding answers to those questions is the reason I became an archaeologist.

A Southern Barbeque

Although she doesn't know it yet, the same goes for UGS. The moderately heated conversation she had with the Southern Pragmatist in the bar has been defused by the time they wander off in search of some Memphis barbeque. They walk and talk, and the Pragmatist reminds UGS about the importance of history, at both large and small scales. At one time or another, he says, James Griffin, Robert Hall, and Alice Kehoe have argued that Mississippian history was contingent on big events, such as contact with Mesoamerica (Griffin 1966; Hall 2000; Kehoe 2005). Now that would be a real historical constraint, wouldn't it? In the same way, some have viewed other native North American cultures as contingent on contact with Cahokia (Dincauze and Hasenstab 1989; Peregrine 1992; Stoltman 2000).

In response, UGS explains that Dr. Science would just as soon believe in the tooth fairy as in any of this. Along with most of the archaeological establishment, he scoffs at such ideas, unsupported by what he believes to be his own thorough reading of the data. "There is no credible evidence," he would say in class, "that significant intercultural contacts ever occurred between Mesoamerica and Cahokia or Cahokia and the Northeast." But UGS, unlike her mentor, is willing to listen and think about the historical possibilities. UGS and the Pragmatist walk on and begin talking about how various Mississippian places might be interconnected in one way or another.

A few blocks later, they catch the scent of hickory and pork wafting from behind a one-room shack named BB's Barbeque. BB is a large woman behind the counter with a note pad. She takes their order and the Pragmatist, once seated, picks up the conversation where they left it off on the street. "So," he summarizes to UGS, "I've heard it said that migrants founded Obion—maybe Cahokians—before moving south, on to Shiloh, just north of Corinth, Mississippi, you know."

UGS knows. Dave Anderson has been digging at Shiloh for the National Park Service. But she is still processing the rest as the Pragmatist continues. "And from there, they might easily have moved into Georgia or Alabama."

UGS hasn't heard of this before and thinks it smacks of old-fashioned thinking, relying too much on migration to explain how ideas—in this case Mississippianism itself—moved from here to there. Of course, it *was* just that. But is that necessarily wrong? As she listens, the voice of Dr. Science plays in her mind. "No!" it reminds her. "The simplest evolutionary explanations are best! There is no incontrovertible evidence for any of this!"

Still, UGS wants to hear more. "What do you mean? Who thinks that Cahokians were behind the founding of all of these Middle Mississippian sites? Isn't that like the old Mother Culture idea of the Olmecs in Mexico that I read about in the *New York Times*?"

At that moment, BB appears at the table with two pulled pork sandwiches, coleslaw, and huge piles of baked beans. The Pragmatist, realizing that he is finally getting across to UGS, smiles. "I don't know what to think about this yet," he says. "There may be more to that Mother Culture idea than we've realized. Think of it," he wonders aloud, "there was nothing else like Cahokia . . . ever . . . at any time before or after. You mean to tell me that it didn't have an effect unlike any before or after? It's like I told you earlier," he said, "you've got to think big, outside the box Dr. Science has put you in." After a moment the Pragmatist adds, "Start by rereading anything ever written by Robert Hall (1997). In my grad school days, we all thought he was a little too far-out. But," he says, "it turns out that Bob was just far-out ahead of his time. After you do that, look at the recent stuff by Ken Sassaman and Charlie Cobb. Then get some of your own data in hand and rethink the possibilities for yourself. Yep," the Pragmatist concludes, "forget the old chiefdom scenarios. Even if it's not what Dr. Science wants you to think."

It certainly isn't. Dr. Science emphatically argued against using the concept of city, Mother Culture, and "Cahokia-centric" views being pitched to UGS across the Formica table in BB's Barbeque. Where is the cycling in such interpretations? How about corporate network strategies? Or chiefs? Perhaps, UGS thinks, the Pragmatist's migration theory isn't so far removed from Service's views of how chiefdom-level societies expanded (Service 1962). But otherwise, there is a Grand Canyon of theory separating Dr. Science from the odd mix of old and new ideas the Pragmatist has been bouncing around.

In recent years, one or two people have tried to bridge that canyon. "You really should be thinking about culture contacts and migrations," the Pragmatist later suggests. They had walked back to the conference hotel and night was now upon them. UGS is attempting to cut out, but the Pragmatist keeps talking. "You know, John Blitz and Karl Lorenz (2002) have done some rethinking of the migration issue, coming up with a solid argument in support of Frank Schnell's (1981) suggestion that Mississippians intruded into the Chattahoochee River area around A.D. 1100."

"I didn't know that," UGS says, beginning to flag from the day, the beer, the pulled pork, and all those beans. How, she wonders, can this old guy keep going?

"They've turned up Moundville-like pottery and Tennessee-Cumberland–style long-stemmed ax heads ("pole spuds") at palisaded Rood-phase frontier sites, including Cemochechobee and Cool Branch (Blitz and Lorenz 2002; Schnell et al. 1981; Pauketat 1983). It's just like what Gordon Willey, James Griffin, A. R. Kelly, and others argued for the Macon Plateau site up in Ocmulgee (Hally 1994). Down on the Chattahoochee, it seems that the newcomers inserted themselves into a no-man's-land between two non-Mississippian groups. It should make you wonder about Obion."

"Yes, it does," UGS feigns.

The Pragmatist does not respond, his attention being distracted, it seems, by something or someone behind her. UGS takes it as her opportunity to wish him a good evening, and she slips through the hotel's revolving door. Looking behind her, she sees through the rotating glass the Southern Pragmatist looking rather cross as he approaches a man loitering in the shadows outside the hotel entrance. She recognizes the loiterer as the slimy character from the bar—Darth Evader again.

51

Notes

1. Occasionally a researcher identified with an extreme in one research area assumes an alternate pose in another. Gregory Johnson (1989) advocates centralized tributary economies (chiefdom) models for the Late Ubaid period, placing him on the maximalist side in the Near East (Adams 2003; Yoffee 2005). However, he thinks that Chaco Canyon has an egalitarian basis, placing him on the minimalist side of that debate (Lekson 1999a, 2005).

2. Stephen Lekson offers this corollary to Yoffee's Rule: "If you can argue about whether a case is or is not a state, then it's really interesting" (Lekson, personal communication, May 2006).

BREAKING THE LAW OF CULTURAL DOMINANCE

The great tragedy of science—the slaying of a beautiful theory by an ugly fact.

—Thomas Henry Huxley

That night in her Memphis hotel room, stomach churning with beer, barbeque, and beans, UGS dreams in fits and starts. Two versions of knowing the past—Dr. Science's and the Pragmatist's—slug it out in her dreams, while an ominous presence lurks in the shadows of her own doubts. Is there a right and a wrong? Whose common sense has she invoked? And how can she, in her uncertainty, deduce truth from all the arguments and assertions? Through the long night the characters come to her, spouting intellectual position statements and platitudes, while the specter of the shadowy corporate threat lurks behind her. She needs to step back and gain some perspective on the whole, as we all do from time to time.

We'll let UGS sleep for the next three chapters while we gain some perspective of our own by reviewing pre-Columbian developments in eastern North America. Our review starts with a brief reconsideration of what happened when the torch of chiefdom studies was passed from ethnology to archaeology in the heyday of the New Archaeology. Elman Service, Morton Fried, and other neoevolutionists were attempting to see order in the morass of ethnographies and ethnohistories of the previous century of anthropology. To do this, they identified the common attributes of certain societies and projected how such attributes might have functioned in the past. However, because they (and all ethnologists) lacked historical perspective, the neoevolutionists necessarily explained change not with reference to actual histories but to an abstract model of cultural systems derived from looking at many societies at single moments in time.

Please note that doing this involves a leap of faith that includes accepting a sophisticated delusion—societies are systems that can be explained using what we know from any single moment in time. But here's the rub. Try explaining the politicians, populations, and social problems in the world today through a comparative study of contemporary nation-states. Ignore the history of European colonization and missionization. Ignore the slave trade, transglobal mercantilism, and imperial expansions that linked the Old and New Worlds. Pay no attention to migrations, ethnic cleansing, world wars, and the unequal accumulation of economic capital. Forget social movements, rebellions, and revolutions of the past. Don't consider the Cold War, Sputnik, computers, or the Internet. And then try to explain our present-day world. You couldn't, without deluding yourself (or, were you a politician, without deluding the masses). Same thing goes for ancient eastern North America.

Lost in Translation

Despite what the comparative, neoevolutionary synthesizers say, their conclusions are not entirely consonant with the historical and ethnographic literature on non-Western peoples. A quick review of classic chiefdom studies, for instance, illustrates two salient characteristics of such peoples lost when translated into a comparative synthesis: organizational variability and cultural plurality. Before Service and Fried, anthropologists—even those heavily biased toward systemic or functionalist points of view (such as British social anthropologists)—stressed the multiple sorts and scales of political practices.

Organizational Variability

These earlier anthropologists spoke of low-order political organizations of chieftains and councils, and they documented powerful chiefly overlords with despotic manners. In historic accounts from North

America, Mesoamerica, Asia, and Africa, the rule of these latter individuals might be limited to one or two generations (Powhatan, Lord 8
Deer, Kdam Yi, Shaka Zulu; Barker 1992; Gluckman 1940; Hickey 1982;
Joyce et al. 2004; Rountree and Turner 1998; Service 1975). In Africa,
there were dynasties or would-be dynasties of rulers based on notions of
divine kingship, presumably based in turn on social memories of phara-
onic Egypt (Evans Pritchard 1948; Frazer 1947). In Polynesia, the supernatural status of paramount leaders hinged on their exoticism as "stranger
kings" (Hoecart, cited by Sahlins 1985). Contrast these with the gold-
hoarding hereditary leaders of tiny Coclé provinces in Panama, less se-
curely ensconced in their political offices and emulating what they knew
of both Mayan and South American kingdoms and buying off allies to
stave off being deposed (Helms 1979).

Neither divine nor desperate, political confederacies existed elsewhere
that unified disparate political entities to some degree. For instance, in
early Ireland, chiefdom confederacies emerged composed of "a number
of genealogically related and unrelated chiefdoms which were unified
through coercion or common agreement" and "legitimized through genealogies which promulgated a fiction of common identity through consanguineal links between founders" (Gibson 1995:123). In eastern North
America, similar chiefdom confederacies have been labeled paramount-
cies (Anderson 1994, 1996; Smith 2003). Interestingly, some doubt the
historic accounts that speak of such larger-order formations, presumably
since their archaeological signatures do not include an obvious correlation
with a settlement hierarchy (Muller 1997).

Also interesting are the similarities between descriptions of such
chiefdom confederacies and certain definitions of formative states. According to Henry Wright and Gregory Johnson (1975:267),

> decision-making activities [in states] are differentiated or specialized
> in two ways. First, there is a hierarchy of control in which the highest
> level involves making decisions about other, lower-order decisions. . . .
> Second, the effectiveness of such a hierarchy of control is facilitated by
> the complementary specialization of information processing . . . [which]
> enables the efficient handling of the masses of information and deci-
> sions moving through a control hierarchy with three or more levels, and
> undercuts the independence of subordinates.

That is, a state possesses a bureaucracy while a nonstate society's administration "is not itself internally differentiated" (Wright 1977:381). The bureaucracy is born out of the political dynamics of complex chiefdoms, as reiterated by Joyce Marcus (1999:92). "The state formed in the context of a group of competing chiefdoms when one of those chiefdoms succeeded in subjugating its neighbors, turning them into the provinces of a larger, unitary state. Elsewhere, Flannery and I have presented evidence that the Zapotec state formed in a similar way" (Marcus and Flannery 1996:155).

The state so defined seems to hinge on two distinctions. First, there is the separation of bureaucracy (the state's internal governmental structure) from the process of confederation (an external unification of disparate peoples). Second, there is the fine line drawn between subjugation and incorporation, or what Guillermo Algaze (1993:9–10) calls formal and informal modes of domination (cf. Yoffee et al. 1999:269). But isn't bureaucratization closely related to confederation, and subjugation to incorporation (the latter being, in modern global–political doublespeak, "freedom spreading")? And if they are (or were in certain ancient cases), then don't evolutionist claims that some states were "pristine" while other "chiefdom confederacies" were "secondary" fall apart (see chapter 7)?

Perhaps, in light of the historical overview in chapter 1, we should question the utility of calling any political formation pristine. Polynesian-style governance did not evolve on each island but was spread by outrigger from island to island. Iron Age African states or protostates were composite megacommunities that, more than likely, harkened back to the archetypal kingdoms along the Nile or the Ivory and Gold Coasts (Bondarenko 2004; Stahl 2001). The Araucanian state in Argentina and Chile, south of the Inka empire, emerged from a confederation of territorial divisions administered by a paramount leader (Dillehay 1995). Southeast Asian theater states were structured by the trading kingdoms and empires in Cambodia, Thailand, and China (Coe 2003; Geertz 1980; Junker 2004).

The larger transregional or global history in which each case is embedded means that pristine political development was impossible. Moreover, no so-called chiefdom or state evolved in isolation from the inside out. All were composite formations that, if anything, developed both from the inside out and the outside in (Chapman 2003).

Cultural Pluralism

Archaeological views of chiefdom evolution are based on certain "classic" ethnological or historical studies: the Kongo kingdom of sixteenth-century central Africa, the Powhatan of sixteenth- and early-seventeenth-century Virginia, the Natchez of seventeenth-century Louisiana, the Alur of early-twentieth-century central Africa (Southall 1956), and the Kachin of pre-1940s Burmese highlands (Leach 1965). In each case, there are descriptions of the ethnic or linguistic pluralism *within* the political region being analyzed.

Both the so-called Kongo and Natchez kingdoms were historically wedged between groups within regions suffering overall depopulation. Wracked by the slave trade, the Kongo kingdom's political power was at its maximum as it continuously relocated and incorporated disparate African groups outside its political boundaries into its tributary economy (Ekholm 1972). The same goes for the Natchez polity, and the other puissant provinces of historic-era southeastern North America (Williams 1930; Muller 1997:63). As disease and death in warring took its toll, the Natchez incorporated others into their polity, and were ultimately themselves scattered and reincorporated into the towns of other confederacies (Iberville and Du Pratz, in Swanton 1998; Muller 1997). Historic confederacies and provinces in pre-Columbian eastern North America were multiethnic aggregations that some feel may have been on the road to state formation (Muller and Wilcox 1999:164).

Another historic political formation of note was the Powhatan of Virginia. The Algonquian-speaking Powhatan people might not have been multiethnic, but they were circumscribed socially by other "Algonquian-speaking chiefdoms . . . to the north and south of them, Iroquoian-speaking tribes or chiefdoms . . . in the inner coastal plain to the south of them, and Siouan-speaking tribes or chiefdoms . . . to the west (Rountree and Turner 1998:278; Rountree 1989). They were constantly at war with these outsiders, and Powhatan himself engaged in wars to eliminate these ethnic others, "depopulating and then repopulating" outlying territories with loyalists and training youth outside of kin groups to be aggressive (Rountree and Turner 1998:281, 285–286), in a historical process paralleling the rise of Shaka Zulu in early-nineteenth-century South Africa (cf. Service 1975).

As described in more recent times, both the Alur (and other African polities) and the Kachin (and other Southeast Asian provinces) were fundamentally multiethnic populations. Aidan Southall's (1956) classic study of Alur society, consisting of a series of quasi-autonomous political chiefdoms linked together in what he called a "segmentary state" exemplifies the pan-African pattern of colonial-era political formation comprised of heterogeneous amalgams of assimilated foreigners, captives, and migrants in multiethnic or multitribal and polyglot political communities (Kuper 1965; Read 1970). Likewise, Edmund Leach's account of the dialectical relationship of the Kachin of highland Burma implicates something very similar. There, periods of more centralized *(gumsa)* social relations alternated with less centralized *(gumlao)* marriage alliance networks, a historical situation cited by many archaeologists as the premier example of chiefdom cycling. Presumably such oscillation in political structure was an inherent quality of the pristine evolution of chiefdoms, Mississippian and otherwise.

However, Leach (1965:36) clearly locates the sociopolitical dynamic in the larger historical landscapes of nineteenth-century Burma. Highland Kachin politicos married into prestigious Shan royal families who were strategically situated with respect to trade routes connecting China and Southeast Asia (Friedman and Rowlands 1978). With historic migrations of the Shan well documented and the Kachin suspected, it is difficult today to reconcile historical fact with Leach's (1965:231) ecological explanation: "Kachin society as we know it today is . . . organized to cope with the ecological situation that exists in the Kachin Hills." This despite the obvious linguistic diversity where certain Kachin dialects were "widely scattered and territorially jumbled up with other languages. . . . the intermingling of language groups is often too fine grained to be shown on any small scale map. To illustrate this latter point, I may mention that in 1940 . . . no less than six different dialects were spoken as 'mother tongue' within a community of 130 households!" (Leach 1965:45–46). Such a situation reveals the considerable historical complexity underlying the *gumsa–gumlao* oscillations on which the chiefdom cycling model has been based.

Migration, Identity, and the Mitigation of Diversity

In summary, some classic ethnohistoric examples of chiefdoms betray two related dimensions of a historical process pertaining to the hints of cultural pluralism: (1) population displacement or migration and (2) what I term the "mitigation" of cultural diversity. The first of these includes both local and long-distance relocations of groups such that cultural identities of various sorts and scales (from families to ethnicities) become juxtaposed in ways dissimilar to their points of origin. The latter stems from such juxtapositions and could involve a number of novel social or political arrangements that resolve the initial tensions of the rearranged populace.

Why, if you lived free of centralized government, would you relocate? Any number of reasons were hinted at in the past century of anthropology. They ranged from an old favorite of archaeologists—environmental pressures—to an even older favorite of cultural anthropologists—fissioning to keep order within communities (for a recent Mississippian revival of this idea, see Blitz 1999). But changing the question slightly to, Why not relocate? elicits an even better answer. From our present-day ethnocentric vantage point, we tend to assume that a sedentary lifestyle is the ideal that all people desire. But that's simply not the case (Sassaman 2001).

The political–historical implications of population movement are seldom considered in archaeological adaptations of ethnological chiefdom constructs, with one series of exceptions. Henry Wright (1984) proposed that political alliances among simple chiefdoms and the hiving off of "claimants to office" would have led to emergent class stratification: elites and commoners who identified more with their social stratum than with an integrated chiefly community. I used this idea in my analysis of the pre-Mississippian social landscape of the central Mississippi valley to argue that such emergent stratification provided the basis for the rapid large-scale appearance of Cahokia (Pauketat 1994).

What I did not consider at the time was the possibility that migrations of one sort or another may have been closely related to many incipient and developed forms of centralization. The best-known examples of this come from the American Southwest (Nelson and Schachner 2002). The oral histories and archaeology of Puebloan and Hohokam peoples there link the development of identities, inequality, and ranking (they aren't necessarily different things) to the history of migrations (Bernardini 2005; Clark 2001; Kintigh et al. 2004). That is, migrations allow one or more clans to become ritually or economically superordinate over others. Who were the native-born members of society or community and who were descended from immigrants? From whence did the immigrants come, from a land with a powerful and meaningful history? Or were they stragglers wandering out of the hills?

migrants determining social status

If such cases are a guide, then what they suggest is not that migration itself explains change, as our Southern Pragmatist might have it, but that population displacement, movement, and migration is closely related to the negotiation of the novel social conditions experienced during or subsequent to that movement (Pauketat 2003b). The process of concern is less the movement and more the *identity politics* foregrounded in various contexts of social life.

A number of archaeological studies have recently proffered the view that identities, like traditions, ideologies, or genders, are continuously constructed and projected experientially in all cultural practices, performances, and technologies (Dobres 2000; Loren 2005; Joyce 2005; Silliman 2005). Identities are never unitary and static but are always multiple and dynamic, if not in a constant state of syncretization, creolization, or hybridity (Loren 2005; Alt 2006b), which cannot be understood outside of the spatiality of the social fields in which they exist. These are not identities as shared cultures that are carried around in the heads of culture bearers. They are identities constantly coming into being contingent on the lived experiences of the people projecting those identities "in full view, on the landscape" (Pauketat and Loren 2005:22).

Such processes are not evolutionary ones that occur in certain types of societies. They are *historical*. They are part and parcel of the human condition, and they are contingent on the agency inherent to the social fields of specific times and landscapes (Ashmore 2004)—regardless of whether old neoevolutionary types might label such times and landscapes bands, tribes, chiefdoms, or states. So they could have led to political formations or governmental units that transcended local autonomy—which we all want to understand—*before* the Mississippian period in eastern North America.

Pre-Mississippian Complexity Across the Southeast

The initial wave of chiefdom interpretations in the 1970s applied the concept to periods and peoples that few self-respecting Mississippianists—never mind minimalists—would consider today. There were claims that the famous Late Archaic Poverty Point complex, the Early Woodland Adena mound builders, the Middle Woodland Hopewellians, and Weeden Island peoples were ranked societies if not chiefdoms of some sort (Earle 1987; Gibson 1974; Carr and Case 2005; Pluckhahn 2003).

Few entertain such a prospect today, especially understandable given the atheoretical, downsizing tendencies of eastern archaeologists. Instead, the commonsense synthesis—rooted in the old evolutionary law of cultural dominance (Sahlins and Service 1960:75)—has linked the basic archaeological chronologies with a progression of evolutionary stages: bands, tribes, complex tribes, and chiefdoms (Smith 1986). The link is deeply embedded in the consciousness of today's archaeology, although seldom made explicit. In such putatively commonsense,

> evolutionary terms, simple societies preceded agriculture because it was food production that made environments rich, secure, and expandable, and, consequently, brought the hunter-gatherer lifestyle and its presumed egalitarian ethos to an end. Only in places where agriculture could not expand, the argument went, do we find egalitarian hunter-gatherers existing after food production became a global phenomenon. (Sassaman 2004:228)

From such vantage points, the end of the Pleistocene era (ca. 9,000 years ago) witnessed native hunter-gatherers settling into their landscapes and living, in some cases, rich yet mobile lives. In eastern North America, Archaic period hunter-gather band societies eventually gave way by about 200 B.C. to the "tribal" social organizations of the Woodland period with their small-scale settlements focused around mound building and the veneration of ancestors buried therein (Smith 1986). Finally, with growing populations and the intensification of plant cultivation, Mississippian chiefdoms began to emerge after A.D. 750 in a slow, gradual manner (Smith 1990).

Even within particular periods, this theme of progressive directional change has taken hold of archaeologists. Jon Muller and James Brown have stated that the spread of Mississippian political symbolism was a time-transgressive phenomenon. The resulting southeastern ceremonial complex(es) became increasingly elaborate later in the Mississippian period (Brown 2005a; Brown and Kelly 2000; Muller 1989, 1997). Mary Beth Trubitt (2000), following Brown's and Muller's leads, has asserted that Mississippian political complexity and craft production intensity too increased with time, the initial Cahokian and early Mississippian complexes being less elaborate, communal, or corporate and the later ones specialized, hierarchical, and network-based (Redmond 1998:273, 278).

Warfare too is said to have escalated alongside increased political complexity, not for historical reasons but evolutionary ones (Milner 1999).

But are these accurate summaries of what really happened in pre-Columbian eastern North America? Not according to Kenneth Sassaman (2004:228), who believes that "this remarkably resilient and dominant theme [i.e., progressive evolution] in anthropological discourse has now been thoroughly erased by evidence to the contrary." If only this were true. Unfortunately what keeps Sassaman's optimistic conclusion from being contemporary reality is the common sense of archaeologists. Beneath that common sense lives a deeply embedded ethnocentric progressivism. It is concealed in words such as "complexity."

On the heels of the 1980s attempts to decouple concepts such as hierarchy, complexity, and inequality (Johnson 1982; McGuire 1983), Carole Crumley (1995a, b) suggested that we pay more attention to the effective scale of the cultural processes typically implicated in evolutionary uses of the word complexity. Much of settlement patterning used to identify the three- and four-tiered administrative hierarchies of chiefdoms and states, she suspected, was being misread (Earle 1987; 1997; Marcus and Feinman 1998; Wright and Johnson 1975). Crumley questioned the assumption that patterns of big sites surrounded by smaller sites should always be interpreted as evidence of hierarchical, tributary, dominant–subordinate relations in a single region.

Her alternative is the notion of heterarchy, which Crumley (1995a:3) understands as "the relation of elements to one another when they are unranked or when they possess the potential for being ranked in a number of different ways." As such, these lateral networks or orders can be complex. Indeed, a hierarchy might actually be an attempted simplification or streamlining of such horizontal complexity (Brumfiel 1995; Yoffee 2005).

Too few archaeologists have thought about Crumley's notion of heterarchy as a dimension of complexity (Nelson 1995). Many have merely adapted heterarchy as an alternative to hierarchy or a substitute for the old evolutionary stage of "egalitarian society." It is anything but this, of course. However, it is tempting to use such an alternative concept as an explanation. Remember what Dr. Science told UGS: "Heterarchy is the simplest explanation of the variability documented in the Archaic period mound builders, if not also the mortuary remains of the Middle Woodland period, in the eastern United States." What he fails to appreciate is that heterarchies are not things that evolved owing to certain abstract mechanisms. In addition, heterarchical society is not an intermediate stage of social evolution. Finally, heterarchies are *not* explanations. Instead, they are dimensions of *all* social formations that can only be understood by studies of the contingent histories of the peoples involved. This applies equally for, say, the Inuit peoples of the Arctic as it does for the imperial—and highly heterarchical—Aztecs of central Mexico (Sassaman 2004; Brumfiel 1995).

The idea of heterarchy opens up alternative ways to begin rethinking issues of inequality, polity, and civilization while avoiding the tired search for the first chiefdoms. As we'll see, such a rethinking entails abandoning the idea of society as an organic system and hence dropping old notions that ranked societies will correlate on a one-to-one basis with a certain type of burial program, exchange system, or regional settlement pattern. At a minimum, this leads us to consider alternate forms of social and political formation, including what Norman Yoffee (2005; Yoffee et al. 1999) is labeling "ritualities" (see discussion below). Our mission is to go beyond the notion of labeling into a strange new world of theory where scale and history take precedence over system and structure.

Rethinking Governance in Northeastern Louisiana

In the past, from an evolutionary point of view, monumental architecture was often considered an important hallmark of chiefdoms (Renfrew 1973; Peebles and Kus 1977). So it is with some trepidation that archaeologists have, over the years, accepted a series of new discoveries of pre-Mississippian monumental architecture in the eastern North America. You can follow the series of discoveries and reconciliations by reading a selection of southeastern studies in chronological order: A. R. Kelly (cited by Hally 1994:4), Phillips et al. (1951), Gibson (1974), Steponaitis (1986), Sears (1992), Russo (1994), and Knight (2001). These all lead up to the crown jewel of pre-Mississippian discoveries: a 5,600-year-old monumental complex at the Watson Brake site in northeastern Louisiana (Saunders et al. 1997).

What could such a discovery mean? Were there complex societies in North America before anywhere else in the New World? Possibly, depending on what is meant by complexity. However, changing people's minds isn't as simple as changing their underwear (although perhaps they should do it

63

almost as often). The fact that there are large-scale monuments throughout the pre-Mississippian eastern Woodlands is thus seen from an evolutionary point of view as a sign that monuments are not terribly demanding in terms of energetics, and are clearly within reach of "egalitarian" societies (Milner 2004). They don't actually take much labor investment to build, and hence don't mean much in terms of how we interpret the past.

Oddly, the discovery of Middle Holocene, Archaic period monumental landscapes or the realization that many large four-sided earthen pyramids dated to the Middle Woodland era actually reinforced the minimalist position that monuments ≠ hierarchical society (Milner 2004, 2005). So, the logic goes, if they don't mean hierarchy at 3600 B.C., then they don't necessarily mean hierarchy for the Mississippians either. After all, "few, if any, special skills or tools are needed to dump dirt in a pile. The labor needed to build mounds is quite modest" (Milner 2004:305).

Contrast this logic with that of Kenneth Sassaman (2004). He sees considerably more in the Archaic mounds of Louisiana, which are, as far as we know, the oldest known monumental architecture in the New World (Russo 1994; Saunders et al. 1997). Dating from 3600 B.C., there are at least eleven Middle Archaic mound complexes in the lower Mississippi valley (Sassaman 2004:258). "The tallest mounds in complexes of 3 or more are also in the range of 4–6 m, with the exception of the 7.5-m-high Mound A at Watson Brake. All sites that have been adequately tested show evidence for staged construction in at least one mound. Finally, mounds excavated to date have included some sort of architectural components at their bases" (Sassaman 2004:259).

Sites such as Watson Brake and Insley, among others in northeastern Louisiana, feature oval, loaf-shaped earthen mounds arrayed around open "plaza" spaces strongly suggestive of an attempted if not realized complex social order. Sassaman (2004:261) argues that, like the many monumental "shell rings" along the Atlantic coast, the "central spaces or plazas created by the circular or elliptical arrangement of mounds may have been especially significant in reproducing hierarchy, as they continue to do today among Xinguanos of central Brazil" (citing Heckenberger 2005; Heckenberger et al. 1999, 2003). He argues that emergent hierarchy and central social orders are evident at such preplanned and fairly rapidly constructed places (Russo 1994, 1996, 2002; J. Saunders et al. 1997; R. Saunders 1994, 2002). In their construction, they spatialized and hence infused social relations with principles of vertical and horizontal opposition and asymmetry (Sassaman 2004:259–262). All of this at 3600 B.C.

The best example of such a spatialization of opposition and asymmetry dates later in the Archaic period, 1600–800 B.C.: the Poverty Point site in northeastern Louisiana (Gibson 1996, 2000). Poverty Point's amphitheater-like arrangement of mounds and plaza forms the centerpiece of an enigmatic monumental landscape covering 5 square kilometers and composed of 750,000 cubic meters of mounded earth (Sassaman 2004:253, 2005:338). Gibson (2000:96) suspects that most earthen construction at the site—including the bird-shaped twenty-one-meter-high Mound A—took place during the first three centuries of its radiocarbon-dated range. Sassaman (2005) suspects a considerably shorter construction span.

These archaeologists take the accumulated evidence to indicate that Poverty Point was North America's first town, built over—and hence commemorating or coopting—an earlier Middle Archaic moundscape (Clark et al. in press; Sassaman 2004:260). Many archaeologists had always suspected that the loaf-shaped mounds were platforms for housing, although whether that housing was substantial or ephemeral remains uncertain given the modicum of architectural evidence excavated to date: a few post molds, hearths, and pits (Gibson 2000). Gibson's conclusions are based primarily on the "extensive midden and . . . secular-looking trash" on and around rows of loaf-shaped mounds (Gibson 2000:105). Built in successive stages, the six rows of concentric loaf-shaped mounds form an arc around an open plaza in the center of which were raised large upright posts (figure 3.1).

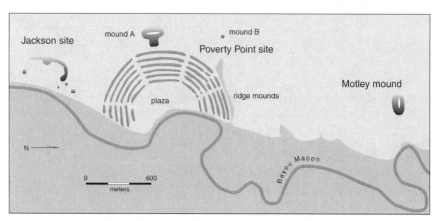

Figure 3.1. Poverty Point site plan map (after Kidder 2002a:figure 3)

The loaf mounds contain stratified construction fills into which were dug fire pits. These were probably used for cooking, and the fact that some are stacked stratigraphically one atop the other suggests to Gibson (2000:103–104) that loaf mound construction was rapid, continuous, and not purely ceremonial. If he's correct, then the Poverty Point site does seem dissimilar to earlier Archaic mound sites, and possibly later Woodland era ones, many of which appear to have had few if any permanent residents. Presumably—and this is a big presumably given the lack of significant archaeological work at many of these sites—their midden assemblages were accumulations of intermittent "feasting and related ceremonial activity" by people who otherwise lived in outlying hamlets (Sassaman 2004:263).

Tristram Kidder's (1991) survey of an outlying region revealed a settlement pattern of lesser sites clustered around larger ones. He interpreted this as evidence of a Terminal Archaic period settlement hierarchy. And while a similar settlement distribution was not clearly evident around other large Poverty Point period sites, including Poverty Point proper, the scale and possibilities of sedentary domestic occupations have theoretical implications. What happens as part of the process of living together under such conditions? That is, might community itself be a malleable construct? This idea was susceptible to politicization in the past and might hide itself from the eyes of archaeologists wanting to see egalitarian hunter-gatherers. Ken Sassaman (2005) now concludes that Poverty Point was just such a community "reflecting literally the histories of migration, diffusion, and colonization that linked [other] communities of people across regions and generations" and that "symbolically incorporate[d] other times (events) and broad-scale social geographies" (Sassaman 2005:337). Its people brought together disparate memories, designs, and meanings of real or fictive ancestors, immigrants, and distant allies.

Clearly the refuse of Poverty Point and a series of lesser Poverty Point culture sites is suggestive of two aspects of communalism that require close scrutiny: intensive cooking of quantities of food and the production of bodily ornaments, religious fetishes, and nominally utilitarian objects from exotic raw materials. The exotic raw materials—stones and doubtless a wide variety of organics long since lost to decay in this moist, hot environment—were acquired from the southern Appalachians to the Missouri Ozarks to east Texas. The acquisition of these materials, followed by the manufacture of objects from them—seems poorly served by standard notions of exchange or trade (Pauketat 2003b). So too is the production of finished objects from these materials misunderstood using standard craft production and prestige goods models.

The Poverty Point craft products include elaborate net weights, chipped-stone projectile points, necklace beads and spacers, stone bowls, and a whole host of baubles and fetishes, with shapes appearing to depict avian and earth monster creatures, along with other living beings: cicada nymphs, lotus pods, spider webs, and so on. Even baked clay artifacts—the famous Poverty Point objects (PPOs) used to cook food in bags—are made in shapes suggesting abstract concepts. There are indications of upper and lower world creatures along with animals and plants that bridge the worlds of water, sky, and earth (much like later Mississippian shamanic imagery).

Regional Order in the Scioto Valley

Some would say the mound centers of northeastern Louisiana were but one episode in a long mound-building tradition in eastern North America (Milner 2004). This is true, in a grossly descriptive sort of way, at the same time that it is deceptive. People lived, embodied, and practiced their traditions rather than receiving them passively from a long line of ancestors (Pauketat 2001a,b). In actuality, there are many short traditions of monumental construction that build on (i.e., appropriate) the traditions of earlier peoples (Pauketat and Alt 2003). The burden of explanation, in my short-tradition view, rests on each construction.

After 50 B.C. in south-central Ohio, the Early Woodland period Adena mound-building practices—burying people in accretional and occasionally impressive conical tumuli—were giving way to a new tradition of great earthen enclosures. Among the earliest was a single enclosure and elaborate effigy burial structure and mound complex at the Tremper site at the mouth of the Scioto River (Carr and Case 2005). Here the Middle Woodland people "may have recorded the beginning of the Scioto Hopewellian tradition, in which multiple communities in a region *gathered* together at an earthwork to bury their dead together" (Weets et al. 2005:533, emphasis added). Another early site, aptly named Mound City, was "an array of at least twenty-four mounds surrounded by a quadrilateral embankment . . . quite different from the dozens of previously used [mound sites] in the immediate vicinity" (Seeman 2004:67). By A.D. 50

these novel Scioto macrocommunities had transformed the earlier scattered "sacred" ritual and burial sites into a focused Scioto valley landscape consisting of over a dozen prominent sacred enclosure localities in the central area (Seeman 2004:figure 26; Carr and Case 2005).

The Scioto valley earthwork localities consist of sets of squared, circular, and octagonal enclosures (figure 3.2). These sets, built over generations (part

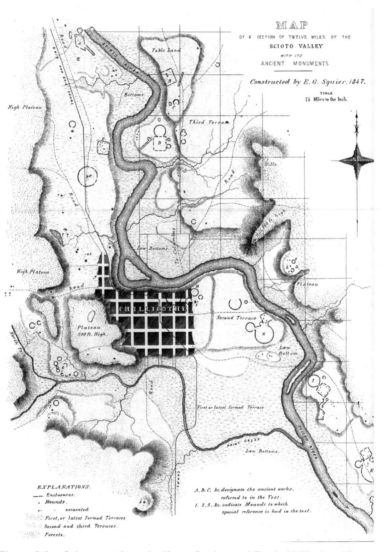

Figure 3.2.   Scioto earthworks (from Squier and Davis 1848:plate II)

of the point of such construction), nonetheless betray moments of abrupt large-scale building efforts that encode someone's cognized principles—including sophisticated astronomical and geometrical principles—into the spatial–social realm (Lepper 1998, 2005). Such agentic moments can be said to have channeled (or, for you Foucault fans, "disciplined") the movements of the many bodies of people gathered in the Scioto localities, as evidenced by embanked roadways leading pilgrims to and from monumental enclosures through natural places and the night sky (Carr 2005b:589; Lepper 1998, 2005:77). Certain of these Hopewellian roads extended for several kilometers; the "Great Hopewell Road" might have stretched forty-eight kilometers from the Newark earthworks to the numerous enclosed spaces of Chillicothe, Ohio (Lepper 1998:129; 2005:79).

Notable among these are five regular tripartite geometric sets each encompassing about thirty-one hectares, minimally indicating architectural canons (Lepper 2005:74) and maximally the exclusive engineering knowledge of political–ritual leaders, members of "a comparatively advanced form of regional alliance" (Carr 2005c:314). The political centrality (if not also the heterarchical complexity of the regional order) seems attested by mortuary events at the Hopewell site, "a burial place generally reserved for persons of much prestige," compared to other ritual places made up of "cemeteries for a broader spectrum of society" (Carr et al. 2005:510). Opulent caches of carved-stone pipes, exotic chipped-stone bifaces, bead necklaces, and human remains clearly were commemorative offerings of communities, even as high-status persons in key mortuary events embodied those communities.

Was the Scioto valley organized as a chiefdom? The question has been repeatedly asked by archaeologists of an evolutionary bent in their attempts to explain Middle Woodland archaeological complexes in the Scioto, the Illinois valley, and the lower Mississippi valley. As Jane Buikstra (1976) first opined decades ago based on limited mortuary data, these researchers find sufficient reason to identify social ranking (in Fried's sense) but seldom argue for stratification or strongly centralized chiefdoms (Carr 2005a). In addition, the population of the Scioto valley and elsewhere during the Middle Woodland period was not strongly centralized but dispersed among many gardening hamlets. We do not know enough of the small residential sites to be able to estimate the population, but it certainly was not as dense as certain Mississippian regions later in time. Thus the law of cultural dominance stands, and commonsense evolutionism prevails.

From my own vantage point, the question of what the Scioto phenomenon represents in political terms would seem unanswerable until we retheorize a single dimension of the Hopewell experience: community. What exactly was it? Conceptualizing the Scioto formation in a manner not unlike Sassaman's (2005) sense of Poverty Point, Christopher Carr (2005b; Carr and Case 2005) implicitly adopts philosopher Martin Heidegger's notion of gathering. For existentialist philosophers, a gathering is an experiential moment in which diversity is brought together (Heidegger 1986). Unity is forged from plurality through the physicality of passage, association, ritual deposition, and periodic construction (Pauketat and Alt 2005; Pollard 2001; Tilley 2004).

Carr sees this in individual mortuary events, ceremonial deposits, and monumental centers, if not also in the entire landscape of the Scioto valley. His idea of a tripartite alliance, for instance, adds a pan-regional spatiality to the Scioto experience. It was a greater imagined community or, to borrow a phrase from the Chacoan Southwest, an idealized "community of communities" (Pauketat 2000a [*sensu* Anderson 1983]; Toll 2004). There were Scioto movers and shakers for sure. But their agency was not a rationalist strategizing sort (was it anywhere?). Instead, it was embedded in a sense of personhood not easily detached from community (Gillespie 2001). And yet community itself may have been something considerably more encompassing, regionally inclusive, and even politicized in many places during the Middle Woodland period than it had been.

For present purposes, we need not interpret this any further. The take-home point is sufficiently profound: community building, polity, and personhood were mutually constitutive. All were realized at a regional scale and in multiple experiential dimensions that cannot be reduced to correlates of a certain type of society and isolated in single cemeteries or villages.

Reinventing the Traditions of Their Coastal Forbearers

As the earlier builders of Poverty Point appropriated an age-old mounded landscape, so the later people of the lower Mississippi valley commemorated the traditions of the ancients, whose monumental earthworks were so readily visible in northeastern Louisiana. Although native Louisianans would never again achieve the grand scale of Poverty Point, later architects were persistent in their attempts. As with their northern Ohio and Illinois counterparts, these native southerners constructed sacred centers of impressive platform mounds, burial tumuli, and circumferential enclosures. The best known of these were at Pinson in Tennessee and Marksville in Louisiana.

In Georgia, Middle Woodland era (Swift Creek) mound builders were the precursors of the so-called Weeden Island people of southern Georgia and northern Florida. Between A.D. 350 and 850, foraging and gardening people built impressive ceremonial sites that, unlike earlier phenomena elsewhere, included modest resident populations. The largest site, at Kolomoki, covered about fifty hectares and had nine mounds, including a seventeen-meter-high flat-topped rectangular pyramid. If the single house excavated at Kolomoki is representative, then up to five hundred sedentary people built small, semisubterranean keyhole-shaped sleeping huts around an open plaza covering approximately five hundred hectares (Pluckhahn 2003).

A smaller Weeden Island center, the McKeithen site, is well-known for the remarkable findings of Jerry Milanich and his coworkers conducting salvage research there in the 1970s. The three-mound site had a resident population of about one hundred people. They lived around an open plaza and between three earthen mounds all sited with respect to a tripartite plan. The northern and southern mounds included a burial mound and a platform alternately interpreted as a mortuary-processing platform—"the body of a dead individual . . . is dismembered and the head is removed . . . while the viscera . . . are discarded" (Milanich et al. 1984:99)—or the substructure for a scaffold (Knight 2001). The central mound, which faced the summer solstice sunrise, was surmounted by a building that contained the body of a singularly significant adult, interpreted to have been laid out in state prior to the abandonment of the site (Milanich et al. 1984). The excavators interpreted the site to have been organized around this individual's persona, perhaps the one in charge of mortuary rituals and interments on the other two mounds. With the death of the individual, the body and building on the central mound was covered with earth in the last commemorative construction project.

At the now destroyed site of Troyville in east-central Louisiana, later Middle Woodland (Middle Baytown) period devotees built an impressive monumental center at the confluence of the Tensas, Ouachita, and Little Rivers (Walker 1936). It was one of several mound communities in the area and surrounding regions of the lower Mississippi valley, where the mounds were primarily mortuary features where virtually all members of society were interred (Kidder 1998:134). Its potential historical significance was recognized by Phillips and colleagues (1951:441), who thought that if the "germs of theocratic control may be deduced" from the "appearance of temple mounds in middle Baytown, we have a possible explanation of the machinery by which the later middle Mississippi cultures were extended so widely over the eastern United States."

The Troyville site covered over 160 hectares as originally demarcated by an earthen embankment over three meters high surrounding at least seven mounds, with several more outside the enclosure (figure 3.3.). The largest of these was a substantial earthen pyramid, square at its base and up to twenty-four meters in height, built in three stacked terraces covering three-tenths of a hectare. Based on salvage excavations in 1931, the central rectangular pyramid appears to have been built up in stages by clay construction fill alternated with thick layers of cane, the latter sometimes supplemented with wooden planks and matting staked into the earth with vertical wooden posts. Around the base of this particular pyramid was a possible palisade of vertical posts (Walker 1936). Each of its four corners may have had a buttress-like extension and yet, except for the conical clay edifice atop it (removed during the Civil War for the construction of a rifle pit), Winslow Walker found no evidence of associated surmounting architecture in his salvage excavations of the basal remnant in 1931. Indeed, Kidder (1998:134) believes that the "fastidiously clean" flat-topped mounds here and at other such middle Baytown centers were used to cover over burials. He concludes,

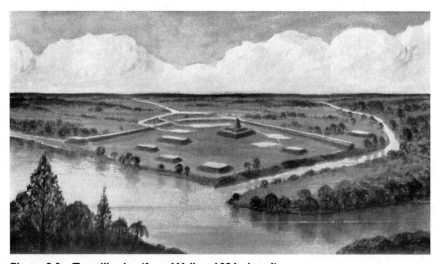

Figure 3.3. Troyville site (from Walker 1936:plate I)

"There is no evidence that the community plan of mounds around a plaza was a means of one group's excluding or metaphorically turning its back on the community. In fact, the totality of the Troyville community plan and its functions suggests an attempt to include the broader community."

Some of the same inclusive "communal" qualities apply during the subsequent so-called Coles Creek period—dating between A.D. 700 and 1100 or so—from the mouth of the Arkansas River south to New Orleans (Kidder 1998; Phillips et al. 1951; Phillips 1970). Lacking the singular qualities of Poverty Point or the Scioto, the various Coles Creek centers are modest in scale (figure 3.4). And there was no apparent interaction

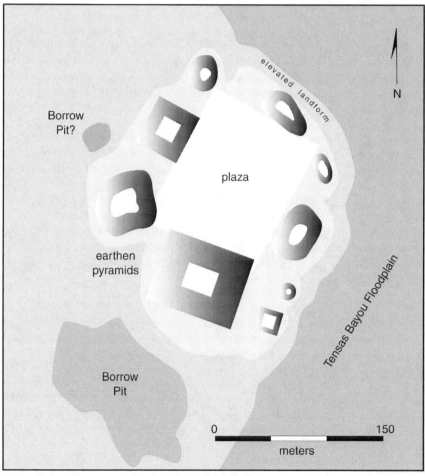

Figure 3.4. Diagrammatic plan view of the Raffman site, a Coles Creek center in northeast Louisiana (after Kidder 2004:figure 2).

sphere that surrounded Coles Creek centers, unlike the transregional Poverty Point culture and Hopewellian interaction sphere. Until some-time after A.D. 1000 and probably more likely during the twelfth century, Coles Creek period people ate little to no corn (Kidder and Fritz 1993). They didn't acquire the sorts or quantities of exotics known from before or after. And they built no houses or temples on their flat-topped pyra-mids. In fact, hardly anyone did before the beginning of the Mississippian period (Knight 2001; Lindauer and Blitz 1997). Outside of Poverty Point (or perhaps the charnel house at McKeithen), truncated earthen pyramids appear to have been stages for performances, platforms for the dead, or substructures for scaffolds—some used in the cooking of food for public feasts (Knight 2001).

However, at least some of the Coles Creek ceremonial centers, while perhaps housing few residents, were landscapes constructed to *exclude* cer-tain elements or aspects of society. Up to several earthen platforms were built, in stages, around central plazas that were also artificial features, con-structed using earthen fill to raise and level their surfaces (Kidder 2004). And yet, while there were numerous "multimound communities . . . there does not seem to be strong evidence that any particular mound community achieved absolute preeminence in its particular region" (Kidder 1998:140).

Importantly, in the Lake George and Greenhouse sites, the flat sum-mits of earthen pyramids were used for a series of exceptional mortuary rites (Williams and Brain 1983:45). These included several containing adults buried with numerous children. As a series, many of the burials exhibit an "obvious lack of order. The dead seem to have been treated inconsistently and often with minimal care" at death, revealed by their irregular horizontal layout and alternating supine or prone positioning (Williams and Brain 1983:45).

And while some of the adults were buried several days to weeks after they died, the same seems unlikely for the children, who may have been dispatched as part of the mortuary ceremony. Take, for example, one "extended, prone adult male . . . accompanied by the bodies of thirteen infants" in Mound C at Lake George. Or take another adult male, buried in a supine position in the middle of a platform mound at the Mount Nebo site, interred with a possible deer headdress and "two adult females on either side and three children. One of the females . . . had a quartzite projectile point embedded in her right tibia" (Kidder 1998:135).

[Alex] Barker (1993) observes that of the 180 burials reported from Mound C at Lake George, seventy-nine were infants. . . . If we exclude infants, the remaining burials "fall neatly along the mortuary demographic profile we would expect for a small population…" [with no] statistical bias toward mound burial for one sex or the other. . . . Barker (1993:8) concludes that these burial data "are consistent with the interment of all individuals from a select portion of society, with the inclusion of additional infants from the remaining sectors of the population that did not qualify for mound inhumation. (Kidder 1998:136)

Were these Coles Creek remains the exclusive central grounds and elaborate mortuary rituals of pre-Mississippian chiefdoms (Barker 1999)? That depends on how we understand community identity—as an imagined and politicized ideal—here in the Coles Creek heartland (see below). This is true with respect to the pre-Mississippian Archaic and Woodland period developments in the Midwest and South, and it is true, we will see, with respect to the rise of Cahokia and the later so-called Mississippian provinces. Chiefdom models of complexity are unable to cope with this all-important and historically contingent dimension—identity. To appreciate what I mean, we must extend our review into the Mississippian period.

Conclusion: Intransigence and Alternatives

Based on a brief review of a few ethnographic and historic cases, I stated earlier that we should question the utility of calling any political formation pristine in an evolutionary sense. The pre-Mississippian complexes of eastern North America are good cases in point. In some ways, each seems precocious relative to what happened around and after it. However, even the Watson Brake site now seems to be one of a series of roughly contemporary Middle Archaic complexes of earthen tumuli or mollusk shell mounds around open social space constructed, according to Sassaman (2004), to inculcate complex social relationships. Most people would not feel comfortable calling Watson Brake, or any Middle Archaic mound site, the center of a chiefdom. Some archaeologists would not feel comfortable labeling any of the above a chiefdom. The question is, Were these different enough from what follows, the Mississippian, to think of the latter as a case of "independent pristine process of social transformation" (Smith 1990:1)? The distinction seems at least as sticky as separating chiefdom confederation from incipient state bureaucratization.

Although there are many unknowns, the potential existed in each pre-Mississippian case for considerable organizational variability if not also cultural pluralism that would seem to call into question the typical evolutionary assertion that political institutions in these societies evolved in such a way as to structure the social fabric and the transsocietal cultures or interaction spheres of Poverty Point, Weeden Island, Coles Creek, or Hopewell. Indeed, the controversies surrounding what to label each of these Archaic and Woodland era complexes stems in large part from the inability to locate the correlates of presumed political organizations and institutions that archaeologists have always assumed lie at the heart of any political phenomenon.

One evolutionary solution would be to assume that if these institutions were there, we'd see them. Since they're not visible (with the possible exception of Coles Creek mound centers), one could assert in a minimalist vein that these pre-Mississippian peoples were noncentralized people, their apparent heterarchical complexity due to their elaborate kin organizations and sodalities (following Service 1962). Their case might be bolstered by the risk-minimization logic of some neo-Darwinists, who believe that communal labor investments such as mounds were a waste of human energy that nevertheless imparted a selective advantage to the mound-building group—integrating people in ways that enabled them to outlast their neighbors during periods of stress (Dunnell 1989).

Their case may also seem warranted by their own labor estimates—ignoring the culture-specific particularities of labor allocation (never mind the many other related laborious tasks surrounding mound building)—which suggest that a few people could build even the largest earthen tumuli over a period of years or decades (Milner 1998, 2004; Milner and Schroeder 1999). Never mind the flaws in such estimation procedures or the empirical evidence that no one ever built a mound in this fashion; the biggest error of these minimalist solutions is their tacit assertion that mounds are an *outcome* of an evolutionary process that in turn happened outside the material and spatial dimensions of the human experience (Pauketat 2003b).

Another approach, slightly modified from this minimalist version, is to appreciate that the Archaic and Woodland era cultural complexes were in all likelihood centralized social formations, but were not based on the sorts of political institutions commonly recognized by classic evolutionism. Instead of political organizations, perhaps they were based on ritual heterarchies. This is the rituality model developed by Norman Yoffee (2005), although he typically applies it to the American Southwest or the Mississippian Southeast, not pre-Mississippian eastern North America.

Elsewhere I have stated that the rituality model "implies that all producers were autonomous, and suffers from chronic theoretical underdevelopment" (Pauketat 2004:182). It seems to assert—despite Yoffee's (2005:173) statements to the contrary—that there were essential qualities of ritual, to which native North Americans in particular were prone, which, contrary to anthropological theories of ritual, did not involve politics. However, all rituals are inherently political (Bell 1997; Kertzer 1988). Cultural complexes don't simply develop owing to the "ritual pull" of some places (contra Kelly 2002:145). Such a view fails to explain why there was a ritual pull *then* and *there*.

A third solution rejects the minimalist position and yet remains wedded to an evolutionary logic. This option involves the recognition that archaeologists might not be able to find the correlates of chiefdoms in the classic sense, owing to the other axes of variation—heterarchies again—that would prevent politicos from expressing themselves in life or death through conspicuous displays. Our own Uncertain Graduate Student, for instance, correctly compared such a situation to the absence of obvious royal tombs at the great Mesoamerican city of Teotihuacán. In dual-processual terms, we might say that Poverty Point, the Scioto formation, or any number of Coles Creek or Weeden Island regions could have been organized as corporate chiefdoms (*sensu* Earle 2001; Peregrine 2001). Clearly labor was mobilized for central purposes or people. Equally clear is the fact that archaeologists working with a number of cases—in North America including the Powhatan polity and the Coosa paramountcy—seem unable to find the correlates of the complicated regional hierarchies unambiguously attested in historic documents (Anderson 1994; M. Smith 2003). Unless we assume the position of doubting any historic observations that do not fit with the minimalist stance, we are forced to consider the possibility that our correlate-based approaches are missing something.

Perhaps the pre-Mississippian complexes are telling us that the missing something is a fuller investigation of the relationships between centrality, monumentality, community, and culture making. Might it be useful, for instance, to consider communities as identities rather than building blocks? If so, couldn't we imagine any number of kinds and scales of community identities dependent on the circumstances of how people gathered at particular times and places? And might mound building be the materiality and spatiality of community building and culture making? Might more mounds concentrated in smaller regions indicate a consolidation of community at any number of scales and alternate political, economic, or religious modes?

In this vein Ken Sassaman (2004) suggests understanding even the earliest Middle Archaic centers (such as Watson Brake) as emergent hierarchical orders. In such a vein, Christopher Carr's (2005) pan-Scioto political alliance inference assumes new meaning, as does T. R. Kidder's (1991) suggestion of possible terminal Archaic polities in Louisiana. That is, community itself might have become the medium of political consolidation (Pauketat 2000a,b). Community itself, or at least select aspects of it, may have been promoted or commemorated by those whose political interests were served by those aspects or memories (Pauketat and Emerson 1999). Might this explain the emphasis we see at places such as Poverty Point on community-building feasts and "secular-looking trash" (Gibson 2000:105)? Might this be commensurate with the apparent parochial character of Coles Creek economies? And might it help explain why the ritual and the political seem isomorphic at places such as Kolomoki and McKeithen?

If you answered yes to any of these questions, then you are one of a growing number of people willing to walk away from the naive evolutionary logic of a Dr. Science in order to embrace a historical or practice-based logic (Pauketat 2001b). According to Christopher Carr and Troy Case (2005:32), this

> follows broad trends in Anglo-American archeology over the past 20 years to invest views of the past with people, to evoke their intentions and decisions from material remains, and to explore the richness of the content of particular cultures contextually and historically. . . . Like other current attempts to humanize the archaeological record, thick prehistory [as they call it] is an active counterbalance to formulating abstract, functional, and/or structural models of cultural systems comprised of

mathematical variables and relationships among them . . . to classifying prehistoric cultures in homogenizing evolutionary-societal types . . . and occasionally to openly ridding archaeological interpretations of human actors and intentionality by applying some narrow brands of neo-Darwinian selectionist logic.

You may agree with Carr and Case (2005:33–34) that people in the past actively created traditions by drawing from collective memories and projecting their version of them into social spheres. And you may see, in the monumental platform mounds and plazas or earthen enclosures, stages and amphitheaters for the projection of such traditions or planned convergences of supernatural forces and cultural experience that would most certainly have had some long-term historical effects on political affiliations and cultural identities.

Pre-Mississippian centers were the sites of cultural construction and production, quite literally, and so the history and scale of such creations—not the structure of political institutions or the systemic qualities of whole societies—become paramount in understanding the subsequent cultural history of eastern North America. From this point of view, the ugly facts of the Archaic and Woodland American Indians have shattered the law of cultural dominance. Standing amid the shards, we need to take a long, hard look at so-called Mississippian chiefdoms.

CHAPTER FOUR

PARSING MISSISSIPPIAN CHIEFDOMS

The mounds or pyramids appear to me to belong to a period different from the others. They are . . . easily distinguished from the barrows, by their size and the design which they manifest. Remains of palisadoed [*sic*] towns are found in their vicinity, which may be accounted for from the circumstance of the mounds occupying the most eligible situations for villages, or from the veneration of the Indians.

—Henry Marie Brackenridge, 1814

The greatest barrier to understanding Mississippian chiefdoms may be Mississippian chiefdoms themselves. Used separately or together, the ideas of Mississippian and chiefdom can imply a cultural homogeneity and uniform political structure rather than a plurality and diversity of organizations, identities, and historical experiences. Used too loosely, they flatten several centuries worth of human history—the experiences of hundreds of thousands of people across much of eastern North America—into a few social roles and types of behaviors or institutions. Finally, unknown to many researchers, these concepts invariably load the scientific questions that archaeologists ask with commonsensical biases. As common sense, biases are not only *not* questioned, they are not even recognized as biases that can be questioned. Isn't this a problem?

The answer to that question lies in the answer to another question: What is Mississippian? To answer this second question, we need to parse the accepted Mississippian construct into macroregions, phases, and particular historical moments. The goal of our parsing is to evaluate the degree to which conceptual biases derived from our definitions and pre-conceptions have skewed our understandings of pre-Columbian eastern North American history.

Defining Mississippian

We have to start somewhere, and identifications of research problems rely on definitions. The recognition that something worth labeling "Mississippian" characterized a large portion of pre-Columbian North America originated with armchair pottery studies in the late nineteenth century (Holmes 1903; Willoughby 1897). Early-twentieth-century scholars observed correlations of the pottery with other architectural and settlement pattern evidence. And they taught their students, who taught us what most archaeologists today agree is Mississippian:

> As originally conceived, the term Mississippian referred to late pre-historic societies of the Mississippi River valley whose members made shell-tempered pottery and built wall-trench houses and earthen plat-form mounds. . . . Since then, maize cultivation and chiefdom social organization have been added to this definition, while shell-tempered pottery and a focus on the Mississippi River floodplain have been abandoned by most archaeologists. . . . we define Mississippian as late prehistoric societies of the Southeast and Midwest that were organized as chiefdoms and whose members practice maize agriculture and con-structed earthen platform mounds. (King and Meyers 2002:113)

Defined thus, the how and why questions of Mississippian archaeol-ogy boil down to, What were the effects of the appearance of maize-based economies? and Why did they lead to chiefdoms? (Muller 1997:386).

The next step, taken by any number of researchers, is to draw a line around societies that fit the definition. The boundary is justified by a series of pan-eastern comparisons of polity size, settlement hierarchy, population density, social relations, maize-friendly environments, volume of mound fill, distribution of exotic goods, and degree of producer specialization, among other things (Anderson 1999b; Cobb 2003; Holley 1999; Milner and Schroeder 1999; Muller 1997, 1999). Researchers frequently characterize Mississippian political economy, society, architectural grammar, leadership tactics, household organization, and iconography in unitary terms, as if there were one Mississippian people, one Mississippian household, or one Mississippian iconography. For example, "What were the military capabilities of *Mississippian townspeople*? . . . War leaders were not equal to the task of such ambitious undertakings as siege operations or the concentration of forces to breach stockade walls" (Stout and Lewis 1998:175, emphasis added). "What are the salient features of *a generalized Mississippian 'political economy'*? From the data on the central riverine area, we see that these social formations were classless societies" (Muller 1997:44, emphasis added).

Some archaeologists include more explicitly cultural or ideological criteria into their definitions of Mississippian, namely, the presence of so-called warfare cosmogony, platform mound, and temple institutions (Knight 1986). Definitions based in part on such a "shared set of religious cult institutions and iconographic complexes" preclude a series of peripheral populations—who otherwise would be identified as organized into chiefdoms—from the status of Mississippian (Scarry 1996:13; cf. Muller and Stephens 1991). These include the Timucua and Calusa of peninsular Florida, the Powhatans and Monacons of Virginia, and the Fort Ancient folks of southern Ohio (among others).

An often unspoken warrant for this move consists of a presumed language barrier: many of the true southeastern Mississippians were Muskogean speakers of one sort or another (Waring 1968). And if Mississippian ideals were embedded in language, the logic might go, then perhaps the ideas of political and religious leaders were representative of the entire population's ideas. That is, the ideologies of Mississippian elites would have also been the culture of all Mississippians. There was no difference according to such a conflated logic. And where there was no dissent or resistance, language and ideology led perfectly to reality. Elite strategies were commoner realities. There were no alternatives and no unanticipated outcomes. Resistance was inconceivable; the decisions and strategies of one were the decisions and strategies of all.

Dual-processualists love it, since their theoretical approach hinges on the idea that two sorts of strategies were implemented at the societal level.

> The dual-processual model has at its core two forms of leadership strategies: corporate- and network-based. Leaders using one strategy over the other draw upon different funds or sources of power. . . . A corporate

strategy is one in which power is derived from a local group and individual prestige is de-emphasized. . . . By contrast, the network strategy
derives power from individual networks of leaders . . . [and] is therefore
more exclusionary. (Mills 2000:10–11)

While there is utility in identifying and *describing* the degree to
which some private or public *practices or places* appear inclusionary, group
oriented, and corporate versus exclusionary, individualizing, and self-
aggrandizing, the power of these terms is *descriptive* only. It is a huge
and unwarranted leap of logic to then assert that such practices or places
were somehow also the strategies of society's movers and shakers. Why
a few leaders alone had the wisdom and the power to decide the fate of
all people, why their strategies are assumed to have been uniform, or why
these strategies are assumed to have been perfectly realized is never addressed in dual-processual models.

Ultimately the entire theory breaks down over the question, Where
did corporate and network strategies come from in the first place? One
who addresses that question by developing a historicized sense that the
corporate or network-based modes were negotiated results of interest groups accommodating each other has already transcended dual-
processual theory and is now using some sort of agency-based social
theory. One who simply avoids the question (of where the strategies come
from in the first place), as do dual-processualists, assumes an innate tendency among leaders to aggrandize and exert power over others. It's the
same old evolutionism, just more nuanced.

Like other social evolutionary models, dual-processualism tacitly re-
lies on an elite-centric view of long-term change. Ordinary people don't
actually do much that matters. Their unofficial or vernacular histories are
curiosities at best. Such definitions of Mississippian go hand in hand with
a heavy emphasis on chiefdom political structures. In other circles, such an
approach is known disparagingly as the "dominant ideology thesis" (Abercrombie et al. 1980). The thesis is conceptually flawed, say the critics. But
then few of these critics are Mississippian archaeologists.

"Most southeastern archaeologists don't wear their theories on their
shirt sleeves like you do," the Southern Pragmatist said to me once. "It's
impolite." They prefer to leave unstated and ambiguous their own theoretical positions so as not to unintentionally criticize their peers. However,

I was advised long ago by the guru of eastern North American archaeology, James B. Griffin, that "criticizing each other is the way archaeology improves itself." Dr. Griffin, as I addressed him ("Jimmy" to his peers), had just heard one of my less memorable conference presentations and pulled me aside for a lecture on clarity and content. We must criticize each other to move ahead, he'd said. Not to do so is to hide our theoretical biases and stultify archaeology. Today I'd add that it exacerbates the crisis in Mississippian archaeology.

My own bias is that Mississippian is not a political system. It's not a cultural system. Nor is it, strictly speaking, a kind of "chiefdom society." It's something much more than this, captured by the realization, among some, that the Mississippian world transcended "linguistic and cultural boundaries as substantial as the differences between medieval Poland and Spain" (Lewis et al. 1998:1). Mississippian is probably better considered a transregional spatio-cultural phenomenon—an "ethnoscape" in Arjun Appadurai's (1996) terms—much like "civilization" and "globalization."

Explaining Mississippian, then, is more about seeking to understand Mississippianization—an uneven historical process in which people politicized maize-based agricultural landscapes and cosmologies in ways contingent on their pasts and on each other. To seek precision beyond that admittedly wordy, vague definition is to impose strict a priori terms on a historically dynamic and locally divergent phenomenon. Don't do it.

Regional Historical Variants

Senior archaeologists have long recognized the inherent difficulties in trying to define something as big as the Mississippian world. Even Jimmy Griffin erred on the side of caution in almost every synthetic statement he made about pre-Columbian Mississippians. Of course, owing in part to his explanatory caution, he was criticized severely by a couple members of the younger generation who sought general scientific explanations in their lifetime (Binford 1972; Taylor 1983). But Griffin's broad, cautious descriptions of the Mississippian world remain the place to start for a general historical overview.

In 1967 Griffin identified four major subcontinental variants of Mississippian culture in eastern North America based on a broad array of unevenly weighted material—cultural, architectural, spatial, and iconographic attributes, probably tinged with historical linguistic evidence (figure 4.1.).

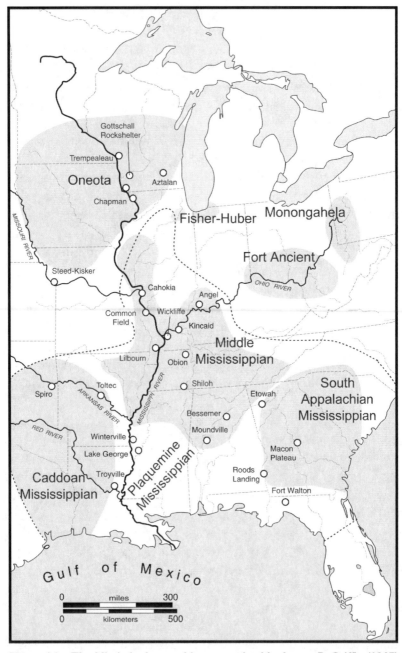

Figure 4.1. The Mississippian world, as conceived by James B. Griffin (1967)

Of these, he suspected that the Middle Mississippi region, particularly around Cahokia, was an early center of cultural development (Griffin 1952; Phillips et al. 1951). The so-called Middle Mississippians lived from the Illinois River valley south through the "American Bottom" and the confluence of the Ohio and Mississippi Rivers to Memphis. From there, Middle Mississippians were identifiable eastward to the Angel site in Indiana and southward through the Nashville basin in Tennessee to Moundville, Alabama.

Since then, others have extended this macroregional tradition south to the Gulf, with multiple indications of migrations into Georgia (Blitz and Lorenz 2002; Scarry 1999; M. Williams 1994). David Anderson (1999b) has added a historical dimension to it with his charting of the spread of terminal Late Woodland and Early Mississippian chiefdoms (Anderson 1997; Pauketat and Emerson 1997). Charles Cobb (Cobb and King 2005), Adam King (2005), and James Brown (2005a) have implied that the Etowah site also experienced a Middle Mississippian phase of development (which conveniently is both a chronological middle and a cultural middle). In short, one can begin to imagine, without straying too far from Griffin's (1967) general Mississippian area designations, how the east was Mississippianized. David Anderson (1999b) believed it began as an emergence and spread of chiefdom organizations (figure 4.2).

Before we can address directly the question of Mississippianization, however, we need a better sense of the places we label Mississippian. To that end, I will break the Mississippian monolith into areas of early and late Mississippian towns, highlighting the best-known or possibly key places and reviewing both commonalities and differences. For this review, I draw on excellent overviews by David Anderson (1999b) and George Holley (1999), as well as surveys and summaries by James Griffin (1952, 1967), Jon Muller (1997), Philip Phillips et al. (1951), Nelson Reed (1977), John Scarry (1999), and Cyrus Thomas (1985).

Foundations

The earliest Mississippian towns range in size from what George Holley (1999) classifies as the megacenter of Cahokia to a suite of modest to small towns and ceremonial centers, from Aztalan, Wisconsin, to Lake

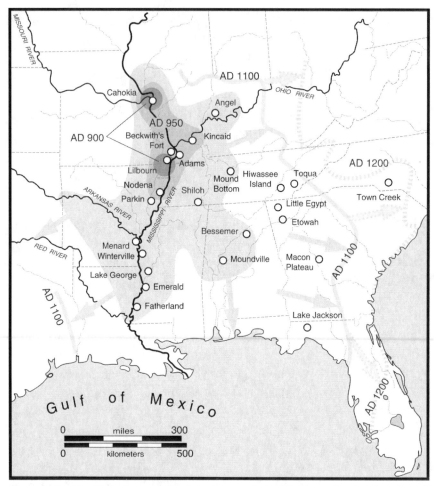

Figure 4.2. David Anderson's "inferred spread of chiefdoms in the Southeast" (after Anderson 1999b:figure 15.5)

Jackson, Florida. We will leave Cahokia for later. Unfortunately the total number of such early towns is unknown, and probably unknowable given site destruction or lack of investigation in some areas. They number easily in the hundreds, most found in the primary river valleys that empty into North America's primary natural and historical artery, the Mississippi River.

Of course, towns are only one part of a regional settlement pattern. Most people lived in smaller villages, frontier settlements, or dispersed farmsteads (Rogers and Smith 1995). These sites do not have platform mounds and must be identified through labor-intensive surveys. Even in the most intensively studied Mississippian regions, archaeologists are lucky if 10 percent of the habitable land has been surveyed, never mind sites excavated. There is much we do not know.

By some conservative estimates, there were at least fifty sizable centers and their political territories in the Midwestern and southern United States in the twelfth and thirteenth centuries A.D., the larger ones probably separated by open no-man's-lands (Holley 1999:figure 2.3). If we were to include the smaller, intermediate, or ephemeral provinces and political units, this number might be easily doubled if not trebled (Williams and Shapiro 1996:148). However many autonomous localities or regional polities there were, it is likely that most of the towns were built over one to ten human generations, the final appearance of many such sites being the cumulative result of decades of construction and reconstuction projects by many hundreds to many thousands of human lives. That's a lot of mound stage construction and plaza leveling, but even more wooden-compound and palisade-wall building, marker-post emplacement and replacement, and pole-and-thatch architectural construction and reconstruction. This is especially so since the total population of all Mississippiandom at any one time between the twelfth and sixteenth centuries must have numbered in the many hundreds of thousands.

Town Plans

Given the nearly pan-continental scale of the so-called Mississippian world, it is no surprise that there was structural variability in the layout of towns. Amid this variability, some have identified specific types of Mississippian towns, based on both size and spatial arrangement (Holley 1999; Phillips et al. 1951:309–344). In the Lower Mississippi alluvial valley, Phillips and colleagues (1951) differentiated between small and large ceremonial and habitation town types, noting that the large Winterville and Lake George settlements constituted a subtype, as did rectangular St. Francis-type villages with thick midden deposits. In the years since, archaeologists have found that most of Phillip et al.'s (1951) vacant ceremonial centers were not actually vacant. And archaeologists have recognized structural similarities between other adjacent towns, such as Kincaid and Angel, in southern Illinois and Indiana, respectively, or the adjacent Turk,

Towosahgy, and Adams sites in Kentucky and Missouri. Yet no two Mississippian centers are exactly alike.

So what is it that causes Mississippian places to look alike in some ways, and different in others? First, the formal similarities between some adjacent towns suggest that builders had the plan of another town in mind when laying out their own. Then again, analysts have recognized the importance of environmental constraints and inducements in the placement or layout of major town sites (Phillips et al. 1951; Schroeder 2004; Stout and Lewis 1998:161). Native builders clearly situated some of their towns with respect to local landforms and waterways at the same time that there are unambiguous monumental orientations to the cardinal directions and the movement of the sun, moon, and stars through the sky (Benchley 2000; Stout and Lewis 1998; Sherrod and Rolingson 1987). In short, there is good evidence for the existence of collective memories and archetypal models of places.

But they were not inviolate. Memories and models never are. The same is seen in many different historical contexts, from the great houses of Chaco Canyon to the early cities of ancient Mesopotamia, or even the divergent layouts of modern airports and major league baseball parks that supposedly serve the same functions.

For some, the plazas and mounds constitute the basic elements of a Mississippian "architectural grammar" (Lewis et al. 1998; they also identify boundaries, usually walls or ditches, associated with one or more access points or gates). This grammar arguably referenced the earlier Coles Creek centers of the Lower Mississippi valley (Pauketat and Alt 2003), if not Mesoamerica (White 2005; Williams and Brain 1983). But clearly there are some important differences between the post-Coles-Creek Midwestern and southern towns as well.

Following the distinction first used by Phillips and colleagues (1951), George Holley (1999:30) concluded that size matters. Thus most small towns consisted of a single plaza demarcated by mounds surrounded by the residential occupation and local cemeteries, which may or may not have been enclosed by a palisade wall or ditch (figure 4.3.). Large towns, however, were not just bigger than the small ones; they were also "*much* larger than other settlements within their region" (Holley 1999:31, emphasis added). They were more than just first among equals.

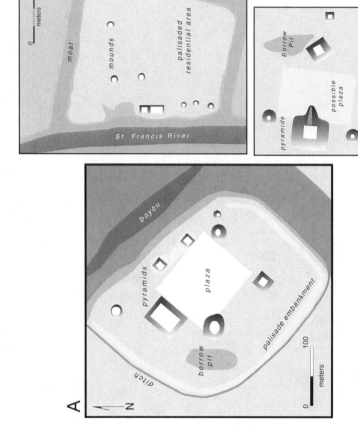

Figure 4.3. Diagrammatic plan views of Mississippian centers: a, Towosahgy (Missouri); b, Parkin (Arkansas); c, Arcola (Mississippi) (after Lewis 1991 and Phillips et al. 1951)

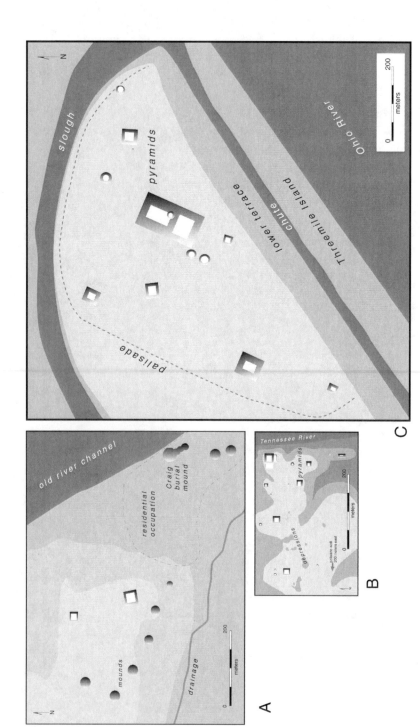

Figure 4.4. Diagrammatic plan views of Mississippian centers: a, Spiro (Oklahoma); b, Shiloh (Tennessee); c, Angel (Indiana) (after Brown 1996; Welch 2006; and Black 1967)

In addition, each of these substantial places had at least two mound and plaza groups and other features that made them *more elaborate* than their smaller counterparts. For instance, Angel and Kincaid in southern Indiana and Illinois, Etowah and Macon plateau in north-central Georgia, and Lake George and Winterville in western Mississippi have special arrangements of smaller mounds bounding inner precincts (figures 4.4–4.6). In addition, these large towns also have exceptionally large central pyramids, which in turn are often comprised of two or more elevated terraces.

Regardless of size, however, the central plazas, not the surrounding earthen pyramids, were the anchoring features of these central built landscapes (Dalan et al. 2003; Holley 1999:24). It is worth contemplating exactly who designed these spaces, and then who built them (Pauketat 2000b; Pauketat and Alt 2003). This is especially important to know,

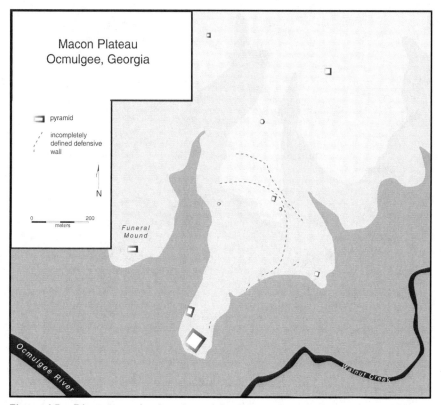

Figure 4.5. Diagrammatic plan view of Ocmulgee, Georgia (after Hally 1994)

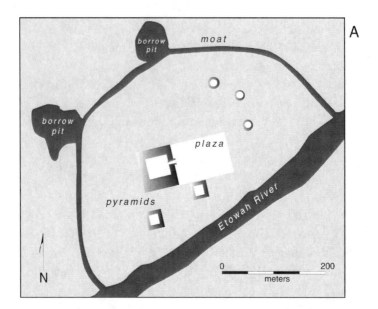

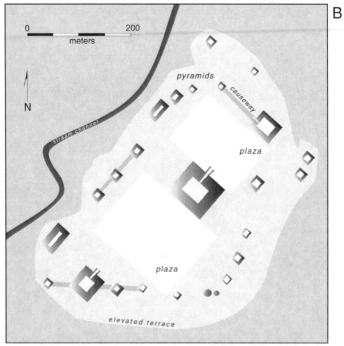

Figure 4.6. Diagrammatic plan views of large Mississippian centers: a, Etowah (Georgia); b, Winterville (Mississippi) (after Brain 1989 and King 2003)

since elevated earthen platforms bounding open highly structured spaces could have imparted a sense of social order depending on who or what was included or excluded from participation. Contemplating that question is made even more urgent because of recent discoveries in the history of planned constructions.

Based in part on the geophysical and archaeological work of Rinita Dalan and George Holley at Cahokia (Dalan 1997; Holley et al. 1993), researchers now conclude that plazas were often designed, engineered, and built at the very inception of a Mississippian town (Stout and Lewis 1998). As Dalan and Holley discovered at Cahokia, plaza construction was an impressive, labor-intensive undertaking involving the coordinated mining of sediments from natural levees followed by the infilling of low-lying swales (Kidder 2004; Pauketat et al. 2002). In addition, once the plaza surface was created, important public buildings and large upright posts may have been built into certain plazas. The act of construction and all subsequent bodily experiences in the plazas were doubtless grand collective social fields highly charged with symbolic meanings and memories.

And the plaza, as Dalan and Holley discovered, was the primary design element of these built landscapes, established at the very inception of various towns. Obviously they had to be, since the construction of earthen pyramids around such spaces would comprise an immediate and substantial constraint to future town growth (Stout and Lewis 1998:161). Not surprisingly, even the early Spaniard conquistadors recognized this design reality: "On the plain at the foot of the hill . . . [i.e., the main platform mound], they make a square plaza corresponding to the size of the pueblo that is to be settled, surrounding which the nobles and chief men build their houses" (Stout and Lewis 1998:159, citing Garcilaso de la Vega; Clayton et al. 1993). Thus the implication is that "unless town planners left room in which the plaza could grow, the length-width proportions of plazas and their areas relative to the principal mounds could not have been preserved without radical surgery to the earth architecture of the town" (Stout and Lewis 1998:161). In the end, community size was "fixed by design fairly early in the history of a town" so that "big mound-and-plaza complexes started out big, small mound-and-plaza complexes started out small, and they all pretty much stayed that way" (Stout and Lewis 1998:161).

One of the only design caveats around such developmental constraints would be the construction of a secondary plaza. Charles Stout and Barry

1. Central plaza
2. principal pyramid

Lewis (1998:163) feel this option explains a possible secondary plaza opposite the large pyramid (with opposing steps) at the Adams site in Kentucky. It very well may explain the two plazas at Winterville and Lake George, especially since a single mound and plaza complex had been established at both during the preceding Coles Creek period. The complex we see today was a result of a planned Mississippian expansion of both towns around A.D. 1200 (Brain 1989; Williams and Brain 1983).

Following the plaza, the next most important element of almost every town, large or small, was the principal pyramid. Among multiple mound towns, there was almost always one platform larger than the rest that dominated the group (Phillips et al. 1951:325). Believing most to be vacant ceremonial centers, Phillips, Ford, and Griffin (1951) interpreted them as the substructures for temples. More recently, Holley (1999:28) identified these most often as elite residential substructures.

> I interpret these prominent monuments as supporting a chief's compound that encompassed a host of functions. Excavations uniformly document the presence of encircling palisades and large buildings. . . . The chief's mound displays features that separate it from the remainder of the mounds: different morphology and mass . . . larger size; a position that dominated the main plaza; and the summit of which supported the center's largest building, typically a multi-room compound. Internal differentiation and the considerable size of these buildings—more than twice the size of other buildings—indicate that they accommodated a large number of people, such as retainers and select audiences. (Holley 1999:28–29)

Importantly, these residential domiciles were *not* usually the same as the Mississippian temples or charnel houses, as some mistakenly assume (Yoffee 2005:174). In addition, within the Cahokian "metroplex" (to borrow a word from Stephen Lekson [personal communication, 2005]), elite compounds were not restricted to the tops of platform mounds. Nor were they limited to single large houses. For instance, in one portion of the sprawling Cahokia complex (called the East St. Louis site), one composite compound consisted of one or more earthen platforms, multiple large domiciles, and storage huts or granaries (Pauketat, ed. 2005). Again, George Holley has gone to some lengths to distinguish the temple mound from the elite residential platform, perhaps the best excavated example being that on Mound F at the Angel site (figure 4.7). He states that the "second primary feature in the Mississippian town is the temple. Temples, also on platform mounds, served charnel and other ritualistic functions. . . . Temple buildings are, like the chief's compound, distinguished (often) by two-room partitioning and palisades that limit access" (Holley 1999:29).

However, the summits of many earthen platforms, at least those in the Middle Mississippian area, are best described as dynamic and multi-purpose. For instance, on Cahokia's Kunnemann mound, Preston Holder documented an array of contemporary and sequent constructions that covered the gamut of building sizes and shapes. There were large and small rectangular, circular, and T-shaped buildings, such that several likely

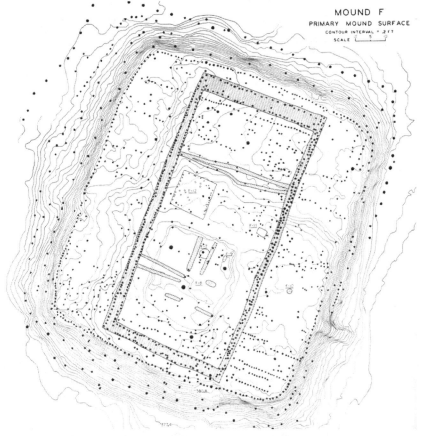

Figure 4.7. Temple on Mound F at Angel (from Black 1967; used with permission of the Indiana Historical Society Press)

occupied the multiterraced summit at any one time (Pauketat 1993). Here, and at the above mentioned East St. Louis site, there were buildings that can be labeled temples, domiciles, storage buildings, council houses, sweat lodges, and, perhaps, meeting halls (Alt 2006a). The same now appears likely for the slightly less elaborate Mound A at the Shiloh site in Tennessee (David Anderson, personal communication, 2003). Thus who and what was represented by mound-summit architecture likely varied by political or kin affiliation and changed through time. Accordingly, determining the function of any one pyramid and its surmounting buildings may be a silly quest, subordinate in any case to understanding the history of construction, maintenance, and renewal of the mound-top architecture.

I have concluded elsewhere that, for both Cahokian and other Mississippian earthen monuments, the repeated act of construction and renewal was a large part of the reason for pyramids (Pauketat 1993, 2000b). Where recent excavations exist in the Middle Mississippian area, it appears likely that construction of the pyramid complex—ranging from the addition of new construction fill to the repair, replastering, or reconstruction of mound-top pole-and-thatch architecture—was a regularly recurring, perhaps annual, affair. In addition, our excavations into a number of mounds around greater Cahokia, recent excavations of Shiloh's Mound A, and careful readings of a suite of older excavations reveal evidence of considerable ongoing maintenance of the earthen pyramids in addition to their periodic renewal and enlargement (Anderson and Cornelison 2002; Williams and Brain 1983).

The mounds were not simple piles of dirt left to sit and erode during the year. More engineering skill and human labor went into them than some have supposed. And once built, they were cared for. Such care, along with the greater investments in creating the central landscape, always seems overlooked by those whose estimates minimize the labor required to build a mound. Ostensibly a means of appraising regional population or political power, the estimates never consider the actual periodicity or amplitude of the group labor invested in the surmounting architectural reconstructions, in the acquisition of the funds and the production of foods to support the construction effort, and in the ritual trappings of each annual project (Williams and Shapiro 1996:147; Wills 2000). Building an earthen pyramid was about much more than digging, carrying, and dumping dirt.

Consider what was being maintained. Excavations reveal that, while towns were occupied, the earthen pyramids were well-proportioned quadrilateral constructions with sharp-angled corners and terraces. They were not grass-covered, eroded lumps of earth but packed-earth pyramids. My own excavations into four pyramids at and around Cahokia, as well as two other well-documented cases at Cahokia (Mounds 11 and 51), uncovered no indications of humus lines. Instead, there were clear signs of many microerosional events—probably summer thunderstorms or winter snow melts—and small-scale maintenance patches of damaged pyramid faces. Very little water-laid silt was allowed to accumulate at the base of the steeply angled pyramid faces, typically dipping 45 to 55 degrees downward from the horizontal summits. David Anderson came to similar conclusions at the Shiloh site in Tennessee.

In other words, these mounds were probably not allowed to sustain a vigorous growth of vegetation, certainly not the green, manicured European grasses shown in today's museum murals or illustrated on the covers of recent books (Lewis and Stout 1998; Pauketat and Emerson 1997). Around Cahokia, dark brown to black, silty clays were sometimes used to cap mounds and presumably control erosion (Dalan et al. 2003; Pauketat 1993). At Shiloh and elsewhere in the South, the silts and clays used to cover the mounds were both reddish and whitish in color. Thus we might imagine that the blackness, redness, or whiteness of Mississippian monuments great and small would have stood out from the green leafy landscapes in which they sat. To those earth tones, we need to add the brown shades of debarked wood and the golden yellow hues of bundled thatch.

Palisades and Compound Walls

Walled enclosures were common but not universal features of Mississippian towns. And, unlike various earthen pyramids, they seem less ambiguous with respect to function. Here, it would seem, were boundary elements that delimited and protected principal and secondary pyramid or compound spaces (Holley 1999; Lewis et al. 1998). Some walls, as at Angel, were associated with buildings and mound-summit surfaces (figure 4.7). Fences shielded mortuary buildings and their yards from view or passage, and walls surrounded the platform mounds or the special buildings and seating areas on their summits. Elsewhere, vertical-log walls also surrounded open, nonmound spaces, as seen in the 278-square-meter premound-stage compound at Cemochechobee (pronounced *Sam-o-chee-cho-bee*), in Georgia, or in the over 600-square-meter bastioned compound (probably daubed and painted red) on Tract 15B at Cahokia (Pauketat and Alt 2004; Schnell et al. 1981). Such walls, fences, and enclosures *divided* settlements, simultaneously protecting ritual space, if not also private elite grounds, from the outside world even as it excluded some segments of that outside realm from routine access of their interiors.

These may be distinguished from the palisade walls or the ditches that surround settlements, or substantial parts of them (figure 4.8). Most of these unquestionably served in the defense of the precincts within, especially obvious since the bastions that line the curtain walls at many settlements were spaced an average twenty meters apart, the ideal distance for an effective enfilade of arrows shot in defense of the wall from each of the bastions. The walls at Cahokia and at Moundville, in Alabama, were massive. Others, as at Angel, were equally impressive (if enclosing a smaller space), built with logs and daubed to create a formidable barrier to would-be intruders (Black 1967). Despite attempts to minimize their military significance (or reinterpret them as ritual walls), comparisons with the walled garrisons or forts of the young United States reveal some Mississippian walls to have been far superior fortifications in many respects. Perhaps this is because most pre-Columbian walls protected more than just military outposts. Since Mississippian towns were also sacred places, the palisade walls guarded, as it were, heaven on earth.

Such walls also had the effect, anticipated or not, of accentuating intracommunity social stratification, since imposing walls would have impeded the access of some residents to, or their movement through,

Figure 4.8. Aerial (Infrared) photograph of the Common Field site (large mound, individual burned houses, and portion of palisade wall appear as large central white oval, dozens of small black dots, and angled subtle light line in lower right, respectively). Courtesy F. Terry Norris, U.S. Army Corps of Engineers, St. Louis District

the town's most important plaza and mound precincts. I cannot believe that palisade walls were built originally to demarcate ceremonial space, a point of view common among those who would pacify the past (Keeley 1996). However, social distance, or stratification, could have been an un-anticipated outcome of an enclosure process involving the construction of palisade walls, compounds, and even fences around house lots or yards (Pauketat and Alt 2004; Johnson 1996). The stratifying effects of such walls may have been especially pronounced where palisades did not en-circle the entire residential occupations, potentially leaving some residents outside during an attack (Holley 1999).

Unlike the plaza, however, walls were not necessarily foundational or deterministic elements of Mississippian town design. Indeed, when or where palisade walls were constructed or dismantled may reveal a town's social and political history in ways that plaza-and-mound construction does not. For instance, in eastern Tennessee, the recon-struction and relocation of palisade walls "have been used to argue for episodes of village expansion (e.g., Hixon, Hiwassee Island, and Loy) as well as reduction (e.g., Toqua)" (Schroedl 1998:77). A palisade wall was not a feature of the Cahokian capital in its first century of existence. By contrast, palisade walls seem to have been built at the founding moments of many other Mississippian centers, large and small. The large encircling wall at the Moundville site was erected at its inception as a regional administrative capital (Knight and Steponaitis 1998:15). And walls were probably built as soon as the "intrusive" settlements in Georgia were founded (see below).

Clearly the reasons for building or not building walls are to be sought in the larger transregional history of Midwestern and southern violence rather than in some generic idea of a Mississippian grammar. In any case, palisade walls were not the same insurmountable obstacles to the design or redesign of a town. After all, they were subject to rot. They could be dismantled. They could be breached.

Housing

A final characteristic element of Mississippian towns was domestic housing. Unlike the presumed case for many pre-Mississippian centers, people did live at most Mississippian towns. *Perhaps* several sites in the

Lower Mississippi valley or the South Appalachian area were vacant throughout most of their history (Holley 1999:37; Williams and Shapiro 1990:172–173; Williams and Brain 1983). However, as often as not, vacancy is an assertion not founded on actual excavations of potential residential areas but on hunches based either on old biases or on the lack of obvious accumulations of refuse on the site surfaces. Unfortunately surface visibility and refuse deposition are always tricky matters in eastern North American archaeology, and so the hunches remain just that (before large excavations in 1960 and 1961, the heavily populated Cahokia site was thought to have been a vacant ceremonial center). In addition, there is an obvious problem with how archaeologists delimit sites within cultural landscapes that might have been perceived quite differently by pre-Columbian people.

In any event, there is ample evidence of moderate to dense residential occupations at any number of large and small centers, with houses often disposed in an orderly fashion and, about half the time, rebuilt in the same location at least once (Holley 1999:30). "For nearly all Mississippian towns, the single family dwelling was the minimal social unit. Most of these structures range in size from 15 to 42 m^2. . . . These households were probably not independent—their disposition suggests that they formed larger functioning units" (Holley 1999:30). Such functioning units seem evident in the arrangement of houses around open courtyards or in sets or clusters (Mehrer and Collins 1995; Sullivan 1995). The latter may include various rectangular and circular buildings, implying functional, seasonal, or social variability (Emerson 1997a,b).

The arrangement of domiciles at some, but certainly not all, Mississippian towns was nonrandom, implying that households conformed to some larger sitewide order. Presumably there were rules and referents that affected how one sited one's house. Depending on the time and place, there likely were similar rules and referents delimiting how and when one built a house or what materials to use in the construction (Simon 2002). Unfortunately there are shockingly few modern excavations of entire domiciles, never mind multiple houses (but see Rogers and Smith 1995). For this reason, today's Mississippianists (outside of Cahokia-area researchers) seldom analyze the packing, standardization, permanency, and construction cycles of eastern North American housing (figures 4.9–4.10).

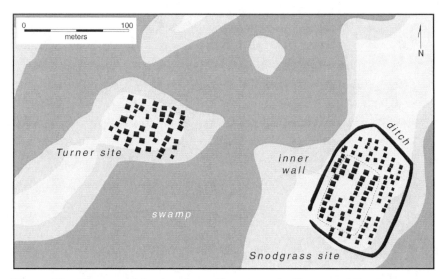

Figure 4.9. Diagrammatic plan view of houses at the Turner and Snodgrass sites, southeast Missouri (after O'Brien 2001)

Were there any other domestic occupations like Cahokia (see Chapter 6)? Cahokia's founding around A.D. 1050 witnessed the establishment of a rigid "master plan" or "Cahokian grid" that Melvin Fowler (1975) has determined was aligned to marker posts and mounds, if not also other cosmological referents (Sherrod and Rolingson 1987; Stout and Lewis 1998). Its founding also saw an abrupt and nearly total conversion of house construction styles that I have discussed elsewhere (Pauketat 1994, 2000a, 2004). At Cahokia in A.D. 1050, the wall-trench construction style—once used as a defining attribute of Mississippian culture—was introduced (and possibly innovated).

> Wherever one looks among the excavations at Cahokia, evidence abounds that the new houses built during the urban renewal events of AD 1050 were assembled in a new architectural style characterized by "wall trenches." The wall posts of pre-Mississippian buildings were set in individually dug postholes. . . . More than likely, the wall posts were saplings bent over and tied off in the center to fashion an arbor-shaped roof. . . . Contrast these to new wall trench domiciles built to house Cahokia's booming population. While these retained the rectangular semi-subterranean look, the use of trenches (dug using . . . stone-bladed hoes) rather than individual postholes makes it possible that walls were

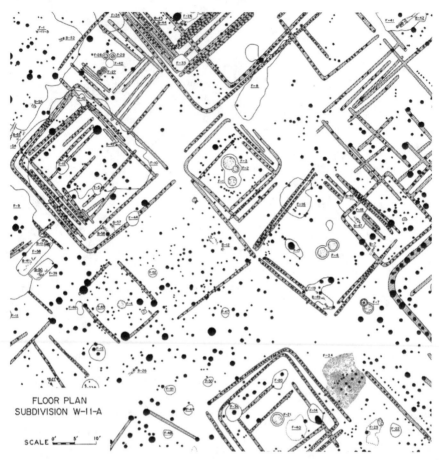

FLOOR PLAN
SUBDIVISION W–11–A

SCALE 0' 5' 10'

Figure 4.10. Wall-trench houses excavated at the Angel site, Indiana (from Black 1967; used with the permission of the Indiana Historical Society Press)

prefabricated on the ground and then set into place at once. For a rect-angular house, this means that the roof would probably have been a separate construction . . . a thatched hipped roof. (Pauketat 2004:80)

The rate and scale of this architectural shift led me to suggest nonfamil-ial work crews possibly taking responsibility for a short-term labor-intensive building effort, not unlike the leveling of Cahokia's main plaza (Pauketat 1994:172–173). Outside of the central complex within the greater Cahokia region, the conversion was uneven and less dramatic, involving a transitional faux wall trench construction style at a few settlements (Alt 2001; Pauketat 2003a; Pauketat and Alt 2005). I suspect that similar home-building projects might have taken place at other large centers, with knowledgeability lags in their corresponding rural zones (on the order of years or decades).

Why? It is likely that new housing was a logical concomitant of the founding of powerful places, with their new monumental pyramid-and-plaza spaces and all they were meant to convey to the people. Consider that a thatched hipped-roof house might have looked quite different from various pre-Mississippian structures. Thus a series of them would have potentially added a whole new golden yellow look to the earth-toned monumental landscape of the center. In addition, housing construction practices embody the intersection of politics, community identity, and daily practice (Pauketat and Alt 2005). Consider John Blitz and Karl Lorenz's (2002) analysis of the first wall-trench architecture along Georgia's Chattahoochee River:

> Concurrent with the appearance of the Middle Mississippian ceramic tradition in these regional phases is wall-trench architecture. . . . We consider improbable the pan-regional dissemination of wall-trench architecture by the mechanisms of long-distance diffusion or independent invention. Wall trenches are signatures of a structurally specific architectural form, the details of which were not easily transmitted by casual observation or indirect sources. . . . Folk architecture carries a high symbolic load often emblematic of cultural identity. . . . For these reasons, we think wall-trench architecture was one element of the cultural blueprint carried by the Middle Mississippian pioneers. (Blitz and Lorenz 2002:124–125)

The lack of sufficient excavated architectural samples, chronological controls, and high-level theorizing in Mississippian archaeology would explain why some might find it "hard to see why this [work crew or blueprint idea] is necessary, since there was an equally rapid adoption of this [wall-trench construction] technique, even in isolated farmsteads, all over the Mississippian world" (Muller 1997:294 n.). Unfortunately, besides overlooking the issue of the projected scale of specific towns (especially the Cahokian metroplex) or the fact that adoption was *not* "equally rapid" within regions (Alt 2001; Blitz and Lorenz 2002), such a minimalist view fails to appreciate that we are talking about changes over, at most, decades (figure 4.11). It also fails to provide a counterexplanation of an established archaeological pattern. Why did wall-trench architecture spread across much of the Midwest and South, over a period of about a hundred years, if either the construction style or the novel house form were not a politically and symbolically charged practice?

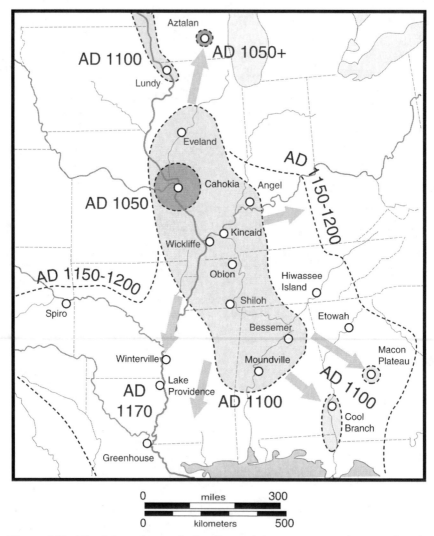

Figure 4.11. The inferred spread of wall trench house construction practices, in calibrated radiocarbon time

In the end, given the bounded, ordered, and planned character of many Mississippian towns large and small, we should, minimally (but not minimalistically), question on both empirical and theoretical grounds any assertion stating that Mississippian household economy was "not scaled down" from centers (Muller 1997:192). Instead, we need to investigate the reasons for Holley's (1999:29) conclusion: "The appearance of towns in the Southeast had a profound impact on domestic life."

CHAPTER FIVE

THE X FACTOR

A French writer has fancifully observed, that civilization arises, *de la fermentation dune nombreuse peuplade.*

—Henry Marie Brackenridge, 1814

Introduced and local cultural traits were quickly welded together to produce [Mississippian] traits that appear unlike the items from which they were derived. . . . This is what we have designated as the X-factor, the contributions made by the culture to its own development.

—Phillips, Ford, and Griffin 1951

Investigating the relationship between the appearance of towns and domestic life is about understanding how different people caused, accommodated, or resisted change. It is about understanding how collective memories were negotiated, remembered, and forgotten, how traditions were invented and reinvented continuously, and how politics and daily practice intersected (Connerton 1989; De Certeau 1984; Hobsbawm 1983; Kertzer 1988). Theory suggests that such intersections happened in the guise of community, where community was (and is) an open, malleable, materialized, and spatialized field of cultural identity formation. Communities weren't static. They never are. They were subject to politicization, cooptation, or reinterpretation by politicos, factions, and hidden (or unofficial) interests at local, regional, and even transregional scales (Scott 1990; Trouillot 1985).

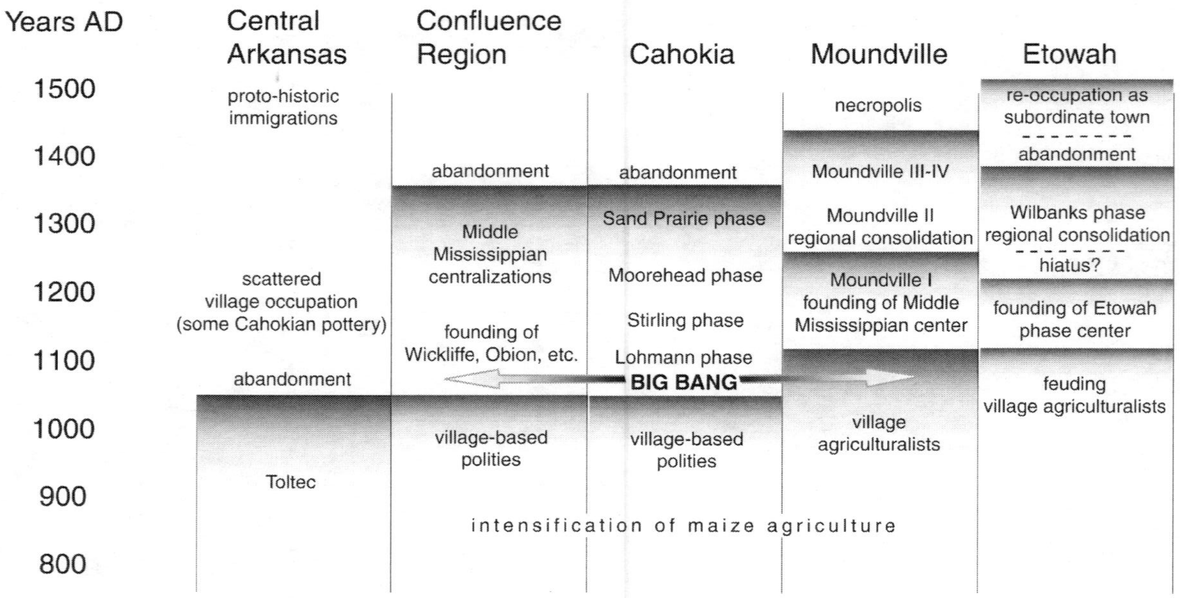

Figure 5.1. Comparative chronology of events from Cahokia to Etowah

To investigate these processes, I review several cases of Mississippianization in different portions of eastern North America. Each case is hindered by the lack of key archaeological information. However, there are sufficient data with which to compare each regional development with an eye toward rethinking Mississippian chiefdoms (figure 5.1). Such a comparative archaeo-history, based in the principles of contemporary social theory, is the key to transcending the problems associated with the commonsense vestiges of social evolutionism and systems thinking in contemporary archaeology.

Along the Arkansas River

As noted earlier, the Coles Creek centers of southeastern Arkansas, southwestern Mississippi, and northern Louisiana seem in their construction to have integrated specific political communities, with the largest (at early Winterville or Lake George) merely being first among equals (Kidder 1998:140, 2002a:87–89). However, there was one nearby exception, the misnamed Toltec site, just to the north in the central Arkansas River valley. Toltec is strategically located "20 km southeast of the point at which the Arkansas River emerges from the interior highlands into the alluvial plain of the Mississippi River" (Rolingson 1990:27). This well-placed site emerged in the ninth through eleventh centuries A.D. to become by far the largest center of its sort (Nassaney 1991, 1994, 2001; Rolingson 2002). "Here we seem to have a good example of a community that, by its size and presumably authority, eclipsed its nearest neighbors (or competitors) in virtually every measure of power, wealth, and status" (Kidder 1998:140).

As a ditched and embanked forty-two-hectare space enclosing eighteen earthen pyramids up to fifteen meters high, the densely packed Toltec site both mimics and supersedes its Marksville, Baytown, and Coles Creek precursors to the south (figure 5.2). A rich layer of feasting debris has been found around the base of some of the platforms, mixed with bits and pieces of sumptuary goods that testify to the religiosity of public mound-top performances (Rolingson 1998). Michael Nassaney's (1994) survey and excavations in the rural Plum Bayou culture landscape around this center located at least two outlier settlements and an array of small habitation sites, farmsteads of a sort, with objects in their possession link-

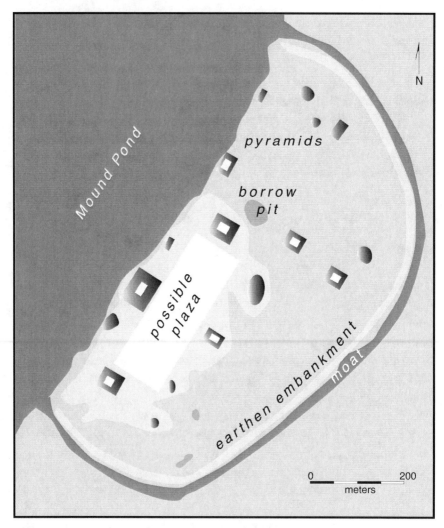

Figure 5.2. Diagrammatic plan view of the Toltec site, Arkansas

ing them to Toltec's central if communal economy: goods probably moved into the center and the Toltec hosts probably reciprocated with religious and political services. For Rolingson (2002), this pattern indicates a simple chiefdom. Nassaney (2001) stresses the novelty of a corporate social order where authority was, to some extent, subsumed by a regionwide community that in turn was created through public events hosted at Toltec.

Such a regional political–communal order was not unique on the Arkansas River at the time, as a series of more modest Late Fourche Maline and Early Caddoan Harlan phase sites are found upriver in eastern Oklahoma (Bell 1984; Schambach 2002). At places such as Spiro, Harlan, and Reed, sparsely populated mound centers were the sites of mortuary ritual for people who grew starchy seed crops and, after A.D. 1000, maize (Fritz 1990; Rogers 1996). Although dates and data are muddled, it seems likely that, until the early twelfth century, none of these sites—and certainly not Toltec—would be labeled Mississippian by archaeologists. Yes, there were centralized political–communal orders of some sort (some would call them chiefdoms), and there were imposing earthen pyramids and modest possible plazas. But something was missing.

What it was appeared, at least in hybrid form, later (A.D. 1250–1400). Let's look west, up the Arkansas River in present-day Oklahoma, where the Spiro site and its outliers grew to singular proportions, at least for the upper Arkansas River valley. There subsequent generations of people appear to have commemorated the ancestral Early Caddoan place by adapting a new Mississippi valley agriculture that involved the politicization of crop production and the domestication of ideologies of power. Spiroans, most living outside the sparsely populated ceremonial center itself, constructed additional earthen pyramids around an open plaza, now with pole and thatch temples and residences atop the flat summits.

Never as large as its southern counterparts at Etowah or Moundville, the Spiro center's political–cultural prominence is evident in its mortuary remains. Latter-day Spiroans buried their elite here with hoards of material objects and elaborate ritual garb. The most notable interments were those in the Craig mound's great mortuary chamber, constructed and buried at about A.D. 1400, perhaps in one last vainglorious attempt to lionize their heritage (Brown 1996).

But Spiro's inhabitants were peripheral players in a game centered far to the east. James Brown (2005a:120) now concludes that "Spiro, which started receiving precious goods from Cahokia in the twelfth century, was also the most influenced by Cahokian ideology." Indeed, for our purposes, the most significant historical events in the Arkansas valley did not originate at Spiro at all, but at Toltec. Of these events, the most noteworthy was the final abandonment of Toltec. While cause and effect are too intertwined to dissect given the data at hand, clearly the Plum Bayou culture evaporated and Toltec proper, along with the entire central Arkansas River valley, was emptied of its people during the eleventh century (Nassaney 2001). The population went elsewhere, perhaps into Caddo country. Others probably moved north, joining the cast list of Cahokia's political theater that, we shall see, was the principal reason for Mississippianization (chapter 6).

Into Georgia

Migration, in addition to being a major component of Mississippianization scenarios elsewhere, is difficult to avoid given evidence from the south Appalachian region. New evidence from the Chattahoochee River basin in southwestern Georgia complements that long known from the central Ocmulgee region, completing a picture of a dynamic transregional political–cultural landscape studded by the great Etowah center in the north.

The history of Mississippianization in various parts of the south Appalachian region seems written on the land as alternating town constructions and, by inference, fluctuating political fortunes. In river valleys between northeastern Georgia and southern South Carolina, the cycling model of David Anderson (1994, 1996) describes well the apparent political–historical flurry of alternating pyramid construction sequences and settlement histories (Hally 1996). Starting as early as the twelfth century in some places, there was considerable physical movement and population displacement between regions, the long-term historical effects of which need to be more closely examined (Blitz 1999; Cobb and Butler 2002; Pauketat 2003a).

For instance, in the Oconee River basin, the sequential developments appear to have involved paired towns, one following the other in time (Williams and Shapiro 1990, 1996). In another case, the Savannah River basin was initially carved into upper-, middle- and lower-valley political territories, each one centered on a major town around A.D. 1350. However, later population movement resulted from or led to political consolidation elsewhere (Anderson 1994; Hally 1994). Even in the Etowah valley and northwestern Georgia, the fall of the great Etowah center was followed by a reconsolidation at the King site. There the indigenous lords of the large province they called "Coosa" met the army of Hernando de Soto (Hally and Kelly 1998). After A.D. 1350 or so, the archaeological expression of these various provinces in the South Appalachian area are described as phases of a greater Lamar Mississippian phenomenon (figure 5.3), a

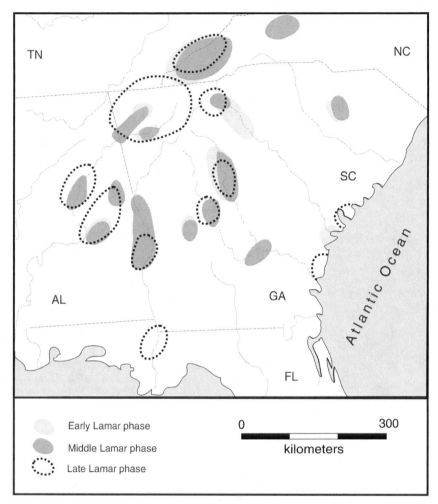

Figure 5.3. Lamar phase complexes through time, A.D. 1350–1550 (after Hally 1994)

ceramic complex which appears, after A.D. 1550, to have an ethnic reality as well (Hally 1994; Saunders 2001).

Rood Phase and Macon Plateau Culture Contacts

The south Appalachian provinces known to European explorers seem to have originated in a series of culture contacts between early Mississippians from the northern and southern Woodland peoples. Currently the best documented case of such culture contact consists of the Rood phase, an intrusive movement of people into the lower Chattahoochee River valley in southwestern Georgia. Sometime at or after A.D. 1100, an outside group of people bearing unmistakably Middle Mississippian ceramics seem to have moved into the formerly uninhabited buffer zone between two adjacent non-Mississippian Weeden Island populations (recognized as distinctive settlement patterns and pottery styles; Blitz and Lorenz 2002). At this time, a palisaded frontier town centered on a single platform mound was constructed at the Cool Branch site, complete with wall-trench houses and pots that bear "a striking resemblance to ceramic assemblages from the Bessemer . . . [and] Moundville I phase" (Blitz and Lorenz 2002:127; see below).

Unlike the culture contact and colonization at Macon Plateau, the Rood phase people stayed and built additional large towns later, as at Cemochechobee, which Frank Schnell and colleagues (1981) date from A.D. 1100 but David Hally (1994:table 14.1) places at A.D. 1200. Indeed, John Blitz and Karl Lorenz (2002) make a convincing argument that the local–foreign culture contact experience produced the early Fort Walton Cayson phase and was a historical precursor to the later well-known Apalachee people so important in the European colonization of Florida.

The case was slightly different at Macon Plateau, an impressive center consisting of eight earthen pyramids in a planned quasi-pentagonal area covering about seventy hectares (Hally and Williams 1994; see figure 11). From the beginning of excavations in the 1930s, and based in part on the ceramic affinity opinions of James B. Griffin (1994), archaeologists understood the Macon Plateau site (Ocmulgee) in central Georgia as possibly the best example of a "site unit intrusion" known in North America (Williams 1994). Here, as at Cool Branch, colonizing foreigners—Mississippians from the north and west—established a new province. The founding of Macon Plateau likely saw the new residents constructing a central precinct from scratch. Their new ceremonial complex included special earth-embanked circular council houses, a large fifteen-meter-high pyramid, a probable plaza on a hill, and a defensive wall and ditch (Hally and Williams 1994:88).

At that time, the hill immediately to the west was established as a cemetery, and several elaborate crypt burials of specially processed and entombed bodies—perhaps of the town's founders—were laid into log-lined chambers (Fairbanks 2003; Powell 1994). These singularly important people were interred with, among other things, thousands of shell beads or bead-studded garments near the beginning of the site's occupation history.[1] Successive charnel house–mound construction fills blanketed this mortuary area, each layer with additional if less elaborate burial interments (Powell 1994). This funeral mound and the other, apparently later outlier mounds might have been components of separate walled pyramid and plaza precincts all tied into a master plan (Hally and Williams 1994:94).

Arguably, the Macon Plateau complex and a cluster of seven other known nearby settlements were founded sometime early in the twelfth century by people most likely hailing from eastern Tennessee who left their homeland for reasons unknown (Pauketat 2005:208 n.; cf. Hally 1994). The arrivals possessed ceramic technologies—shell-and-grit tempered smooth-surfaced globular jars, bowls, bottles, and (sometimes fabric-impressed) pans—like those of Tennessee but totally different from the stamped pottery of either the preceding Late Woodland period or subsequent Mississippian occupations in central Georgia (Cobb and Garrow 1996; Williams 1994:131–136). "On the other hand, the *later* non-Macon-Plateau (but still "Mississippian") ceramics from contiguous regions show many similarities in vessel shape, decoration techniques, paste formula, and firing methods to those of the [preceding] late Woodland" (Williams 1994:137). That is, the early Macon Plateau Mississippians were outsiders who came, saw, and left. Once Macon Plateau was abandoned—probably close to A.D. 1200—the locality was not reinhabited, suggesting a lingering fear of the place, taboos linked to its former inhabitants, or bad memories of events that happened there. Local folks avoided the locality for generations (Williams 1994:137).

Etowah

The founding of another large center in Georgia north along the Etowah River was perhaps less dramatic (see figure 4.6). The initial town is known only from some feasting midden and several large wall-trench structures. Based on this meager evidence, the early center is presumed to have consisted of two small pyramids and a plaza (King 2003, 2005). Although convention dates the beginning of this, the Early Etowah phase from A.D. 1000, four of the seven radiocarbon dates from four Early Etowah phase features have intercepts of AD 1160 to 1238. The one-sigma range of all seven dates falls between AD 899-1275 (King 2003:table 8). Given the small excavated sample and limited structural evidence, the one hundred year "Late Etowah" phase (AD 1100-1200) may in reality encompass the entire early Mississippian component. (Pauketat 2005:208 n.)

Indeed, the radiocarbon dates suggest that such a beginning might postdate A.D. 1150. If so, then the subsequent Early Savannah phase—a time of political collapse and occupational hiatus within the Etowah region (currently dated A.D. 1200–1250)—may need to be rethought, especially as it is based on an absence of datable evidence.

Adam King (2003:112) offers a dual-processual model that sees the Etowah site, the Sixtoe site in Georgia, the Hiwassee Island site in Tennessee, *and* Macon Plateau as emerging chiefdoms that share the same corporate orientation, which he dates from A.D. 1000 (Schroedl 1994, 1998). Such a start date is probably inaccurate, a little too early for any of these places (Cobb and Garrow 1996; Schroedl et al. 1990:table 21), especially since seven of eleven Hiwassee Island dates fall between 1100 and 1280. In any event, following Cobb and Garrow (1996) and Keith Little (1999), Adam King's main point is unaffected by chronology; this corporate orientation may have been a Late Woodland "solution to endemic warfare" in this and other regions (King 2003:114).

The people of the Woodstock culture (immediately preceding the Etowah phase) built walls around their settlements, including that of the type site Woodstock Fort near Etowah (Cobb and Garrow 1996). Clearly the "available evidence points to a general climate of social circumscription, endemic warfare, and resource stress afflicting a large section of the Southeast" at this time (Knight and Steponaitis 1998:10). Thus, perhaps "early Mississippian chiefdoms in northwestern Georgia were formed as alliances forged between once hostile subgroups and were maintained through action for the common good" (King 2003:115).

Apparently a political reconsolidation of Etowah proper in A.D. 1250 followed closely on the heels of (if it didn't in some ways exacerbate) a presumed Early Savannah phase occupational hiatus in the larger Etowah valley. King (2003) prefers to see the subsequent Wilbanks phase (A.D. 1250–1375) as a period of network-based strategizing by Etowah elites. However, the labor-

Figure 5.4. Etowah's Mounds A and C, view to south

intensive boom in monumental (corporate) constructions—dramatic building stages added to Mounds A and C, a newly paved and rock-lined plaza, compound wall constructions, a circumferential palisade and moat—here and at as "many as five secondary centers . . . established in close proximity to Etowah" (King 2005:153) indicate less a network strategy and more the transregional preeminence of Etowah's people (figure 5.4).

Key to this preeminence, King (2005) notes, was the adaptation of a foreign mythology consisting of what James Brown (2005a)—following Paul Radin (1948) and Robert Hall (1989, 1997)—calls the Morning Star legend, the mythical struggle of a superhuman bird-man with the forces of death and darkness. That legend is traceable in some ways to the Middle Mississippian peoples near or at Cahokia. That's important, and seems equally so at other southern centers (e.g., there's a huge modeled clay effigy of a bird-man, complete with the characteristic forked eye, on the floor of a burned earth-embanked circular building at Macon Plateau). Etowah's Middle Mississippian period is hence both a chronological and a political–cultural unit in Georgia.

Etowah elites during this time appear to have established fictive kin alliances with distant neighbors (an idea that closely parallels Robert Hall's

[1991] analysis of Cahokia's transregional interactions). Such alliances included likely ties to the south with the inhabitants of late Rood phase sites (e.g., Cemochechobee) and the Lake Jackson site complex. These alliances were created by giving away actual pieces of the mythological story to these distant peers and political wannabes. These pieces of Etowah included the so-called Braden A copper plates, some of which were cut into smaller pieces for the manufacture of special headdresses (King 2005; Jones 1982; Schnell et al. 1981). Previously such alliances were identified as a long-distance exchange corridor where southeastern ceremonial complex objects moved from place to place (King 2003:123; Brown et al. 1990). But now, it seems, economic exchange has given way to political history.

During the Wilbanks phase Etowah was to its neighbors what Cahokia had been to Etowah previously (Brown 2005a). Middle Mississippian in Georgia was the "idea of Cahokia writ large" (Anderson 1997). With the apparent burning of the palisade wall and the likely sacking of the Etowah site around A.D. 1375, the elaborate retelling of the Middle Mississippian narrative through art and mortuary theater came to a rather ignominious end (King 2005). Bird-man or Morning Star referents are few to nonexistent in the later Lamar Mississippian complexes. The legitimating story seems to have been intentionally forgotten. By whom? Apparently the masses of people not schooled in the arts and stories of foreign would-be rulers.

Moundville and the Mid-South

Prior to the establishment of the first Mississippian towns in west-central Alabama and east-central Mississippi, there is clear evidence of a situation much like the pre-Mississippian Etowah valley (Knight and Steponaitis 1998:10; Powell 1992). "Riverine settlements are closely spaced, site sizes are large" and evidence of warfare and subsistence stress is found in "each of the crowded valleys" (Knight and Steponaitis 1998:11; Little 1999). And like the Etowah valley far to the east, the initially modest Mississippian developments appear to have mitigated these problems to some extent.

A couple decades after A.D. 1100, a small center consisting of two separate Moundville I phase pyramids and surrounding residences was established at what would later become the Moundville megacenter (Knight and Steponaitis 1998; Knight et al. n.d.). Lubbub Creek's small earthen pyramid sixty kilometers west of Moundville was under construction to the west by about the same time (Blitz 1993; Welch 1990). To the north, another similar town was founded at the Bessemer site in the early twelfth century, minimally consisting of three pyramids and a series of oversize wall-trench buildings (DeJarnette and Wimberly 1941; Welch 1990). And much farther north in western Tennessee, the Shiloh, Savannah, and Obion sites were founded at or slightly after this time (D. Anderson, personal communication, 2003; Garland 1992; Welch 1998a, 2006).

The next phase in the political development of the contiguous regions around Moundville, however, was abrupt. Sometime around A.D. 1225, an expansive new town design was superimposed over the former early Moundville center (figures 5.5–5.6). It consisted of at least twenty-nine earthen

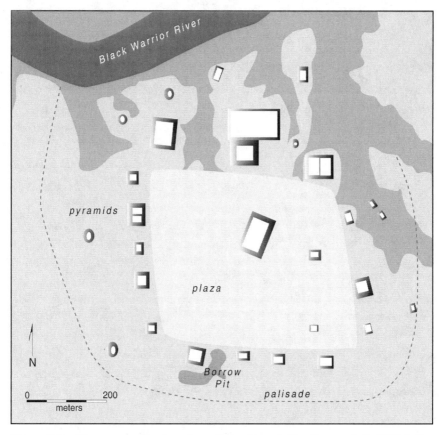

Figure 5.5. Diagrammatic plan view of the Moundville site, ca. A.D. 1250 (after Knight and Steponaitis 1998)

Figure 5.6. **View of Moundville's plaza and Mound A (center) from Mound B**

pyramids and a large plaza (covering up to 20 hectares). Importantly, not only was the town's plaza designed to accommodate giant gatherings, the layout of the new grounds was highly structured in ways "deliberately arranged . . . to evoke and reinforce key social distinctions" (Knight and Steponaitis 1998:60). According to V. James Knight (Knight and Steponaitis 1998:60), these included an attempt at fixing the rank ordering of local kin groups while the placement of the largest elite domiciliary pyramid, Mound B, "reveals the paramountcy as symbolically transcending a reciprocal dual organization." As well as having historic parallels in the arrangement of Chickasaw towns, according to Knight, this diagrammatic center, in its oddly trapezoidal configuration, appears duplicated, at least in outline, by the intrusive frontier Rood phase site of Cool Branch mentioned earlier (figure 5.7).

Moundville's regional preeminence is difficult to deny, as were its effects on domestic life within and beyond the Black Warrior River valley in which it sits. The new center appears to have attracted local people, who moved to it or to one of the many farmsteads nearby (Welch 1998; Wilson 2005). Vincas Steponaitis (Knight and Steponaitis 1998) estimates a max-

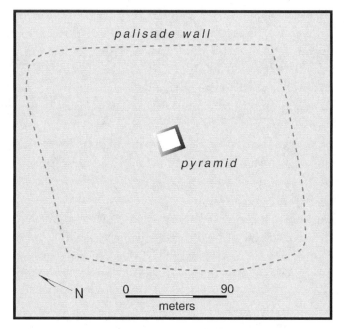

palisade wall

pyramid

N
0   90
meters

Figure 5.7. Cool Branch site plan (after Blitz and Lorenz 2002)

imum of a thousand people at the seventy-five-hectare Moundville site during this time. In addition, the old "nucleated communities gave way to smaller and more dispersed farming settlements" so that most people, after A.D. 1225, lived in farmsteads (Knight and Steponaitis 1998:12). And these people were, according to Mary Lucas Powell (1992, 1998), healthier than their ancestors had been.

But perhaps life was not as idyllic as all that, at least for those categorized as outsiders during the Late Moundville I and Early Moundville II phase (A.D. 1225–1300). After all, the founding of the expansive new Moundville capital included the construction of one of the longest bastioned palisade walls ever built in the pre-Columbian Southeast (Vogel and Allan 1985). It enclosed about seventy-five hectares, encompassing most of the site's residential buildings, and was rebuilt at least six times in the thirteenth century (M. Scarry 1998:79–80). Given its massive size, prominent rectangular bastions, and reconstruction, most would agree that it was a defensive feature.

Let me explain what I mean by "defensive." Some years ago Vincas Steponaitis (1991) noticed that between Moundville and the large towns of Lake George and Anna, just over 300 kilometers to the west, there were no significant Mississippian towns that could have competed with Moundville for control over access to key resources or transportation corridors. To the northwest, the next largest complex was Etowah, 300 kilometers away. Based on his quantitative analysis of prestige goods in the small Pocahontas polity, he suspected that the newly consolidated polities of Moundville, Lake George, and Anna in A.D. 1200–1250 "may have actively *precluded* the emergence of similar centers in the Pocahontas region, by diminishing the availability of the very tokens that were needed by local leaders to enhance their power and prestige" (Steponaitis 1991:226; but contrast Wilson 2005; Wilson et al. 2006).

We may accept the gist of Steponaitis's analysis while wondering if the Moundvillians (or perhaps Mound-villains, depending on one's perspective back then) might have employed physical force rather than insider-trading schemes to obtain the same result.[2] As I've previously noted, following the warfare studies of Ross Hassig (1998), such fortifications were not simply passive defenses against attacks (which are usually viewed as correlating with rather than causing chiefdoms; contrast Carneiro 1981, 1998b). A wall (or an imposing bounded center or walled pueblo) could have been perceived as an offense to outsiders, a threat by the builders in opposition to any number of neighbors (Blitz and Lorenz 2002; LeBlanc 1999; Pauketat 1998). This is because it enables aggressors to minimize the number of defenders (mostly archers) that would need to be left behind to effectively defend their own hometown. A bastioned palisade permits the people living within the wall to project a large fighting force into distant lands. Had their hometown been unfortified, they would have needed to leave behind more defenders.

And what was there to defend while attacking one's neighbor? As demonstrated by the Casquíns with Hernando de Soto's aid, and to the horror of Pacahans, the most important resource was the town's central ancestral temples. Defiling them or removing the bones of the ancestors who legitimated the town's history would have undermined the raison d'être of the community, including the elites who embodied its sacred powers and organizational center. Lesser worries might have included capital investments and food stores. One possible attack (or ritual incineration) at the East St. Louis site—part of the central Cahokian complex—took out at least fourteen and up to fifty storage huts and other buildings around A.D.

1160 (Pauketat, ed. 2005). Finally there was the potential loss of people as casualties or prisoners of war. Given historic-era practices, it is likely that victors took captives as slaves, wives, or sacrificial victims earlier in the Mississippian period.

That Moundville's inhabitants probably controlled a sizable portion of the Mid-South may need to be rethought in all of the above terms. The fact that lesser, semiautonomous regimes existed, perhaps even prospered, within Moundville's striking distance—as seems the case in the Tombigbee valley's Summerville polity west of Moundville—does not run contrary to this view (cf. Blitz 1993). Rather, like the implication of King's (2003, 2005) sense of long-distance political alliances (and Robert Hall's fictive kin adoptions; Hall 1991), we need to realize that there are more consequences to organized violence and transregional hegemony than meet the archaeological eye. It is not simply a matter of direct control over all aspects of daily life, differential access to prestige goods, or extractions of tribute from beyond the region, as per a typical minimalist stance (Muller 1997). We might instead take a cue from early twenty-first-century American international policy: *international peacemaking and the spreading of cultural ideals, often through strategic state-sponsored violence, effects a level of extrasocietal control sufficient to enhance a group's indirect control and influence, all of which allays common resistance at home.* It's not conquest warfare, but some effects aren't so different.

The powerful Moundville phenomenon in the Mid-South was not sustained in the same way after A.D. 1400, perhaps owing to its mode of consolidation and perhaps to communal resistance. Unlike Macon Plateau, people appear to have altered their political realities by commemorating Moundville and their Moundvillian ancestors, albeit in ways that decentralized government. Certainly, as the administration was decentralized, hiving off to the surrounding, formerly subsidiary outliers, the old capital was converted into a necropolis and the once powerful stories and icons of elites communalized (Knight 1986, 1997; Knight and Steponaitis 1998:19; Welch 1998b:165; Wilson 2005; Wilson et al. 2006). Henceforth, it slowly faded into history, barely noticed by Hernando de Soto's wandering army in later years. Elsewhere the struggle—a literal struggle—for the hearts and minds (and muscles) of the masses continued.

The Confluence

When Hernando de Soto's army crossed the Mississippi River in 1541 near present-day Memphis, clever local native politicos positioned themselves to redirect the foreigners' destructive power at their own enemies, with some success (as with Casquí against Pacaha; Clayton et al. 1993). Thus it might appear that the rise and fall of late pre-Columbian Mississippi valley polities can be explained with reference to networking native elites, sometimes with help from their European counterparts (Smith and Hally 1992). And yet this greatly oversimplifies the social realities of the times.

For our purposes, those realities began around A.D. 1200 as Cahokia, that most powerful neighbor to the north, loosened its grip on the Mississippi River. Beginning at that time, it seems likely that a series of new fortified towns was established along the Mississippi from Ste. Genevieve, Missouri, south through the wide river floodplains to Memphis, Tennessee. Prior to that time, and reminiscent of Moundville's shadow effect, there were no large centers along that stretch of river and hence no large numbers of warriors to challenge what I have elsewhere called Pax Cahokiana (Pauketat 2004:124).[3]

A few important settlements were founded around A.D. 1100 in the central Mississippi valley, Wickliffe being one (Wesler 2001). Located at the confluence of the Ohio and Mississippi Rivers, Kit Wesler's (2001) admirable long-term investigation of this unusually shaped and compact site, which includes long overdue attention to chronological refinement, stands as a model for the rest of us. Unfortunately there is little else of comparable detail with which to compare Wesler's conclusions. And it is unclear, at the beginning, what Wickliffe represents (see chapter 6).

There are early Mississippian towns up the Ohio, for instance at Angel and Kincaid. Angel appears to have been founded at around A.D. 1100 (Hilgeman 2000). Kincaid, on the other hand, may have a pre-Mississippian occupation, or at least an Early Mississippian one, although whether this constituted an actual organized town is not clear. Indeed, Kincaid is only now beginning to see renewed attention after lying dormant since 1930s excavations by the University of Chicago (Cole et al. 1951). Kincaid was much larger and more complex than anyone previously thought, with a developmental history that complements Cahokia's (Paul Welch, personal communication, 2006). Unfortunately, despite attention to regional survey in the 1970s, we know appallingly little about who did what where and when in the region, called the Ohio River's Black Bottom (Butler 1991; Muller 1987).

The same might be said of the vast stretch of floodplains and ancient Pleistocene age terraces in Missouri's Bootheel region. Here, immediately south of the Ohio–Mississippi confluence and along with the bordering hills of Kentucky and Tennessee to the east, were twenty-five major towns that date to the period A.D. 1200–1400. In an area of some 4,000 square kilometers, this works out roughly to be one Mississippian town per 160 square kilometers (figure 5.8). Yet our knowledge of even basic occupation histories and regional settlement patterns is almost nil. For anyone who already presumes to know what caused and resulted from the founding of such places, much

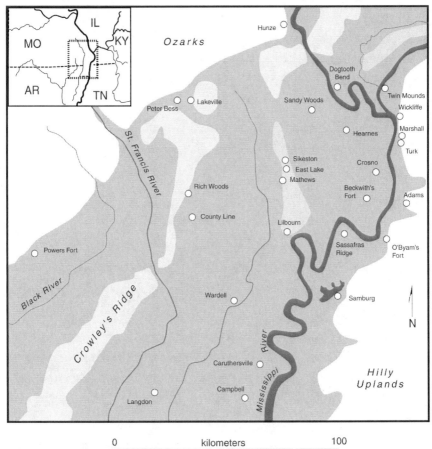

Figure 5.8. Mississippian fortified towns in the Ohio–Mississippi Confluence region (after Lewis 1991; O'Brien 2001)

more than this might not be necessary. Indeed, as modern land leveling and uncontrolled development continues, much more than this might become impossible.

What can be gleaned from the few problem-oriented archaeological projects and fortuitous anecdotal lines of evidence suggests that fortification was a defining feature of towns in the region. Considered theoretically, we might wonder if fortification—not as a thing but as an ongoing practice of constructing and reconstructing walls—was not also a defining feature of community identities (Pauketat 2007). Maybe families that built walls together stayed together, migrated together, or perished together. Patchy information from southeast Missouri makes this point.

Consider the Common Field site, just eighty kilometers south of Cahokia (see figure 4.8). Judging from surface finds and minimal excavations, this fortified site was probably built by A.D. 1200 and burned by A.D. 1400. When a Mississippi River flood scoured the site in 1981, Corps of Engineers archaeologist Terry Norris walked across the surface after the farmer plowed the field, finding more than a hundred exposed burned buildings with their disturbed charred structural timbers and household

Figure 5.9. Common Field site, Ste. Genevieve County, Missouri, in 1981 showing large burned house stains and plowed earthen pyramids. Courtesy F. Terry Norris, St. Louis District, U.S. Army Corps of Engineers

debris (figure 5.9). Unfortunately the archaeologists contracted to evaluate the extent of the damage were unable (or did not think) to map the locations of and collect the artifacts from all of the possible burned buildings at the site, even in this once-in-a-lifetime condition. Then, violating an agreement with the farmer and landowner, they dug into the site. The angry farmer drove them off. We are thus unable to evaluate the intrasettlement diversity and, pending additional data, compare it with those who might have resided outside the walls of this doomed town.

Presumably farmsteads or modest subsidiary villages surrounded some towns (Rogers and Smith 1995). While existing data on population density is insufficient, we might presume that some but not all residents of the founding populations of approximately A.D. 1200 moved into the region, perhaps from the Cahokia region to the north, known to have been losing population at the time. And while some might argue that natural population dynamics may explain the initial growth and subsequent fluctuations, others feel strongly that, based on artifactual–stylistic evidence, there were localized migrations or relocations of sizable population segments at various times in the past (Mainfort 1996; Morse 1977; Williams 1990).

Thus the question that must be asked but few have answered in the central valley, concerns the social consequences of such movement (Cobb 2005; Cobb and Butler 2002; Pauketat 2003a). Whatever the origin points, the predispositions of the migrants would have considerable impact on the organizational potentialities and historical contingencies of their respective regions. How were people disposed on the landscape initially, later, and finally at the end?

Consider a localized intrusion known as the Powers phase in the Little Black River lowlands of southeast Missouri (O'Brien 2001; Price 1978; Price and Griffin 1979). Powers phase people founded the central town of Powers Fort at about A.D. 1250. Based on one completely excavated palisaded, outlying village, portions of an adjacent unpalisaded village, and circumstantial evidence from Powers Fort itself, it seems clear that the people of this region were subject to a general assault at about A.D. 1350 (Price and Griffin 1979). Powers Fort was sacked and the outlying villages—called Snodgrass and Turner—and probably other such settlements—were burned to the ground (figure 4.9). As to the extent of the killing of residents we are unaware, and presumably the Powers phase folks, like their northern Common Field counterparts, regrouped elsewhere.

My sense is that organized violence of this sort is only poorly explained by the popular (and generally evolutionist) generalizations about chiefly warfare (Pauketat 2007). These explanations commonly hold that warfare (not war) was either (1) an outcome or correlate of chiefly institutions or (2) an elite tactic, one of many drawn from the quiver of strategies that, we are told, typify Mississippian chiefdoms (Dye 2005). The problem is, wars as discrete historic events (not warfare as generic epiphenomena) had immediate and long-lasting impacts on the social fabric and cultural identities of everybody's lives.

In the central Mississippi valley, deleterious effects of the escalating intergroup violence in the region seem attested in two ways. The first of course is physical. Human populations suffered great traumatic stress leading, instantaneously or in drawn-out fashion, to radical demographic changes. The second deleterious effect is social. When a town such as Powers Fort or Common Field was destroyed, people didn't relocate en masse to another place, transferring their social relations to other people and places intact. No. Things must have been mixed up, with cultural standards and referents abandoned and reformulated and daily practices adjusted to new realities in other places.

In other words, wars eliminated or displaced people and, in that way, cultures. The survivors necessarily reconfigured their daily social lives in new or altered environments. Wars change history through an "awful arithmetic," to quote Abraham Lincoln, who recognized the tremendous alterations in the social fabric and cultural identity that wars produce. Yet archaeologists seldom theorize about warring as historical process.

Great social change on the scale of whole regions is apparent in the general abandonment of large portions of the central Mississippi valley. Perhaps initiated by the evaporation of Cahokia after A.D. 1300, much of the central Mississippi valley became a vacant quarter (S. Williams 1990; see also Cobb and Butler 2002). There were no substantial settlements of any kind in this contiguous series of vacated regions. However, to the south, opposite Memphis, Tennessee, the St. Francis-type towns appear to have become entrenched within their defensive walls. People didn't bother (or perhaps feared) to leave their settlements to discard refuse and human waste. At these sites—one of which, Parkin, was known to Hernando de Soto's chroniclers as the town of Casquí—the midden produced from rotting organic compost, human waste, and discarded possessions reaches depths—even today after centuries of settling—of 2.5 meters. The middens also reveal in precise geometric detail the outline of the town's defensive moat and wall (Morse and Morse 1983; Phillips et al. 1951:329–334).

After A.D. 1300, the social lives and cultural environments of people in the central valley were reconfigured almost daily, a process that accelerated with European contact. Muller (1997) observes that historic-era towns were continuously incorporating stragglers and migrants from elsewhere. He assumes that people were attempting to maintain viable population concentrations in the face of death through violence and disease. Whether this was the goal or not, stragglers reattached themselves somewhere, and doing so could have dramatically altered the sociality of town life if not the degree to which people identified with the place (or any place).

Depending on town history, we should expect varying kinds and degrees of cultural hybridity that Susan Alt (2006b) believes would have constituted social and political change simply through the novel circumstances in which people found themselves. Such change might have resulted from the experiences of specific people in social fields—even at specific gatherings—or might have resulted from the mix of experiences within or between Mississippian towns. In 1814 Brackenridge alluded to this as civilization's fermentation. In 1951 Philip Phillips, James Ford, and James Griffin called this the X factor, the historical process whereby foreign and local cultural practices "were quickly welded together to produce traits that appear unlike the items from which they were derived." The X factor, they said, encompasses the "contributions made by the culture to its own development" (Phillips et al. 1951).

Here at the confluence, the Late Mississippian towns may be the perfect examples of how domestic life, cultural identity, and politics were fermenting. As we've seen, the St. Francois settlements were very nearly self-contained polities without outliers or rural farmers. Daily life in one of these towns was simultaneously political and military, the citizens of the towns living in a perpetual state of war with their enemies in other towns. Traditions, memories, and community identities were negotiated, reinvented, and engaged everyday and with political and military overtones unlike any other Mississippian place in eastern North America. What would come of all of this? Some have suggested that if de Soto's army had not arrived when it did, a very different political reality—a

Mesopotamian-style state—might have arisen near the confluence (following Wright 1984). Certainly, distinctive ethnicities seem to have congealed in the process.

Conclusion

If Mississippian history in the central Mississippi valley ends with ethnicizing populations meeting the onslaught of European-induced change, then it probably began with politicized communities punctuated by the demise and abandonment of the pre-Mississippian Toltec site—suggesting something more than an evolutionary emergence was going on (chapter 6). Here was hybridity, fermentation, and the X factor at work.

Eastward across the coastal plain and piedmont of western Mississippi, Alabama, and Georgia, the so-called rise of chiefdoms around A.D. 1100 looks fairly unimpressive, consisting of small confederations of people latching onto a new solution to the disarray of the terminal Woodland lifestyle. Several decades into the process, this new solution was sometimes imposed as a package from the outside, as the Rood phase along the Chattahoochie River shows best. Later developments at Etowah reveal that such solutions were not so much imposed as they were adapted versions of Middle Mississippian ideas and legends.

Whatever the story, our comparisons of the archaeo-histories of several regions attest to the interregional contingencies that impinged on the people who formed, politicized, or negotiated community. As identities, communities were always being remade, and migrations and subgroup relocations always necessitated a reconfiguration of kin ties, status categories, political alliances, work groups, and legitimating legends. We see evidence of such things in several Mississippian historical disjunctures: Macon Plateau, Cool Branch, the abandoned central Arkansas valley and, later, the entire central Mississippi valley.

We should also assume that similar community-formation processes were a dimension of every Mississippian town's establishment and abandonment, if not every wall-trench house construction. After all, towns were aggregations of many people, and once they dissolved or were split asunder, the people necessarily reformed elsewhere with others, in different physical landscapes, and under different historical conditions. Wall trenches, at least initially, embodied new post-Woodland sensibilities of identity, cosmology, and polity. Explanations that appeal only to administrative cycling simply do not come close to capturing this all-inclusive historical process.

Consider two different forms of "communalization" reviewed above, and the divergent historical outcomes that each produced, even while nominally organized as chiefdoms. First, there were towns founded in which community building was accomplished through acts of great, inclusive (we could say "corporate") monumental constructions, such as Moundville or Wilbanks phase Etowah. Second, there were particular places or historical moments when communalization involved the apparent decentralization of large towns but the recentralization of many smaller ones, such as we see in late Moundville times, across much of the Lamar landscape, or in the post-1200 world of the central Mississippi valley. In the first instance, huge pyramidal mounds were built in planned arrays requiring both a design and the labor of many people throughout their respective regions. In such instances, walls were also built, and they were at least as labor-intensive as any mound. What's more, they bounded communities in more ways than one.

What the construction of walls seems to represent particularly well is a mode of community identity formation involving the construction of "us" from "them" (Emerson 1997a,b). Those sorts of boundaries were simultaneously communal and political. And such boundaries in the earth are projections of a community at the same time that they may be offensive threats to "them" in the larger world beyond. What varies in the communalizing effects of people collaborating to construct a huge wooden palisade is scale, and that scale, as the Mississippianization histories point out, must be understood in terms of a big pan-eastern history. The difference between Moundville—with its dispersed farmstead landscape and its political–military shadow—and Parkin—with its holed-up, densely packed population—cannot be adequately explained with reference to a certain type of corporate or network strategy. Those little functionalist explanations beg the big historical questions.

The big historical questions involve understanding how Mississippianization in the Southeast related to the domesticization of the supernatural, the politicization of the everyday, and ultimately the ethnicization of social relations not seen in pre-Mississippian ceremonial centers. I assert that almost all of these phenomena happened through the media of community, a malleable and negotiated field of politics and cultural identity with a dynamic generated from within. Explaining that dynamic—the X factor—means going back to the founding of a most unusual and grand of pre-Columbian places, Cahokia.

Notes

1. The unique qualities of these burials are lost in the presence/absence statistics presented by Adam King (2003:112).

2. Besides, according to Gregory Wilson (personal communication, 2006), most of these Moundville prestige goods actually postdate the rise of Moundville as a regional polity (Wilson 2005; Wilson et al. 2006).

3. This statement is contradicted by archaeologists who seem to assume that the sites were occupied continuously for many centuries, despite a lack of hard evidence (Lewis 1991; O'Brien 2001). There may be earlier occupations on the landforms where the later towns were built, but there is no evidence that the towns themselves were laid out before A.D. 1200.

YOFFEE'S RULE AND CAHOKIA

The history of Mississippians is the history of Cahokia writ large.

—David Anderson, 1997

I hope that my emphasis on the people, places, and things of Mississippian political–cultural movements, community building, and identity formation—instead of models of political–economic cycling and institutional evolution—is not misread. I do not seek to dismiss out of hand the existence of certain architectural, technological, cosmological, or even administrative similarities among the so-called Mississippian peoples of the Midwest and Southeast. Quite the opposite. I know there are patterns, and some highly interesting ones. I think these patterns owe themselves primarily to a big pan-eastern, political–cultural history. And that big history, arguably, begins at a big place, Cahokia.

And I do mean arguably. In fact, all of the conceptual issues gnawing at our main character, the Uncertain Graduate Student, have already come to a head in the sometimes heated debates between rival Mississippianists during the past three decades. These debates have centered on how to interpret the wealth of archaeological data from the greater Cahokia region (Mehrer 1995; Milner 1998; and Muller 1997; versus Emerson 1997; Kehoe 1998; Pauketat 1998; Pauketat and Emerson 1997). Some of these debates have been constructive. Other debates have turned political, with individual researchers refusing to cite the works of the others or, worse, attempting to block access to research collections or archaeological sites for political reasons. It happens.

133

So it's no wonder UGS isn't sleeping well. She awakens early from confused dreams of Dr. Science, the Southern Pragmatist, Obion, and the shadowy character in the corner of her mind. She needs her morning jolt, and in the hotel coffee bar, UGS jots down what she recalls about her conversations yesterday of migrations, Mesoamerican contacts, Cahokia, and the flaws with chiefdoms and dual-processualism. And there, getting her caffeine fix, UGS can't escape one final nagging question that, depending on the answer, will redirect all of her other answers and ultimately make her rethink her planned dissertation research at Obion.

What Was Cahokia?

UGS visited Cahokia a couple of times and climbed the 150 steps up the face of its largest pyramid, Monks Mound, twice (figure 6.1). In her espresso-induced hypersensitivity, UGS can still remember how it felt. It is a palpable memory that has stuck with her and now informs her thought process. For her, the Cahokia site (or "Cahokia mounds," as it is locally known) seems as awesome as it did for the first European American to describe it in print, Henry Marie Brackenridge (1814). He was "struck with a degree of astonishment" at the breadth and thirty-meter height of Monks Mound. And he surmised that "a very populous town had once existed here, similar to those of Mexico, described by the first conquerors" (Brackenridge 1814:187–188).

Figure 6.1. Monks Mound at Cahokia, view to west

History of a Question

But debate over "what was Cahokia?" had already begun before Brackenridge's visit. It was the larger debate over the mound builder myth (Silverberg 1968). Aided by an apparent lack of native cultural memories of places like Cahokia, prominent scholars—Noah Webster being one—denied that American Indians could have built anything that required sustained group effort, never mind a monument as enormous as Monks Mound. Many people wanted to believe that somebody—anybody—besides Native Americans built the mounds of the eastern United States (Pauketat and Loren 2005). Even into the 1920s, well-known geologists denied that Cahokia's pyramids were anything but natural remnants of Pleistocene age sandy terraces (Kelly 2000).

Now that's minimalism. And it was based on the common sense of the nineteenth and early twentieth centuries—that American Indian nations could not have accomplished anything worthy of note. Today some worry that this national legacy can still be seen in contemporary archaeological theorizing: consider the dehistoricizing evolutionist constructs, such as the chiefdom, or the out-of-hand dismissal of historical complexity via Occam's Razor (Kehoe 1998; Patterson 1995). The issue has come to a head over Cahokia, a place Alice Kehoe (1998) has noted is "hidden in plain sight" because of the cumulative biases of our intellectual heritage.

So, is it possible to give an honest, unbiased answer to the question, What was Cahokia? Perhaps not. The question is about the same as asking someone to explain the history of Chicago or New York. The explanation depends on one's perspective. But pigeonholing Cahokia as just another Mississippian chiefdom does not feel right to a lot of people. For one thing, Cahokia was huge even by archaic-state standards. For another, it precedes by decades and in some cases centuries all other well-dated Mississippian towns. In part for this reason, Cahokia's dead weren't buried with the standard southeastern ceremonial complex art objects—which has been said to heavily favor masculine, sky-world, bird-man themes—as seen at Moundville, Spiro, or Etowah (Knight et al. 2001). Cahokia's craft objects and iconography as often suggest feminine, fertility themes (Emerson 1989). Even Jon Muller (1997:386) admits that Cahokia is exceptional, with a "possible 'statelike' organization."

Like other apparent precocious places, Poverty Point or Chaco Canyon, Cahokia doesn't seem to fit one's expectations of a typical anything.

In recent years, some people have simply left Cahokia out of their summaries of the Mississippian world (Steponaitis 1986). After all, notes V. James Knight (1997:229), Cahokia's "untidy bulk tugs forcefully at the seams of text-book-variety generalizations by which its lesser counterparts might be accommodated." In short, Cahokia was too big, too early, and too far north to fit easily within the ordinary explanatory framework of some Mississippianists. Given this, why cram it into the Mississippian mold at all? Perhaps the summaries that left Cahokia out of the Mississippian realm were correct. Cahokia really was too extreme to be called a Mississippian chiefdom.

Indeed, the Pragmatist's generation of archaeologists did not hesitate to call Cahokia a state—a highly centralized society where rulers were vested with governing powers that transcended kinship, including absolute force to discipline and punish, a standing army, and some sort of tributary or taxation system (Conrad 1991; O'Brien 1991, 1993). Guy Gibbon (1974) and Patricia O'Brien (1989) called it the "Ramey state," after a prominent nineteenth- and early-twentieth-century family that owned and protected the central precinct before it was purchased by the state of Illinois. Their conclusions were based in part on important research spearheaded by Melvin Fowler, who not only had the site mapped in its entirety but fielded crews and graduate students to document its internal complexity by excavating along the palisade wall and into Monks Mound and Mound 72 (Fowler 1975, 1997; Fowler and Hall 1978; Fowler et al. 1999). What he and his coworkers found was nearly revolutionary: an internally complex urbanizing landscape; hybridity on a grand scale. Fowler and his students documented what they believed to be a four-tiered regional settlement hierarchy (Fowler and Hall 1978), consistent with Wright and Johnson's (1975) definition.

During the late 1970s and 1980s, a massive cultural resource management project got under way in the greater Cahokia region—also identified by the expansive Mississippi river bottom in which it sits: the "American Bottom" (Bareis and Porter 1984). This was the FAI-270 Highway Mitigation Project, and it was staffed by a cadre of young Midwestern archaeologists who would go on to contribute a series of key data monographs that would lead to a new synthesis (Emerson and Jackson 1984; Jackson et al. 1992; Kelly 1990). Their interpretation of Cahokia, what I've elsewhere called the third-generation synthesis, was heavily influenced by the ecological and progressivist evolutionary paradigm of the New Archaeology, and rejected the Ramey state flat out (Pauketat 2002). There had been some inklings of statehood, given the evidence of far-flung trade, a shell-bead-making workshop, and rural craft localization (Kelly 1991; Prentice 1983; Yerkes 1983, 1991). But such inklings drew heavy fire (Griffin 1992; Muller 1984, 1987, 1997; Pauketat 1987). In the end, Cahokia, it was concluded, had been "no more than a linked series of simple chiefdoms" occasionally orchestrated as part of a weak three-tiered settlement hierarchy (Milner 1996:42).

Lately the debate has boiled down to disagreements over population estimates. Back before the first large-scale excavations at Cahokia in 1960, James Griffin believed Cahokia to have been a largely vacant ceremonial center, like Coles Creek sites to the south (Young and Fowler 2000). The hundreds of houses exposed on excavation tracts in 1960 and 1961 changed all of that, and the next population estimates ballooned to 25,000 to 40,000 people for Cahokia alone (Gregg 1975). With the third-generation research came lower estimates again. In 1998 George Milner concluded that "most reasonable population figures for Cahokia fall in the low thousands." That estimate, he believed, made sense, since the floodplain could support no more (Milner 1998:123).

However, Milner's low-ball figures were partly a result of the fact that he lengthened the critical Lohmann phase—the phase of Cahokia's consolidation—from the standard fifty years to a hypothetical hundred years (Milner et al. 1984). Adjusting for this error, and based on my own studies of the old 1960s excavations, the actual estimates for Cahokia proper at its maximum are 10,000 to 16,000 people (Pauketat 2003a; Pauketat and Lopinot 1997). Of course, this estimate does not account for numbers of people who lived in the two sprawling complexes of East St. Louis and St. Louis (see below). Nor does it include the rural population, which since 1995 we have realized includes significant numbers of people living at villages beyond the floodplain, in the hilly uplands to the east, and probably to the west.

Susan Alt and I have designated one sizable upland farming district the Richland complex (Alt 1999, 2001, 2002). The people living at several large villages, smaller hamlets, and many homesteads appear to have provisioned Cahokia with food and cloth. This not only fits well the now analyzed architectural evidence (all earlier estimates do not; Pauketat

2003a), it also agrees with the gut instincts of Henry Marie Brackenridge, who wrote that "this could never have been the work of thinly scattered tribes." Other archaeologists have likewise estimated that some 10,000 people must have contributed their labor to build Cahokia proper (Reed et al. 1968; Thomas 1907).

What Constitutes a City?

I gave a talk recently at a Midwestern university espousing these population figures and a new story of Cahokia's role in Mississippianization. I used the word "city," and during the question-and-answer period a young Mississippianist repeated what he had heard Dr. Science say recently: "There were no cities in pre-Columbian North America." Begging to differ, I replied, "Well, he's wrong."

In general, I find such all-encompassing minimalist declarations— usually chock-full of negative modifiers—to be based on biased beliefs rather than reasoned, open-minded considerations of all the data. No cities in North America? Why not? If a city is a relatively dense concentration of people disposed in such a way as to reveal central organizing principles other than kinship, then Cahokia (and its adjacent sprawling complex) was a city, at least for about a hundred years (A.D. 1050–1150). Why?

First, there's the simple matter of Cahokia's great scale and the proximity of the people living there. At one time, Melvin Fowler (1975) defined the Cahokia site as a large diamond-shaped complex that covered thirteen square kilometers (figure 6.2.). Even more conservative estimates of the space involved are impressive. For instance, within Fowler's diamond-shaped boundaries, Neal Lopinot and I (1997) have delineated a circular catchment of eight square kilometers that picks up most of Cahokia's pyramids and plazas. But that space is still too large, argue Rinita Dalan and associates (2003), to have permitted routine face-to-face interaction between kin and neighbors. People in one part of Cahokia wouldn't have known what was happening in another part.

Second, there's the issue of Cahokia's actual population estimate. Within that 8-square-kilometer catchment is at least 1.8 square kilometers of high-density residential occupation. When one calculates reasonable estimates of people per house, based on known archaeological counts and sizes, then the population of early Cahokia ranges from 10,000 to 16,000

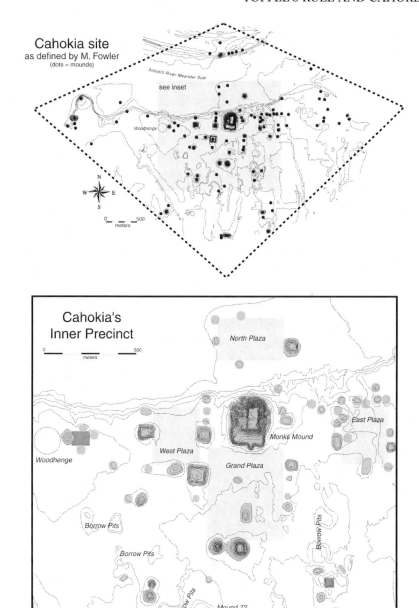

Figure 6.2. Cahokia in plan view (after Fowler 1975, 1997; Pauketat 2005)

people. This means that early Cahokia alone, at 10,000-plus people, was at least ten times larger than Moundville, Alabama. Add in guesstimates of the rest of the sprawling St. Louis and East St. Louis metroplex and the number could be fifteen or twenty times that of Moundville.

However you slice it, Cahokia is larger than the next biggest Mississippian town complex by at least one whole order of magnitude. Using the high-density residential area only—not counting the total area of this complex—it was 2.4 times larger than all of Moundville (using Knight and Steponaitis's [1998:3] figure of seventy-five hectares; Pauketat and Lopinot 1997). Going by number of mounds, Cahokia is four times larger than its Alabama counterpart. If we were to use the total area covered by the central Cahokia complex (ca. 8 to 13 square kilometers), then the main body of Cahokia covers roughly ten to sixteen times more land than the Moundville megacenter. And that doesn't even count the adjacent East St. Louis and St. Louis portions of the central administrative complex (figure 6.3.). In short, unlike Moundville or any other Mississippian center in the American South, Cahokia is city-size (see chapter 7).

Like other early cities, Cahokia seems to have a design that references cosmological order even as the experiences of the city violated that design over time (Carl 2000; Low 1996). Melvin Fowler (1987:ix), among others, suspected a single unit of measurement, the "Cahokia yard" (1.03 meters). And more importantly, within the diamond-shaped area, Fowler (1997) defined eleven principal mound-and-plaza groups and considered the possibility that Cahokia was comprised of distinct residential neighborhoods or barrios. His suspicions are confirmed by suggestive patterns of craft activities or practices more common to one area than another: there are more spindle whorls and broken bits of ax-head-making debris but few microtools on one tract, microtools in abundance on another, microtools and ax-head-making debris on a third, and no concentrations of any of this on yet a fourth (Pauketat 2004:84; Yerkes 1991). And these patterns do not even consider whatever was going on in the rest of what I have elsewhere termed the Cahokian sprawl.

> Cahokia . . . was actually just one of three not-so-discrete archaeological sites within an even larger "central political-administrative complex" that sprawled along an ancient riverbed and hopped across the Mississippi River. . . . To the south was the East St. Louis site, with its fifty earthen pyramids and associated temples, storage huts, and walled compounds. . . . Immediately across the Mississippi from East St. Louis, occupying

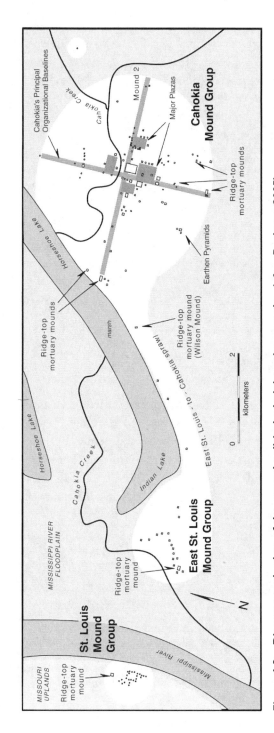

Figure 6.3. Diagrammatic view of the central political administrative complex (after Pauketat 2005)

the western end of the political-administrative sprawl, was the St. Louis or "Mound City" site, with its twenty-six pyramids and 2 ha plaza. Unfortunately, the pyramids of both the East St. Louis and the St. Louis groups were leveled during the nineteenth century. Perhaps for this reason, few written descriptions of greater Cahokia do justice to the scale of the entire . . . complex. (Pauketat 2004:71)

These three pieces of the whole central complex "are unique in North America in terms of both size and proximity, and cannot be easily fitted within a standard spatial model of Mississippian settlement" (Pauketat 2004:164). Taken as a whole, the Cahokia metroplex

seems internally differentiated and suggestive of substantial heterarchical complexity. Various social units represented by pyramid-and-plaza groups at the Cahokia, East St. Louis and St. Louis sites may have been ranked or unranked one to another. . . . Perhaps each of the pyramid-and-plaza groups within the big three sites of the central political-administrative complex was home to families or the scene of ritual performances or social functions not found or conducted at the others. (Pauketat 2004:166)

Was this a city? If Cahokia somehow turned up in another part of the world, archaeologists would answer yes, definitely. That's also what the Pragmatist would say. Indeed, even Mesopotamianist statesman Norman Yoffee—until recently following what he now believes was a minimalist line of thought (Yoffee 2005)—stands ready to accept that Cahokia was a city (personal communication, April 2005). He's less ready to believe Cahokia was at the center of an archaic state, which he defines using a Mesopotamian yardstick (cf. Stein 1998:15). He agrees with Monica Smith (2003:13) that cities "need to be uncoupled from the necessary presence of states." In that, Smith echoes landscape theorist Henri Lefebvre (1991), who believed—like Brackenridge's fanciful Frenchman—that the urbanizing fermentation of cities is what produced societies.

So, for Yoffee and others, the question then becomes, This protourban Cahokian landscape was at the heart of what exactly? A chiefdom, a state, or—what Yoffee (2005) has suggested for Chaco Canyon—a rituality? It's the question UGS was contemplating, specifically thinking about the validity of Yoffee's Rule.

A State?

For now, let's examine the question of statehood and save rituality for later. According to Yoffee's Rule (1993:69, 2005:41), "if *you* can argue whether a society is a state or isn't, then it isn't" (emphasis added). Judging by this standard, at the time of this writing, Cahokia was not a state. However, there's the little problem of who is "you" in Yoffee's Rule. Presumably, the "you" in this appeal to common sense refers to the collective you, not to any one person who—owing to cultural bias, psychosis, or some other character flaw—might argue any point, at any time, or any place. Presumably, if most people agree that something's a state, it's a state. If not, it's not.

I'm almost okay with that characterization, since it correctly locates the definitional process in the present rather than the past. However, let's be clear: even by this standard, Cahokia was a state in the eyes of 1960s and early 1970s researchers, when the collective you mostly agreed on such matters. Since then, Cahokia was not a state, since the chiefdom model has been in vogue at least since the late 1980s. Recent history, however, tells us that popular opinion is malleable. Thus Yoffee's Rule is an arbitrary yardstick.

Population gives us yet another measure. Several researchers have stated that ancient settlements exceeding 2,500 individuals fragmented without higher-order government (Feinman 1999:108, citing Kosse 1990). Certainly this is the pattern in pre-Columbian North America, where the largest towns—excepting Cahokia—have populations less than 3,000 people (Pauketat and Loren 2005). As Gary Feinman (1999) has summarized, other researchers have noted that states tend to be coterminous with regionally integrated populations in excess of 10,000 people. Feinman (1999:97) further notes that, in his earlier comparative study of New World regional societies, middle-range populations (however defined) seldom exceed 30,000 people within a region (Feinman and Neitzel 1984). Presumably, beyond that organizational threshold, states emerged. But again, the watchword in population studies is variation.

Other ways of defining and identifying states are hardly more definitive. Placing all their interpretive eggs in institutional baskets, researchers have posited that states might be identified by the correlates of their institutions and the ways that such institutions governed regions (Flannery 1999a). By the 1970s, the state was thought to be nearly isomorphic with the bureaucracy itself and, following Wright and Johnson (1975), to be expressed as a four-tiered settlement hierarchy through which bureaucracies governed regions. Some took Henry Wright and Gregory Johnson's (1975) insights as law, without paying enough attention to heterarchical complications and the methodology of settlement pattern analysis (Marcus 1999; cf. Crumley 1987, 1995a, b). Others have concluded that bureaucracies and rulers can be identified through the presence of palaces and grand mortuary tombs (Flannery 1999a; Yoffee 2005:229).

However, a lot of water has passed under the definitional bridge since Wright and Johnson codified their thoughts on hierarchy. And while there still exists a shoot-from-the-hip I-know-a-state-when-I-see-one attitude among some, there is also a growing recognition that many presumed states in many places can't be defined using a single standard or checklist of traits (Chapman 2003; Junker 2004:225; Stein 1998:10). This is true to an extent even among committed statists such as Joyce Marcus and Gary Feinman, who acknowledge that "archaic states were a lot more fragile and internally diverse than the archaeological literature would lead one to believe. Born out of tremendous *effort*, they also required a substantial *effort* to hold together" (Marcus and Feinman 1998:12–13, emphasis added). States, I guess, really aren't as stately as some have presumed.

Effort is an important consideration in understanding a people's stateliness, and there are two ways of thinking about this. The first is in terms of regal effort. Some see the state as embodied in the power vested in or displayed through divine rulership. Besides the obvious cases of Africa and Mesoamerica, such divine rule was also pervasive across Southeast Asia. There ideology, ritual, and state pageantry were at the core of otherwise politically unstable regimes large and small that range freely along various axes of political–organizational variability that some analysts might feel compelled to circumscribe, rather artificially, as chiefdoms or states (Junker 2004:226, citing Geertz 1980; Tambiah 1976).

The second way to think about effort and stateliness is through the allocation, disposition, and control of communal labor. Thomas Patterson (1987) has argued for a noninstitutional definition where the state was identified through the specific historical relationship between laborers and those who would appropriate labor. The power to command labor, allocate labor, or dispose of labor—a spatialized power—was real power. Presumably once that power existed, you had a state.

The two senses in which effort can be understood as instrumental in the identification of the state carry through to a recent discussion that happened to be aimed at characterizing the Great Towns and Regional Polities in the Prehistoric American Southwest and Southeast (Neitzel, ed. 1999). I have extracted from the paper by Yoffee, Suzanne Fish, and George Milner (1999:263, 269) the following list of four criteria or tendencies of states (see also Yoffee 2005):

1. "In the rise of many early states, the founding of new sites is an important process through which political power can be disembedded from the structures of kinship and other, traditional organizational formations. . . . Such relocations of the royal court also provided the opportunity for new systems of land tenure and control of other basic means of production to be regulated by kings and other political leaders."

2. "The formation of city-states typically entailed a systematic reorganization of the countryside; indeed, one may say that the process of 'ruralization' is the twin of 'urbanization' (Yoffee 1995a, b). In states, therefore, villages and towns were not residuals of a pre-state countryside, left behind in the centripetal tendencies that resulted in cities. Rather, the countryside was created in the process of state formation, and villages and towns became special purpose settlements that were located in relation to urban central places."

3. "The trajectory of development in emerging states includes an interplay among various and often competing sources of power in society (Yoffee 1993)."

4. "In early states, societal (or ideological) power . . . was typically exercised by persons who manipulated, maintained, and reproduced the symbols by which groups with different cultural orientations were integrated within a larger societal umbrella."

All four criteria pertain in some way to understanding the theatrical displays and labor controls that others have felt define the state and urbanism (M. Smith 2003; Zeder 2003:156–158). They agree with Lefebvre's (1991) sense that landscapes don't make cities, cities make landscapes (Emberling 2003; Yoffee 1995b, 2005; Zeder 2003). That sense is particularly a propos for a contemporary view of the state: it is less an organizational thing and more a pervasive phenomenon that "is both everywhere and nowhere" (A. Smith 2003:79). The state is diffuse, heterarchical, and hidden in the practices of people (Kus 1989). It wasn't in just one place and wouldn't exist except as people put it into action.

That, as noted earlier, is the official secret of the state, said Abrams (1988:77), "the secret of the non-existence of the state." As conveyed by Robert Adams (2003), Susan Kus (1983), and myself (1994), this is the state as a cultural hegemony that was in the past and is in the present, according to Adam Smith (2003:79), "implicated in every aspect of our daily lives, from the production of culture and economy . . . to the creation of personal identities." In this way, the state simplifies complex, heterarchical social relations (Brumfiel 1995; Yoffee 2005). What was Cahokia? Let's answer this question using the four criteria above.

Cahokia Inside Out

Criterion I: Disembedded "New Cahokia"

Like Mississippian towns in the South, Cahokia was a planned center. Melvin Fowler (1975) recognized the design to involve north–south and east–west axes and possible other geometric alignments. Unlike these other places, however, the redesigned Cahokia site of A.D. 1050 (we'll call it "New Cahokia" to distinguish it from the pre-Mississippian village complex) was laid out on a grand scale as part of what I've called Cahokia's "big bang" (Pauketat 1997). Judging from plaza investigations initiated by Rinita Dalan (1997) and George Holley and colleagues (1993), we can be relatively certain that New Cahokia's aptly named grand plaza was the centerpiece of a new city. This vast open space—evidently built in anticipation of the great gatherings to be held there (Lewis and Stout 1998)—was a single public works project that dates to about A.D. 1050, or the beginning of the so-called Lohmann phase.

Based on our excavations in 1997, Susan Alt, Jeff Kruchten, and I now believe that the grand plaza covered at least nineteen hectares and involved dismantling and paving over pre-Mississippian (Terminal Woodland) residences at its northern end (Pauketat et al. 2005). In fact, everywhere excavations have occurred at Cahokia there are Lohmann phase basement deposits (Dalan et al. 2003; Pauketat and Lopinot 1997). Certainly there were even older pre-Mississippian village deposits along the high northern ridge on either side of Monks Mound (Dalan et al. 2003). There might even have been two or three pre-Mississippian mounds and a modest plaza. However, it now seems plausible that Cahokians deconstructed much of this old settlement when they rebuilt Cahokia as a capital city. There are hints in the disappearance of pre-Mississippian courtyards that the deconstruction involved a top-down phasing out of old kin-based collectivities (Pauketat 1994).

Dalan, Holley, and colleagues (1993) also believe, based on their findings, and I agree based on my excavations into Mound 49, that the clay-core stages of the peripheral pyramids were constructed at the same time as the plaza (Pauketat and Rees 1996; Pauketat et al. 2002). Notably, these would have included the leader's residential platform and compound, Monks Mound, initially a large 6.5-meter-high clay pyramid (Dalan 1997:93; Dalan et al. 2003). Importantly, from this point on, the pyramids and their surmounting architecture were the periodic (probably annual) focus of communal labor, as they were routinely enlarged, resurfaced, and refurbished.

As I have discussed at length elsewhere, the end of the preceding terminal Woodland period and the beginning of the so-called Mississippian Lohmann phase is the same archaeological moment—the great Cahokian historical disjuncture—in which several other key alterations were made to the greater Cahokian landscape (Pauketat 1994, 1998, 2003, 2004a). Owing to a fairly rapid in-migration, the population of the center increased from the 1,000-plus people of the Terminal Woodland village of old Cahokia to the 10,000-plus figure of the new city. The same exponential increase probably was experienced throughout much of the immediate Cahokia locality, as about half of the dozen or so pyramid and plaza outliers—numbers vary depending on where lines are drawn—are known to have been founded during the Lohmann phase (i.e., the East St. Louis, Emerald, Horseshoe Lake, Pfeffer, Powell mound, and probably the Rolle-Olszewski sites). We simply aren't sure of the rest at this point (figure 6.4.).

Not surprisingly, this is the same historical moment in which a suite of other social and architectural changes is evident. First, wall-trench housing was adopted, described earlier (chapter 4). Second, domestic practices became differentiated among certain neighborhoods, house-

147

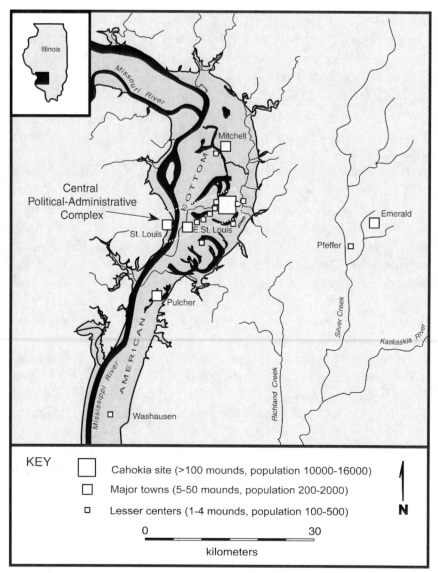

KEY

☐ Cahokia site (>100 mounds, population 10000-16000)

☐ Major towns (5-50 mounds, population 200-2000)

▫ Lesser centers (1-4 mounds, population 100-500)

N

0 ——————— 30

kilometers

Figure 6.4. Major Mississippian sites in the northern American Bottom (after Pauketat 2005)

holds, or locales: we see the beginning of the localization of ritual object assemblages and craft and fabric production (Alt 1999, 2001; Emerson 1997; Pauketat 1997, 1998, 2003b; Pauketat and Alt 2004). Third, new building forms were innovated or introduced from elsewhere at this time, including the circular sweat lodge or council house and rectangular buildings with special (T-shape) porticos. The new buildings were placed in select locations amid residential buildings, which themselves were aligned rigidly according to a site-wide grid (Collins 1997). This fourth observation, the establishment of observable housing rules, also included segregation of high-status kin groups from low-status ones. For example, in one excavated area there are two groupings of houses, a northern cluster of large houses associated with circular buildings and a southern cluster of smaller houses lacking associated circular buildings (Pauketat 1994).

These four changes and the evidence that Cahokians built a new city over an old village meets Yoffee and colleagues' (1999) criterion 1 above. It's not quite the same sort of disembedded capital as described by Richard Blanton (1978) for Monte Albán. However, the founding of New Cahokia, the capital city,

> entailed the creation of a new "spatiality"—a whole new relational environment where people remade traditions. So, after AD 1050 private and public social life was being played out in new space and according to new constraints of locality (who and what was where) and orthagonality (houses sited and oriented to the central precinct). . . . The historical effect may have been to "disembed" cultural practice and governance from a pre-Mississippian sense of space. (Pauketat 2004:94)

Cahokians did what Stout and Lewis (1998) noted must be done to circumvent the constraints built into centers (see chapter 4). They dismantled the old village and superimposed a grand new design.

Criterion 2: Ruralization

This disembedding of the new Cahokian order "from the structures of kinship and other, traditional organizational formations" was extended into the rural zones surrounding Cahokia. Indeed, Thomas Emerson (1997a, b) first observed what has come to be referred to as the replacement hypothesis during his analysis of the floodplain farmsteads of approximately A.D. 1050–1350. That hypothesis states that Terminal Woodland villages and farmsteads in the northern American Bottom were abandoned at the moment of the Cahokian disjuncture, around A.D. 1050, and the area then quickly repopulated according to new Cahokian rules of location and order.

Given the numerous excavated early Mississippian period farmsteads in the northern American Bottom, the evidence for this is not difficult to muster, and yet it is routinely overlooked by those who favor minimalist evolutionary scenarios (Pauketat 2002:154). Here's the evidence: Terminal Woodland rural settlements in the American Bottom were typically villages or hamlets, the best known ones being old Cahokia and the Range site (Kelly 1990; Pauketat 1994). There were a few likely farmsteads or very small hamlets comprised of an isolated series of three or four houses (Emerson and Jackson 1984; Milner 1984; Pauketat et al. 1998). However, these Terminal Woodland small sites are uncommon at, say, A.D. 1000, at least compared to the pattern after A.D. 1050.

In addition to their scarcity, there is another salient attribute of the later Lohmann phase farmsteads. In the floodplain outside of Cahokia, there are no known instances among the scores of excavated farmsteads in the northern American Bottom proper where a pre-Mississippian single-set-post house was rebuilt—presumably by the same family—as a new wall-trench house! Indeed, there are only two or three cases where one could legitimately argue that the same families lived at the site before and after A.D. 1050 (Emerson 1997a,b). Affirmation of this replacement phenomenon is not difficult: we need only look at the population estimates for one rural floodplain locality. They do not begin with the preceding Terminal Woodland phases but with the Lohmann phase. Why? There were no rural pre-Mississippian farmsteads excavated in this analyzed portion of the floodplain (Milner 1986). The farmstead occupation began with the founding of New Cahokia.

The replacement pattern breaks down as one moves out away from the immediate Cahokia vicinity. George Holley and colleagues (2001) and Susan Alt (2002), for instance, have documented the continuum of pre-Mississippian single-set-post to Mississippian wall-trench housing at the upland site of Knoebel southeast of Cahokia (Bareis 1976). A similar situation exists at a number of nearby upland Richland complex sites, although it is uncertain if many of the latter are not simply old-fashioned houses built after A.D. 1050 (Pauketat 2003a). The same might be the case for the southern American Bottom, where Schroeder (2004) argues—based only on surface survey data—for greater locational continuity for the rural people over the Late Woodland to Mississippian continuum. Such decreasing direct control over farmers is as it should be, making even clearer the singular qualities of the Cahokian historical disjuncture. Distinct ruralization does appear to have been the twin of the urbanization of Cahokia. The new rural countryside was probably planned to more efficiently extract food resources from the reorganized agricultural landscape (Emerson 1997a,b; Pauketat 1998).

Criteria 3 and 4: Ordered Pluralism

The construction of New Cahokia not only marked a new order but apparently also involved an unwieldy conglomeration of many quasi-autonomous or heterarchical subcommunities (Fowler 1997) that seemingly attached themselves to the new city, to one of its major sprawling outliers (East St. Louis and St. Louis), or even to certain rural localities (the Richland complex showing evidence of such immigrant subpopulations; Alt 2002; Pauketat 2003a). Such immigration is attested in the regional population levels. Too few to reliably count prior to A.D. 1050 (I'd guess we are talking about a few thousand people in the entire American Bottom region), the regional population between A.D. 1050 and 1200 has been guesstimated by George Milner (1998:figure 6.1) at 12,500 to 50,000 people. As his numbers were generated without benefit of knowledge of the populated Richland complex, and were halved by his lengthening of the Lohmann phase, we could double his minimum calculations: the greater Cahokia region could have been populated during its golden century by 25,000 to 50,000 people, between a fifth to half of which lived in the central political–administrative complex (cf. Pauketat 2003a). However many there were, some large percentage of the regional population probably originated from surrounding regions, near and far.

Many of these people lived in the central sprawl, and we should expect much more cultural diversity in future excavations than most have suspected. Certainly there are numerous distinct pyramid and plaza complexes—each apparently with affiliated residential subgroups—that straddle swamps, a stream (Cahokia Creek), and the main channel of the Mississippi River. Covering such terrain, it is difficult to imagine how this metroplex was integrated, as it has no counterpart anywhere else in pre-Columbian North America, save perhaps the less densely populated Chaco Canyon (see chapter 7).

This unusual "heterarchical segmentation at the top" (Pauketat 2004:166), along with the weak pattern of craft localization at Cahokia, may be evidence—albeit not definitive—of the "interplay among various and often competing sources of power in society" (Yoffee 1993). It is unfortunate that much of the East St. Louis and St. Louis segments have been destroyed, as there are hints of complementarities between the complexes. Henry Marie Brackenridge (1814), for instance, initially indicated that most of the East St. Louis mounds were circular, not four-sided pyramids, and elsewhere I have suggested that circular, flat-topped tumuli were topped by circular council houses (and contrary to a popular misconception, they were not burial mounds; Pauketat 1993). Still others have observed that circular mounds were often paired with rectangular ones at Cahokia (Reed 1977), recapitulating in monumental form the basic circle and cross theme so pervasive to Mississippian cosmologies elsewhere. Recent excavations into what remains of the once-great East St. Louis suburb leaves little doubt that its central precinct was home to high-status families living within walled residential compounds (Pauketat, ed. 2005).

There are also a compelling series of large, elaborate "communal" political–religious rites and ghastly mortuary ceremonies that speak to a new kind of "societal (or ideological) power . . . exercised by persons who manipulated, maintained, and reproduced the symbols by which groups with different cultural orientations were integrated within a larger societal umbrella." That power, here and in many such cases, seems effected through grand spectacle and political theater. Great communal rites are represented in deposits of sumptuary objects and ritual debris mixed with concentrated feasting refuse. Small-scale deposits are known from several outlying towns or village sites, where they have been called green corn ceremonial pits (Emerson 1997a,b). Similar but more extensive deposits were found at the base of a late Lohmann phase platform at the East St. Louis site and adjacent to Cahokia's grand plaza (Kelly 1997; Pauketat, ed. 2005; Pauketat et al. 2002).

Rather than detail these here, I simply need to point to the scale of the gatherings that occurred only meters from and under the watchful eyes of those atop Cahokia's principal pyramid. For instance, one discrete commensal gathering involved the cooking, consumption, and discard of select portions of over 2,000 individual white-tailed deer, the use and breakage of perhaps more than 7,000 pots, the smoking of great amounts of tobacco, the production of craft objects, and the ritual use and disposal of red cedar branches and quartz crystals, among other things (Pauketat et al. 2002:tables 8–9, zone D2). Some of the action might well have taken place atop Cahokia's principal pyramid, if not atop a series of the platforms in conjunction with the great gatherings in the plaza.

Other contexts provide more evidence of the theatrical performances that led to a societal umbrella covering what I believe to have otherwise been considerable social diversity and cultural plurality. These consist of at least ten and perhaps twelve special mortuary tomb mounds, locally called the ridge-top mounds owing to their distinctive hipped-roof-like shape. Most of these are located in visually prominent locations at Cahokia, with the largest located at the southern end of Cahokia proper, three to the west as part of the Powell mound group, and one each—the largest mounds—at the East St. Louis, St. Louis, and Mitchell sites (Ahler and DePuydt 1987; Howland 1877; Kelly 1994; Titterington 1938). Bits and pieces of what was seen when the Mitchell, St. Louis, East St. Louis, and the Powell mounds were destroyed all indicate what I have elsewhere interpreted to be a series of theatrical mortuary rites that materialized or, more accurately, embodied a distinctly Cahokian version of creation (Hall 2000; Pauketat 2005; Young and Fowler 2000). Sometimes-segregated male and female bodies—likely execution victims, honored dead, and accumulations of relatives from charnel houses—were reportedly grouped in recognizable trenches and buried with sacred bundles and a specific set of creation-story objects (chunky stones, copper earpieces, arrows, and beaded capes).

The best-known of these is the Mound 72 remains, especially the famous submound beaded burial and the associated retainers. Two men on and under a falcon-shaped beaded blanket were interred with a host of other adult men and women and the complete array of creation-story artifacts (Fowler et al. 1999; Pauketat 2004, 2005). Among the contemporary and subsequent mortuary rites commemorating the submound burials were the executions of women who, according to their osteological traits, were drawn from a distinctive subpopulation (Rose 1999). They ate more corn and less meat, a substandard diet compared to the better-fed honored dead (Ambrose et al. 2003).

Perhaps these women were captives from far away or the executed wives of a recently deceased lord. However, it is just as likely that they were women from outlying farming villages, specifically those of the Richland complex. There are intriguing hints from isotopic study of their cooking pots that these recently relocated and immigrant farmers cooked more corn than the average Cahokian (Beehr and Ambrose 2004). Whatever their origin, their execution may have been one component of a grim retelling of the creation story through human bodies, enacted at a scale that has no precedent. Such an enactment probably was as much a theatrical event as feasting in the plaza (Emerson and Pauketat 2002). The locations of the ridge-top mounds are anything but hidden. Big Mound in St. Louis, for instance, was situated atop a Mississippi River bluff, with a secondary terrace overlooking the river that might have been a stage for public mortuary performances visible by anyone on either riverbank. Not incidentally, Big Mound was visible from the summit of Monks Mound.

Cahokia Outside In

If the regional-scale evidence above is not definitive, it is also not the only scale at which we can observe the extraordinary phenomenon that was Cahokia. Many people have struggled to understand the meaning of possible Cahokian outposts, colonies, culture contacts, and trade objects or "calling cards," particularly along a northern frontier that stretches from northern Illinois through Wisconsin and into Iowa, southern Minnesota, and the eastern Great Plains (Emerson, ed. 1991; Pauketat 2004; Stoltman, ed. 1991). After all, colonies, outposts, and immigrant enclaves are associated with well-known states in other parts of the world (Algaze 1993; Stein 1998; Marcus 1999:80).

The case for Cahokian colonies and outposts remains contentious. Less controversial are the various clues in this northern frontier of Cahokia-inspired if not Cahokia-caused migrations, intergroup violence, and religious movements (Pauketat 2004). There are several cases of Cahokian site-unit intrusions, similar to the earlier noted cases in Georgia. Among these is a case very similar to the Rood phase example, where Cahokians—and there seems little doubt as to their identity—set up a small outpost along the Mississippi River between two extant Terminal Woodland groups in west-central Wisconsin at or just before A.D. 1050 (Boszhardt 2004). This and similar intrusions suggest that the local Woodland farmer-foragers ceased building the locally famous effigy mounds, presumably an indication that a new socio-religious order had taken hold (Birmingham and Eisenberg 2000; Stoltman and Christiansen 2000; Theler and Boszardt 2000).

A similar, if more radical and controversial example of this same sort of intrusion can be pinned to the Aztalan site, in south-central Wisconsin.

> Before AD 1050, Aztalan was an important place of effigy mounds, conical mounds, an earthen embankment, and a residential settlement along the Crawfish River (Goldstein 1991:215; Richards 1992). Sometime shortly after AD 1050, a new 9 ha fortified village was superimposed over this sacred landscape . . . [complete with] two modest earthen pyramids overlooking a 3 ha plaza. . . . The effects on the people of the surrounding region were . . . profound. Some people, perhaps the enemies of the local Aztalan folk, were displaced northward (Overstreet 2000). . . . Samuel Barrett's (1933) finding of burned human body parts . . . suggested to him cannibalism. (Pauketat 2004:129)

This relatively isolated intrusive site produced some Cahokian pottery, more Cahokian knock-offs, and even more local Late Woodland or hybridized Mississippian ceramic wares. Like several such sites in the north, Aztalan looks to have been established by a group of migrants in league with local people (Emerson, ed. 1991; Stoltman, ed. 1991). The immigrants, either Cahokians or closely related Mississippians from the Illinois River valley, may have been "invited" up north, or at least befriended by local Late Woodland people who fought off an enemy with the help of the immigrant southerners (Richards 1992). It is unclear how long the colonizers maintained communication with their southern allies (Emerson 1991). What is clear is that the settlement wall was burned and the site sacked around A.D. 1200.

Peace in the Valley

There are three reasons to believe that Cahokians established a Pax Cahokiana throughout the Mississippi valley prior to the thirteenth century (Pauketat 2004:124). First is the presence of Cahokian settlers, colonists, migrants, or converts, as noted above, between about A.D. 1050 and 1200. Second is the many early Cahokian material objects—decorated (Ramey Incised) pots, Cahokia-style gaming stones and projectile points, special ear ornaments, redstone figurine smoking pipes, marine shell beads, and more also dating to A.D. 1050–1200—in places as remote as Gahagan, Spiro, and Shiloh in the south to Aztalan, Silvernale, and the Great Oasis sites in the north (figure 6.5). Previously it has been suggested that the ear ornaments and smoking pipes might have been gifts given by Cahokians to their political allies (Hall 1991). Other objects, as I have suggested, might have been visual aids used to tell the Cahokian story of creation (Pauketat 2005).

The final reason to believe in Pax Cahokiana might seem initially counterintuitive. Beginning in A.D. 1050, there is evidence of low-order violence, seemingly directed against Upper Midwestern places more than people, in the form of incinerated sites or domestic structures (Pauketat 2004). This may have been unlike the pre-Mississippian-style feuding we saw previously in the South. It was also unlike the large-scale village raiding and incineration seen in the Upper Midwest after A.D. 1200, when Pax Cahokiana presumably had dissolved. At that time, endemic violence against people began to spiral out of control, culminating in the fifteenth century.

For these reasons, I suspect that Cahokia and allied parties maintained peace and order in the upper Mississippi valley between A.D. 1050 and 1200 through tactical strikes against populations who might have, from a Cahokian viewpoint, stepped out of line. They perhaps did likewise downriver, at least to the confluence of the Ohio and Mississippi Rivers and into southeastern Missouri. This might account for the apparent suppression of significant political competition in this southern locale prior to A.D. 1200 (Anderson 1997). If true, might this have meant that Cahokia maintained a standing army, one of the old magical criteria for statehood? That depends on one's definitions. If a standing army was a group of warriors who routinely received some degree of compensation, perhaps from central storehouses, for services rendered then, yes, it is possible.

Cult of the Rulers

Elsewhere I have argued that Pax Cahokiana was part and parcel of a political–religious cult emanating from the American Bottom (Pauketat 2004, 2005). I will not repeat this argument here, except to point out that local participants in this or any number of localized spin-off cults to the north appear manifested in both the cessation of certain local practices

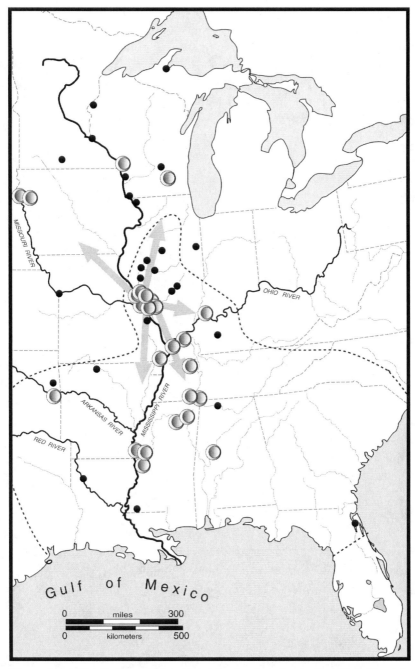

Figure 6.5.   Distribution of Cahokia-style chunkeys (and other Cahokia-style figurines, Ramey pots, and long-nosed god earpieces; after Pauketat 2004)

(such as the construction of effigy mounds in Wisconsin and Iowa) and the construction of new ancestral temples on rectangular earthen platforms (smaller copies of the southern Cahokian pyramids). In addition, from the beginning, this cult appears to have featured personifications of thunderbirds: the bird-man, falcon impersonator, or man-god known variously as Red Horn or Morning Star (Brown 2005a; Emerson 1989; Hall 1989, 1991, 1997; Salzer and Rajnovich 2000).

Some researchers agree that the impacts of Cahokia may have been in the realm of a political–religious cult (Brown 2005a; Hall 2005; Pauketat 2004). Several years ago, David Anderson (1999b:227) said that we must take care

> to differentiate between the . . . spread of chiefdom organizational forms . . . and the spread of Mississippian ideology (Pauketat and Emerson 1997). . . . The latter (i.e., Mississippian ideology and religion) appears to have developed or crystallized in the tenth and eleventh centuries . . . and Cahokia seems to have been the primary center where this took place. . . . [The] origin and spread [of Mississippian] owe a great deal to the early and dramatic emergence of Cahokia.

Following what Thomas Emerson and I were advocating in the early 1990s, James Brown (2005a) now asserts that art–historical evidence suggests that much of what we know as Middle Mississippian or Southeastern Ceremonial Complex art, after A.D. 1200, has its roots at Cahokia (Brown and Kelly 2000; Phillips and Brown 1978). "The scale and depth of the local response to the interaction with Cahokia reminds us that Cahokia's actions may have had an impact on certain southern towns decisive enough to shape their subsequent history. It is hardly accidental that the period of Cahokian impact is about the same across the Southeast (Brown 2005a:119). Of course, as we've seen, Cahokia's impact needs to be understood as more than just an art style. As discussed in chapter 5, aspects of Cahokia's ideology—from wall-trench housing and Morning Star mythology to ideas of governance—are identifiable at Macon Plateau, Cool Branch, Early Moundville, Etowah, and Spiro within just a few years or decades of Cahokia's dramatic historical disjuncture, and probably by the early twelfth century in many places.

Archaeologists who study other times and places "find it remarkable that both large and small Mississippian sites scattered across much of the

southern Eastern Woodlands shared so many easily recognizable organizational features" (Yoffee et al. 1999:269). But the mystery of this remarkable
pattern is reduced if we recognize that Cahokia was more than just another
Mississippian chiefdom. The puzzle for us today, then, is to explain the rate
and amplitude of Cahokia's impact. The rapidity with which a cult of the
bird-man, presumably a Cahokian idea writ large, was transmitted across
the South is startling. So is the amplitude of Cahokia's impact, measurable
as the homogeneity with which this phenomenon spread.

I suspect that Cahokia's statelike agricultural ideology—the know-
how to control labor—was a big part of this phenomenon, at least as it
appealed to would-be rulers at sites such as Moundville, Etowah, or Spiro.
And I further suspect that such Cahokian information was spread by
direct contacts between Cahokians and southerners. We should heed, as
the Southern Pragmatist insisted, Robert Hall's (1991) model of powerful
Cahokian politicos creating alliances through the adoption of foreigners. Certainly Cahokia's calling cards were distributed north and south
(Pauketat 2004). Many of these calling cards appear to be components of
the legends of the heroes of Cahokian creation.

But archaeologists have been particularly bad listeners and have
tended to conflate the signatures of Cahokian culture with the limits
of political control or influence. They were not the same thing. Clearly
boundaries existed—political or cultural—wherein Cahokians might
have sought to oversee agricultural production, extract provisions, moni-
tor debts, and impose their sense of normalcy (O'Brien 1994). These
boundaries were contingent on the transportation and communication
constraints of the day. For instance, hauling large amounts of maize in
from fields a five-day walk away might not have been feasible (then again,
see Benson et al. 2003 on Chacoan corn provisioning and Malville et al.
2001 on Nepalese porters). As we see at Moundville as well, the zone of
direct, daily control was much smaller than the political–developmental
shadow wherein Cahokians might have flexed their muscles from time to
time (compare Steponaitis 1991 with Welch 1998b). So it was for known
political confederacies, like Coosa, in the Southeast. So it was for any
political capital, from Mesopotamian city-states to imperial Tenochtitlan
(Hassig 1985; Yoffee 2005).

Unfortunately, in conflating the greater Cahokian tributary economy
or political hegemony with its sometimes subordinate neighbors or distant

confederates in an outer sphere (Pauketat 1998), we may have overlooked more than many realize, for example, tactical locations or resources on the Mississippi River—little Gibraltars—that Cahokians might have sought, for however brief a time, to take and hold. Eleventh-century evidence from Wisconsin's Trempealeau site area is the best case so far for such tactical control (Boszhardt 2004; Green and Rodell 1994; Stoltman 2000). But there may be other evidence, perhaps including the intriguing contours of the Wickliffe site, thought by Wesler (2001) to have been founded about A.D. 1100.

At the end of the eleventh century A.D., Cahokia was at its political–economic maximum and Cahokians—expert landscape engineers—were building imposing earthen pyramids, leveling great plazas, and reclaiming large low-lying swales at Cahokia and East St. Louis through labor-intensive cutting-and-filling operations (Koldehoff et al. 2000; Pauketat, ed. 2005). There were any number of twelfth-century towns in the Mid-South that show evidence of Cahokian contacts (Pauketat 2004; Welch 2006; Wesler 2001). How important was this southern tier to Cahokians? Might taking and holding the Ohio–Mississippi River confluence have been in Cahokians' interest or, more likely, a group of locals in reaction to the fact of Cahokia? In either case, might these people have sculpted the natural bluff on which Wickliffe sits so that it resembles a huge thunderbird, with principal mounds and a ditch marking the head, wings, and heart (figure 6.6)? Perhaps not, but a hypothetical Wickliffe geoglyph—wild speculation on my part—would be facing northwest at an angle close to the direction of the Cahokia site from there.

Grounds for Reflection

Inspecting the coffee grounds at the bottom of her paper cup, our Uncertain Graduate Student comes up with some of these lines of evidence herself, at least enough to reassure herself that she can face up to the scrutiny that such ideas will surely get from Dr. Science. That one final nagging question—what was Cahokia?—may not be answerable with finality at the moment. For now, it is sufficient to argue that Cahokia was different in a way and on a scale that explains much of pan-eastern Mississippianization, at least if we think about it historically. Besides, UGS thinks, there is one more macroregional pattern that speaks to what

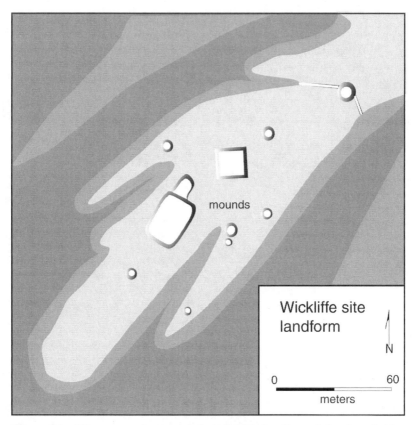

Figure 6.6. Diagrammatic plan of the Wickliffe landform (after Loughridge 1888)

Cahokia was. She writes it on her note pad: "If Cahokia was a singular political–cultural force, copied but never duplicated, then why are there no oral histories of the place?" It's true: after greater Cahokia was abandoned and the vacant quarter emptied out, the great capital city of the north—with its artisans, neighborhoods, huge pyramids and plazas, cult of the rulers, and pervasive pan-eastern influence—was simply forgotten. Dhegiha-Siouan peoples, such as the Osage, Omaha, Ponca, and Kansa, have origin stories that locate them in or near "the greater Cahokia area at one time in their histories" (Hall 2005:102). And there are hidden clues to Cahokians in the Morning Star legends and bird-man artwork. But there are no actual stories of a founding city in legend or lore (contrast Chaco Canyon; Lekson and Cameron 1995).

161

This might seem especially peculiar since one would suspect that Late Mississippian émigrés, presumably numbering in the thousands as they gradually left Cahokia (between A.D. 1150 and 1350), might have passed along stories of their former home to subsequent generations. After all, there wasn't that much time between Cahokia's abandonment and the arrival of Euro-American explorers, missionaries, and historians. "What was there to forget?" writes UGS in a memo to herself. Whatever it was, it was much more than had ever been known to any chiefdom.

WHAT CONSTITUTES CIVILIZATION? COMMUNITY AND CONTROL IN THE SOUTHWEST, MEXICO, AND MESOPOTAMIA

To be vested with enormous authority is a fine thing; but to have the on-looking world consent to it is a finer.

—Mark Twain

As any critic of evolutionary–typologizing approaches would be quick to point out, labeling Cahokia a state doesn't solve any-thing. However, it does punctuate my sense that archaeologists need to reverse the causal arrows of evolutionist thinking in eastern North America: administrative institutions did *not* evolve to constrain societies. No. There are great gaps and discontinuities in the long mound-building histories of the east. And then one great heterogeneous gathering in the American Bottom appears to have given rise to the startlingly homoge-neous Mississippianization of the Midwest and South.

But the rapid, large-scale Mississippianization process emanating out of Cahokia was a grand negotiation of divergent political and cultural interests, conflicting cultural memories, and alternate kin and suprakin allegiances from the inside out and outside in. This was a thick, sticky, and uncertain historical process. Back then, few could have known what was in the offing, certainly not enough for us to take seriously teleological models of strategizing chiefs.

Given this, the questions UGS needs to ask herself are these: Could such a historical process be better understood by looking to other formative developments outside the Eastern Woodlands? Was there anything in the wider world like Mississippianization? If so, in what ways? And, in light of my insistence on abandoning social evolutionary models in both theory and practice, can we derive a set of general principles from comparisons between Mississippian history and that of other world civilizations?

Let's imagine that instead of a comparative seminar on chiefdoms and states, like the one Dr. Science offers, UGS takes part in a comparative ancient history colloquium. Let's further imagine that the course covers comparisons of three big histories intended to expose the commonalities of historical processes (not societal types). The best documented and, for present purposes, most informative big histories from the ancient world include those found in the American Southwest, the Formative period of southern Mexico and the Uruk period of Mesopotamia. There are others of course: Longshan to Shang China, Iron Age Africa, pre-Dynastic Egypt, pre-Roman Europe, and the pre-Incan Chavin through Tiwanaku phenomena in the South American Andes. Since this is a book and not a seminar, however, I must rein in my comparisons. Indeed, I necessarily skim over many of the details even from the three cases I've chosen in order to highlight revealing historical parallels and divergences.

The American Southwest

If archaeologists are some of the best people you'll ever meet, then southwestern archaeologists are among the best of the best. It's evident in their sunny dispositions. They are cooperative scholars and content people. They generally get along with each other and with the descendants of the ancient people they study. And they can date their sites using tree-cutting dates, making them the envy of your average Mississippianist.

That's all nice and good, but, theoretically speaking, perhaps too nice for the good of their interpretations, as it seems to give life to a bias that native people in the past were as happy, evenhanded, and apolitical as themselves. The old normative belief in traditions as unchanging inheritances of the past, rather than as ongoing commemorations in the present, is alive and well in the Southwest. But there are at least two well-known reasons to think twice about what we might call the communal–native bias in southwestern archaeology: Chaco Canyon and Casas Grandes (figure 7.1).

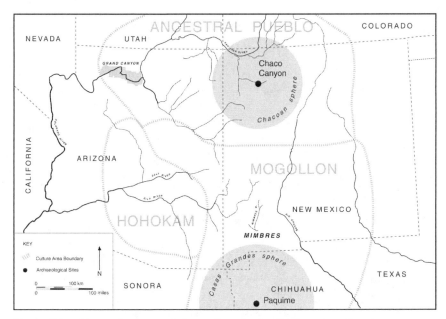

Figure 7.1. Chaco Canyon and Casas Grandes in the American Southwest

Chaco Canyon

Southwestern native people had adopted a sedentary maize agricultural lifestyle long before the first major developments in the remote, semiarid San Juan basin of northwestern New Mexico and adjacent portions of the Four Corners states (Lekson 2005; Mills 2002). In the Southwest, the sociality of such a lifestyle formed around periodic movements of villagers from one locality to another, necessary to cope with droughts (Nelson and Schachner 2002). For reasons we'll leave aside for now, hundred-room masonry pueblos, the first of the "great houses," were constructed at a couple locations in the Four Corners region around A.D. 860. The largest of these was in the Dolores region north of Mesa Verde. Named McPhee pueblo, it was "large enough to house eighteen to twenty families totaling about a hundred people" and "displays remarkable similarities" to three others clustered in Chaco Canyon, 150 kilometers to the south (Windes 2004:16). Like two of the canyon buildings—Pueblo Bonito and Una Vida—the McPhee pueblo has one construction episode dated through dendrochronology to A.D. 861. Something was happening, something involving large-scale community activities and rituals that left behind a lot of trash (Windes 2004:16).

165

However we explain this happening, it presaged an even more dramatic pan-southwestern development. After A.D. 875, farming at high elevations became difficult, and the Dolores area occupation ended quickly, with people relocating to concentrated early great houses at lower elevations, including those along the Chaco wash (Windes 2004). Migration of this sort juxtaposed two groups, native-born and immigrant. Even if there were no intentional attempts to actually alter social relations, things would have changed. Certainly in later historic Puebloan periods, emergent social stratification accompanied such situations, and the people knew it (Clark 2001): those who were there first possessed a higher status than those who came last.

What happened next might be a classic case of what I earlier called the "mitigation of cultural pluralism" and the "physicality of community building." Chacoans old and new built grand statements of their new collective identity. The great houses went up. The construction of Chaco Canyon's monumental pueblos happened in momentous pulses, or what Norman Yoffee dubbed Chaco Canyon's "little bangs" (after Cahokia's big bang) at a School of American Research conference in 2003. There were several "little bang" construction projects in Chaco Canyon dating between A.D. 850 and 1130, each a massive labor investment that produced twelve major masonry monuments, some multistoried, spread out along the floor and mesa tops of the twenty-kilometer-long Chaco Canyon (Windes 2004). Construction accelerated in A.D. 1020, these constructions including the addition of huge subterranean great kivas (Van Dyke 2003), as the canyon became what Steve Lekson (1999a, 2005) calls "downtown Chaco," a veritable cityscape (figure 7.2).

Radiating outward from the canyon were formal roads, some leading to specific populated places, others leading in important general directions or to long abandoned sites. Barbara Mills (2002) has interpreted the roads to have been more than simple transportation corridors. They were roads through space and time, connecting places and peoples in such a way as to construct a specific history more than an economic network. Not that the latter wasn't also a reason for the roads. But joining a procession into Chaco on such a road to attend a ritual event would have been an experience that defined one's relationships with others and with the powerful supernatural forces of the past and present. At least some of those powerful forces might have come to reside in the canyon's great houses.

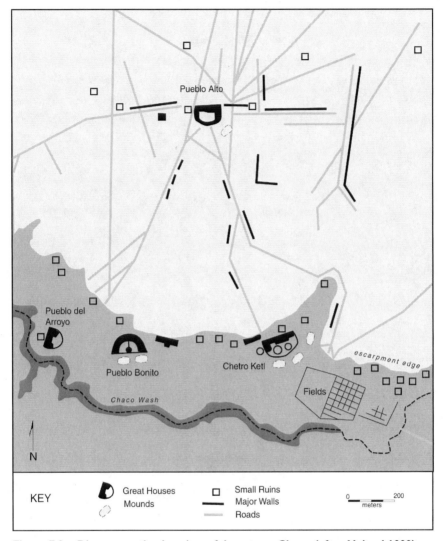

Figure 7.2. Diagrammatic plan view of downtown Chaco (after Neitzel 1999)

According to Stephen Lekson (1999), the canyon's great houses were not just or principally grand houses of communal worship for pilgrims. They were, first and foremost, palaces—the great residences, public meeting places, and storehouses of priestly hosts and rulers (figure 7.3). They were also models of design, individually and collectively, that tapped references to solar and lunar events and to each other (Farmer 1999; Sofaer 1997). Downtown Chaco's great houses, and many of the more distant

Figure 7.3. Pueblo Bonito as viewed from Chaco Canyon's rim

Chacoan outliers, were built according to strict masonry protocols, each seemingly designed around restricted central public and kiva spaces and rows of hard to access storage or ceremonial rooms. By contrast, most of the canyon's farmers lived in small single-family masonry pueblos *not* built according to the public masonry protocols (what in the eastern Woodlands would be called farmsteads).

Some of the great houses, such as the biggest of the big, Pueblo Bonito, were enlarged repeatedly, with subsequent constructions being made according to updated masonry veneer styles (Windes 2004:15). Like the light and dark sediments used to build a Mississippian pyramid, Chacoan masonry veneer construction was not done for mere visual effect, as the entire surface of each great house wall was subsequently plastered over. Thus the technological style of construction is more revealing of a set of rigid design principles—if not on-site construction engineers—who were concerned with each building's deeper meaning (Cameron 1998). My hunch would be that the layers of stones were not only mimetic of the surrounding canyon walls rock strata, but the alternating thick and thin masonry layers (of Types II–IV dating to the eleventh century) symbolized the dualisms of the ancestral Puebloan cosmos and society, here permanently built into the physical landscape.

The great houses were community constructions both in the sense of who did the building and, recursively, of what the ritualized acts of building, rebuilding, and renewal produced (Cameron 2002; Crown and Wills 2003; Van Dyke 2003, 2004). If there is a better case in world history of political authority seamlessly enacted through community-building projects, I can't think of it. For this reason, I think that debates over the nature of Chacoan leadership—ritual or political—miss the point. All formative civilizing developments mix religion and politics (never mind a well-known twenty-first-century American president) through the guise of community. Leadership existed, and the offices that leaders filled presumably were vested with considerable power—attested by the coordinated construction pulses—and sanctioned by a high degree of religiosity. Thus describing the canyon as a "location of high devotional expression," as does Colin Renfrew (2001), may be adequate for some descriptive purposes but is inadequate as an explanation of the society produced by Chacoan construction projects (and most of the sites he uses as examples from other parts of the world).

Consider some of the economic realities behind Chaco's singular experiment in political communalism (which has been suggested for Cahokia as well; Saitta 1994). Chaco Canyon at one point had perhaps 2,000–3,000 people residing in and around the downtown great houses. Considerably more people, perhaps many hundreds to thousands, entered the valley to attend the periodic ceremonial events (Judge 2004; Lekson 2005; Mills 2002:75). This means to me that each event would have had its own economy (think of Cahokia's grand plaza feasts or, if you'd prefer, Woodstock). These people would have needed to eat, and the presumed storerooms of the great houses would require filling.

Food was grown in the canyon, where at least some farmland was publicly managed, as seen in the gridded and gated field irrigated with floodwaters from Chaco wash (shown in figure 7.2; Vivian 2004). But archaeologists now know that much of the corn recovered in the canyon was grown near the Chuska Mountains, about seventy-five kilometers to the northwest (Benson et al. 2003). The same goes for the 200,000 timbers used in canyon construction and for many of the objects, cooking pots, and exotics integrated into the rituals of daily life (Toll 2001, 2004; Windes and McKenna 2001). For some this might indicate Chacoans were unable to sustain themselves. For others, this means that Chacoans had moved to the very precipice of a tributary economy, perhaps hidden to the people of the day—if not also to archaeologists—by the periodicity of surplus mobilization (i.e., once in a blue moon).

Such gatherings had historical effects (again, Woodstock). For one thing, so many people at short-term events focused a great deal of legitimate power at one place and at one time. And such events are prime opportunities for hosts to appropriate that power, if only by seeking to embody the event. If great houses didn't begin their histories as high-status residential quarters, then such might have been an outcome of certain great house powwows (this is also one explanation for how elite buildings came to be built atop earthen platforms in eastern North America). In short, the power potentially conferred on such hosts—perhaps owing to their perceived esoteric knowledge (of things liturgical, astronomical, consanguineal, and political)—could have been great, certainly greater than many of the heirs of so-called chiefdoms or kingdoms known to history (some of whom were—and there's no nice way to put it—idiots).

However politicos were perceived within or apart from the community, the power of this place and its political–religious movement inspired (or required) the construction of numerous smaller versions of it located at distant outlying points.

> The single most important attribute of a Bonito phase Chacoan outlier is the presence of a great house, which is identified on the basis of one or more of the following attributes: larger building size and labor investment than contemporary structures within its community, multistoried construction, symmetry of layout, evidence of planning in the form of large-scale foundation units, core-and-veneer wall construction, and banded masonry. (Mills 2002:81)

Many of these outliers were located on natural prominences or along the Chacoan roads, as if to claim the power of the place. Doubtless, a good deal of autonomy was granted to each outlier, if only by virtue of the sometimes great distances between it and Chaco Canyon (up to 200 kilometers). But the regional data indicate that many of these places were part of a larger political–religious confederacy (Lekson 1999a:55). The degree to which direct political (via religion) controls over daily social life correlated with this confederacy may be indicated by the network of roads linking outliers with the canyon (Lekson 1999a). These roads indicate something more (or less) than economic networking, however, as they seem to link important ancient places and geographical features with traffic to and from the great houses (Mills 2002; Van Dyke 2003). They were, in short, processional and experiential avenues through space and time.

The political ties between localities via such roads were likely ritualized—perhaps explaining Norman Yoffee's (2005) preference for calling the Chaco Canyon polity a "rituality." However, politics and ritual are coterminous everywhere, as Yoffee (2005:173) notes, even or *especially* in the rituals of nation-states (Bell 1997; Kertzer 1988). Whatever ritual paths were followed to this ancestral Puebloan confederation, it was ultimately and unavoidably a political confederation. I submit that the various little bang constructions of the great houses and other great facilities and roads of the canyon, and the construction episodes at outlying localizations, were the physicality of the confederation process itself. The great house projects gathered people and gave them a heritage that linked them into a greater regional economy (that was spatially and temporally discontinuous but uniquely extensive) that continued to shape the history of all people in the American Southwest.

How large a region was confederated at any one time under the umbrella of the canyon's resident (political–religious) elite in the greatest of the great houses remains an open question, but there are good reasons to think that Chaco's confederacy covered much more area—if no more people—than any Mesoamerican chiefdom or Mesopotamian city-state. First, as Steven LeBlanc (1999:184–186) and Lekson (2002) have both observed, there was remarkably little violence in the greater San Juan basin during Chaco's heyday. At the same time there were higher incidences of ritual killings or mistreatments of the dead, perhaps indicative of what both consider potential state-sponsored violence (Wilcox 1993). In Lekson's (1999a:63) words, a "sort of 'Pax Chaco' prevailed, where families could live in small houses scattered around a Great House, without evident fear of violence or thuggery. In the century before Chaco and the century after Chaco, big villages were the rule; only during the Chacoan era was the great majority of population able to live in single-family homes."

Second, as went Chaco Canyon, so went the Chacoan outliers. After A.D. 1130, the array of outliers in the Four Corners area dissipated. Later post-Chacoan complexes at Aztec and Salmon Ruins, to the north, are impressive attempts to re-place Chaco. But they belie a period of great regional change.

Subsequently migration, cultural plurality, increased violence, and the localized reproductions of traditions in ever changing social landscapes seem everywhere the X factor processes that underwrote the coalescence and dissolution of southwestern communities, not unlike the processes behind early Chaco itself (Haas and Creamer 1993; LeBlanc 1999). For instance, beginning at A.D. 1250 in the Galisteo basin south and east of Chaco Canyon, James Snead (2004, 2005) reckons that migrants with diverse cultural backgrounds established composite settlements, some referencing (if not actually symbolically inaugurating) a prominent nearby landmark called Petroglyph Hill. Inhabitants of one hilltop site, situated in a side valley of the Galisteo, added a prominent multistoried square room block just after A.D. 1300, a move Snead interprets as an attempt by residents to make a permanent place in an otherwise precarious and dangerous social landscape. The move, though, could have been interpreted as offensive in nature by others. And it was these others who attacked and burned what we now call Burnt Corn Pueblo, probably one September morning around A.D. 1325, when the residents had spread the ears of corn out on the roof to dry (Snead, personal communication, 2005).

In succeeding decades, people avoided the locality. Snead (2005) concludes:

> The incineration of Burnt Corn Pueblo was not simply a raid or strike against economic rivals but an attack on history—either the real history of a group with deep cultural ties to the area or the "created" history of an immigrant group. In its place the smoking ruins represented a third history, one that persisted long after any direct recollection of the events that created it had vanished. We can't know what that story was, but in Pueblo tradition the destruction of a community was an inevitable correlate of the moral failure of its inhabitants.

Casas Grandes

There were other great historical and economic changes in the southwestern world after Chaco Canyon's abandonment, including the florescence of the classic Hohokam in southern Arizona, the movement of people north into the Mesa Verde region, and the abandonment of the

Mimbres valley of southern New Mexico (Hegmon 2005; Lekson 2005; Nelson and Schachner 2002; Shafer 1999). Of these, the Mimbres abandonment may again indicate the importance of both migrations and the X factor in the rise of the largest and, in the words of Stephen Lekson (1999b), the most "cosmopolitan pueblo" in the Southwest: Paquimé or Casas Grandes in northern Chihuahua (Di Peso 1974; Di Peso et al. 1974; Whalen and Minnis 2001a).

Steven LeBlanc (1983, 1989) argues that the southern Puebloan Mimbres people—best known for their beautiful black-on-white painted bowls—were pulled south into the rapidly emerging phenomenon of Casas Grandes. Indeed, it is noteworthy that "Mimbres Classic Black-on-White sherds [are found] on the surfaces of a few [of the region's] Medio period pueblos" (Whalen and Minnis 2001a:106). In addition, few people lived in the greater Casas Grandes region during the period before the construction of Paquimé, known as the Viejo phase. As evidence, we may look to the 324 datable sites in Michael Whalen and Paul Minnis's (2001a:table 4.1) regional survey universe, where Viejo phase sites numbered fifteen (5 percent of total). The rest date to the Medio period (ca. A.D. 1200–1450), as does Paquimé and the transregional Casas Grandes interaction sphere (Schaafsma and Riley 1999; Whalen and Minnis 2001a,b).

Most archaeologists now agree that Casas Grandes is an ancestral Puebloan, not Mesoamerican, phenomenon (Lekson 1999a; Whalen and Minnis 2001a,b). However, it was probably the conduit for the influx of Mesoamerican stories, icons, and objects into the Southwest as far north as the Mesa Verde region (Cobb et al. 1999; Lekson 1999b; Schaafsma 1999). However, unlike most northern Puebloan complexes, including Chaco Canyon, is the clear-cut evidence of a more typical centralized settlement hierarchy, with the obvious central administrative place being Paquimé itself, which covers nearly thirty-six hectares (Lekson 2005:256).

"Paquimé began as a dozen or more independent, widely spaced, single-story adobe compounds. These were followed by an explosive 'urban renewal' (Di Peso's term) creating the dense, massive structure seen today" (Lekson 2005:257). That massive structure consists of eight hectares of multistoried adobe room-block residences, about six times more "than the next-largest neighboring settlement" (Whalen and Minnis 2001a:140).

The rooms were large, tall, and mostly rectangular, with heavily timbered upper-story floors and roofs. Many rooms were more complex in shape, with 'L'-shapes and even more complicated forms (one room resembles an abstract butterfly in plan). These shapes created small nooks and re-entrants which accommodated shelf-like 'sleeping platforms,' but which may also have served to strengthen and buttress multi-storied walls. . . . Other internal features include small, raised adobe fireboxes sometimes carved into geometric or effigy forms. (Lekson 2005:257)

The multistoried room-block structures were built around a series of small plazas, all arrayed in turn into a larger L- or I-shaped configuration (figure 7.4). In addition, Paquimé featured other large plazas, canals, courtyards with gated macaw or parrot pens, large earth ovens (for processing agave), I-shaped ball courts, "five masonry-faced platform

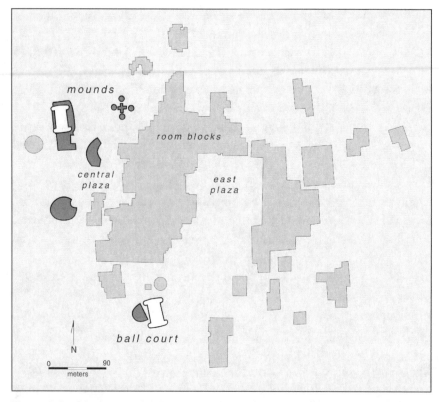

Figure 7.4. Diagrammatic plan map of Paquimé, Mexico (after Lekson 2005 and Whalen and Minnis 2001a)

174

mounds ('pyramids' in Di Peso's terms) and effigy mounds (in the forms of a plumed serpent, a decapitated bird, and a cross) . . . [and] two large reservoirs/settling ponds for water channeled to Paquimé from distant springs" (Lekson 2005:257).

Similar elaborate features and pueblo-style adobe room blocks are known from a variety of outliers within the Casas Grandes inner zone, the area that lies within a day's walk of the urban pueblo. At a number of secondary centers or outliers in this zone are small adobe-walled pueblos, ball courts, birdcages, and large ovens indicative of public gatherings, ceremonies, and, perhaps, an architectural orthodoxy (Whalen and Minnis 1996, 2001a,b). In addition, this inner zone includes more evidence of agricultural improvements—low stone terraces and canals

> constructed all over the upland slopes . . . in what we . . . perceive as soil and moisture conservation features built in an attempt to increase the agricultural productivity of these less-than-prime quality lands lying away from the main river valleys. It was originally argued that corvée labor was used to construct these facilities, the principal purpose of which was to protect the valley floor irrigation systems around Casas Grandes from uncontrolled rainfall runoff. (Whalen and Minnis 2001b:341–342, citing Di Peso et al. 1974:823)

Whalen and Minnis (2001b:342) conclude that the construction of terraces and canals may have been part of a regionwide "productive intensification . . . stimulated by the needs of Casas Grandes, as Di Peso originally argued." Beyond a day's walk from Paquimé, agricultural improvements tail off, and such features as ball courts, birdcages, and large ovens are virtually unknown, indicative of the region's centralized integration. However, Whalen and Minnis (2001b:339) interpret the presence of ball courts, birdcages, and ovens outside the central city in the same vein as the craft production refuse and stores within Paquimé:

> Shell, for instance, was found stockpiled in remarkable quantity in a few rooms. Nevertheless, there was not similarly concentrated evidence of shell ornament production, and the data argue for the opposite situation: dispersal of shell ornament manufacture. Di Peso and his colleagues report "caches of shell in open pits in various rooms scattered

throughout the city" (Di Peso *et al.*, 1974, Vol. 6, p. 402). They further note that these caches contained a large variety of molluscan species and that workmanship in the caches was of higher quality than that displayed in the huge shell stores. Di Peso and his colleagues interpreted these caches as the stores of individual shell workers scattered throughout the community. Assuming this interpretation to be correct, the sizes of the caches argue strongly that shell jewelry manufacture was a small-scale affair, probably carried out by a number of craftsmen in various parts of the city.

[A]viculture was a decentralized activity practiced by a number of people in the community. Turquoise, malachite, and hematite are likewise dispersed throughout the community (Di Peso *et al.*, 1974, Vol. 8, p. 91), and there is no indication of stockpiling or centralized working of any of these materials. (Whalen and Minnis 2001b:340)

Whereas Whalen and Minnis (2001a,b) see craft production debris, birdcages, and other public facilities as "dispersed" within greater Paquimé, the fact remains that, viewed at the scale of the Casas Grandes region, these features are concentrated in and around the central complex. Indeed, the regional centrality, along with the large size of downtown Casas Grandes, may indicate both greater administrative complexity—in heterarchical terms—and a bounded political phenomenon in excess of Whalen and Minnis's (2001a,b) modest thirty-kilometer radius. Remember, as I've argued for Cahokia, the zone of direct pervasive social control and the limitations of native North American transportation—which are real and observable—need not have been isomorphic with the boundaries of a Casas Grandes polity.

In fact, there are three other reasons to suspect a greater Casas Grandes polity: signal stations, entrepôts, and an interaction sphere that stretched for some 200 kilometers in any direction (Fish and Fish 1999; Swanson 2003). The first of these consist of possible hilltop signaling sites that would have been visible from one location to another. Such sites minimally indicate a degree of communicative coordination projected out into the hinterlands. In addition, some hinterland areas contain "large, surplus-concentrating settlements . . . in major ecological or transport corridors of peripheral zones" presumably "positioned for the convenience of the surplus-concentrating elites" (Whalen and Minnis 2001b:349). Such sites stretch into distant lands, such as the Animas area of southwestern

New Mexico (Fish and Fish 1999). Some might lump all such places into a Casas Grandes interaction sphere, but others have interpreted the distant complexes, which include Casas Grandes–style ball courts and Chihuahuan pottery wares, as "a dependent periphery, a series of frontier settlements, or part of a political economy" (Whalen and Minnis 2001b:353, citing Di Peso 1974; LeBlanc 1989).

The days of being content with the nonexplanatory "interaction sphere" should be behind us. If we eschew thinking of culture as a passive, diffused phenomenon, then we must answer the question, How were elements of what appear to be politicized, public practices put into place (literally) in Chihuahua and then transferred to people in the hinterlands? If the equally nonexplanatory "peer polity" idea is invoked (see chapter 1), what was the relationship between emulation by outsiders and the projections of insiders? Indeed, given the continuously constructed character of culture in general, can we be justified in distinguishing the emulations of traditions from insiders' projections? Moreover, what if distant peoples were interacting with Paquimé because they were "related" or "adopted" by those in greater Casas Grandes? The answers to these questions lie in an expanded backdoor approach to identity in archaeology where urbanization, landscape, and polity were inextricably wrapped up in the historical process whereby people were "gathered" and their cultural practices and embodied identities and labor appropriated for the greater good.

Formative Mesoamerica

Answers to these questions might be illuminated by the Early to Middle Formative world of southern Mexico at about 1650–300 B.C. (figure 7.5). That Formative world, where many have looked for the origins of New World civilization, is rich with ancient sites and early cities. In the past, southeastern North Americanists have looked to Mesoamerica for the explanations of Poverty Point, Coles Creek, or Mississippian. Perhaps this has fed Mesoamericanists' egos more than is warranted: archaeological and art-historical discussions of how such civilizations emerged in Mesoamerica have tended to be long on claims and short on data. Besides, one fact is now apparent to all: there were earlier monumental developments in North and South America.

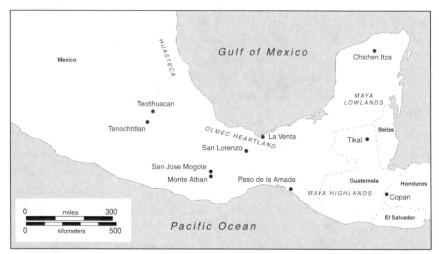

Figure 7.5. Map of Mesoamerica showing select major sites (after Hendon and Joyce 2004)

Lacking eastern North America's long history of elaborate mounded ceremonial centers (dating back to 3600 B.C.), Mesoamerica's earliest constructed monumental center dates to about 1650 cal. B.C.—Paso de la Amada on the Pacific coast in Chiapas (Clark 2004). During its first century and a half of existence, the core of this planned central settlement consisted of at least fourteen central mounds (and various outlying others) surrounding a plaza nearly 200 meters in diameter, with a ball court to one side. This monumental core covered at least 37 hectares, with an additional 130 hectares of scattered residential areas in the immediate greater Paso de la Amada vicinity (Clark 2004:60).

The large three-plus-meter-high mound at the plaza's southern end was built in at least nine major stages, each probably topped by an elaborate elite residential structure (Clark 2004:figure 2.4). John Clark (2004:60) estimates that 2,000-plus people populated greater Paso de la Amada, "20 percent of whom were privileged to reside near the formal core." And like its distant Louisiana Archaic counterparts, Clark (2004) interprets Paso de la Amada's planned construction as the defining experience(s) of a new sort and sense of community. And like any number of southeastern and southwestern examples, he sees this and other early Mesoamerican centers as sites where pilgrims gathered. Paso de la Amada's large plaza, for instance, could have "accommodated over 10,000 spectators on special occasions but probably saw use by much smaller crowds" (Clark 2004:60).

The re-imagining of community in this way eventually led to social stratification, a localized process that was replicated elsewhere in Mesoamerica,
although slightly later than Chiapas.

Agricultural villages had emerged at about the same time in highland
Oaxaca and the lowland Gulf Coast region. The sparsely populated Valley
of Oaxaca was home to less than a thousand souls between about 1700
and 1300 cal. B.C. (Clark 2004:48; Marcus and Flannery 1996:78–79). In
the northern of three valley arms sat the settlement of San José Mogote,
with its 120 to 350 people living on about seven hectares. In this Early
Formative period, even this modest village was first among equals. And
as such, it sported a number of coeval or sequent public buildings, more
elaborate but not much larger than ordinary dwellings. Otherwise, there
was no central planned monumental space until near the beginning of
what is typically called the Olmec horizon (ca. 1300 cal. B.C.).

Long about that time, some contend that Formative villagers in the
distant lands of coastal Veracruz and Tabasco had already coalesced to
construct Mesoamerica's first city and stratified society at San Lorenzo
(Clark 1997:216, citing Benson 1996; Cyphers 1996). Although dis-
puted by Flannery and colleagues (2005:11222), the most recent survey
documents that San Lorenzo covers 500 hectares, making it "10 to 20
times larger than any contemporary community in Mesoamerica" (Clark
1997:216, 2006). John Clark (2006) believes that this size makes it more
than first among equals. San Lorenzo residents, he says,

> sponsored the creation of numerous stone monuments. Colossal stone
> heads, multiton table-top thrones . . . and lesser monuments were
> dragged through the tropical rainforest to San Lorenzo from stone out-
> crops located 60-70 km away. . . . Other public works projects concerned
> the construction of San Lorenzo itself. The central portion of the site is a
> natural, 50-m-high plateau that was intensively and extensively modified
> in pre-Olmec and early Olmec times by constructing a series of massive,
> residential terraces that stepped up from the surrounding plain to the
> summit. (Clark 1997:217, citing Coe and Diehl 1980; Cyphers 1996)

Although the history of this urbanizing process is poorly understood,
the coordinated labor embodied in San Lorenzo's monumental landscape
arguably bespeaks Olmec state making (Clark 1997, 2006; cf. Blanton et
al. 1999:20; Marcus and Flannery 1996). And yet even here or at later

centers (especially La Venta), the Olmec state was not an absolute institution that persisted without continuous collaborative practices from all aspects of society. The Olmec state, as constructed within its few early ceremonial cities, was likely a heterogeneous aggregate of competing interests governed, as Clark (1997) notes, through public works and largesse. Susan Gillespie's (2005) reanalysis of the central commemorative pits and pyramids of downtown La Venta reveals that, between 800 and 400 B.C., Olmec governance was actually an ongoing construction of place and collective memory through carefully orchestrated and meaning-laden earthen and stone depositional practices (figure 7.6).

Viewing the Olmec state(s) in such a way is not to say that it was merely an outcome of a general evolutionary trend in Mesoamerica. Admittedly, like the interactionist views on the Mississippian emergence (see chapter 2), an older evolutionary school of Mesoamericanists prefer gradualist (if not also minimalist) explanations that see the Olmec phenomenon as a pan-Mesoamerican Formative period interaction sphere (Flannery et al. 2005). Local chiefdoms, the story goes, adapted to local agricultural conditions. Accordingly, there could be no Olmec Mother Culture emanating out of coastal Veracruz and Tabasco (Blanton et al. 1999; Flannery et al. 2005). This view is based in a particular theory of social evolution that holds places and material culture to be outcomes or consequences of forces beyond the agency of ancient people (see chapter 1).

And while a common alternative—the diffusionist Mother Culture scenario—is overly simplistic (i.e., all things good and beautiful came from San Lorenzo), the interaction sphere explanation seems increasingly strained by evidence (never mind lacking in social theory) that contradicts categorizations of the Olmec cities as the centers of peer polity chiefdoms with parallel evolutionary trajectories. Instead, the appearance of the classic Olmec art—which doubtless correlates with subsidized Olmec artists at the major Olmec cities—correlates with the truncation of the occupation of Paso de la Amada and, in the Valley of Oaxaca, the restructuring of San José Mogote into the paramount administrative center in the region (Clark 2004). By the twelfth century B.C., the town of San José Mogote was centered on a wide, stone-faced, two-meter-high pyramid featuring opposing carved feline and bird images near its steps. This pyramid fronted a large public plaza, surrounded by other modest pyramidal mounds.

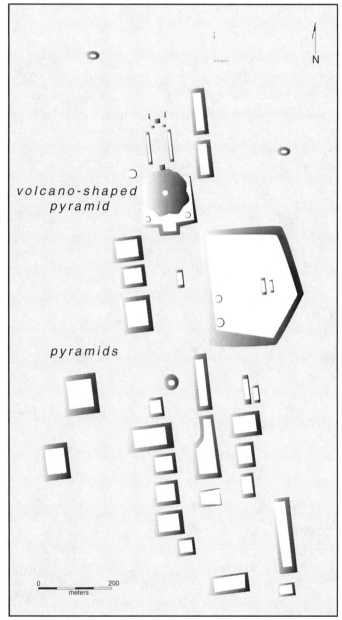

Figure 7.6. Diagrammatic plan map of La Venta, Mexico (after Adams 1991)

San José Mogote's territorial control probably did not extend to the other two arms of the valley (Blanton et al. 1999:figure 2.7; Marcus and

Flannery 1996:108–110). It was also not stable, as noted by Arthur Joyce (2004:196):

> Warfare within the Oaxaca Valley is suggested by a high frequency of structures destroyed by fire and by a sparsely occupied buffer zone separating the Etla arm of the valley from the two other arms which were occupied by competing polities (Kowalewski et al. 1989:70-75). At approximately 600 B.C., a temple on Mound 1 at San Jose Mogote was burned to the ground, suggesting that the most restricted and ritually important part of the site was penetrated by a raiding party (Marcus and Flannery 1996:129). Survey data indicate that San Jose Mogote was losing population, with the site decreasing from 70 ha to 34 ha by 500 B.C. (Kowalewski et al. 1989:72-77). These data suggest that many commoners were expressing resistance, withdrawing support from the rulers of San Jose Mogote, and leaving the community. At the same time, competing centers in the Oaxaca valley . . . were increasing in size.

These developments occurred in the century immediately preceding the dramatic founding of the new administrative center of Monte Albán on a modified mountaintop at about 500 B.C. (figure 7.7). Over the subsequent centuries, Monte Albán rulers extended their grip on the

Figure 7.7. Monte Albán's central mountaintop complex

entire Oaxaca valley and beyond, the best-known conquest being that of Cuicatlán Cañada (Spencer 1982). The armies of Monte Albán burned local buildings, killed locals (and mounted their severed heads on a rack: *tzompantli*), built an outpost, and moved in. Back at Monte Albán, this conquest and others like it were celebrated and commemorated by carved stone panels. Initially these included some 400 Danzante carvings arrayed in a gallery in the southwestern area of the central plaza that show naked and mutilated enemies or captives. Later, they involved more elaborate place glyphs set into the face of a building in the plaza (Marcus 1983).

The shopworn social evolutionary explanation of events goes as follows. The period of unbridled interpolity violence pushed the various competing chiefly elites of the three arms of the Oaxaca valley to innovate a novel adaptive solution, a new kind of government where power was shared (if still led by the San José Mogote elites). They did this in a new place where no faction held an overwhelming advantage and where administration of the entire valley could be efficiently overseen, literally. For all intents and purposes, what the confederates innovated was a state bureaucracy. Their new capital was disembedded from the preceding era's social problems and thus was destined to succeed (Blanton 1978; Blanton et al. 1999; Yoffee 2005:189–192). It grew from an initial population of just over 5,000 people to tens of thousands by the seventh century A.D. owing, presumably in large measure, to the expansionistic tendencies of the state (Blanton et al. 1999). In a rapid demographic surge not unlike Cahokia's (chapter 6), the entire valley went from a pre–Monte Albán population of perhaps a couple thousand to an early Monte Albán period population of nearly 15,000 (Kowalewski et al. 1989). By "the Late Formative (300-100 B.C.) the city grew to cover 442 ha with an estimated population of 17,242 . . . and the population of the valley as a whole increased an estimated 27-fold" (A. Joyce 2004:196-197, citing Blanton 1978; Kowalewski et al. 1989).

While there is much in this shop worn evolutionary scenario with which to agree, we should question the inferences about when and how the state arose. Arthur Joyce's (2000, 2004) idea of resistance gives us reason to think beyond the social evolutionary biases concerning the formation and putative expansionism of the Monte Albán state. Consider these nuanced or alternative interpretations. First, rather than the inherent weaknesses of chiefly administrations, the violence witnessed at San José Mogote prior to the foundation of Monte Albán might have stemmed from internal resistance to the attempted emulation of Olmec archetypes by Oaxacan wannabes. This possibility gains additional importance if we consider another alternative: the new administrators of Monte Albán, as many intimate, were drawn mostly from the old elites of San José Mogote.

Hence, as Charles Spencer (1982) once inferred, the founding of Monte Albán might not have been a *consequence* of the creation of a new institution, the state (which, from a social evolutionary vantage point, would have happened behind closed doors—out of sight and unrecoverable by archaeologists; see chapter 1). Instead, the founding of Monte Albán would have constituted the first step in the spatialization and materialization of a cultural hegemony that interpenetrated every facet of daily life—accentuated by the displacement of many hundreds of people to a new city and the fact that the relocated rulers could see, and the new city could be seen from, practically any location in the valley. Archaeologists can see and recover the process of state making in this case. And this particular political gathering certainly seems top-down, at least in its mountaintop construction.

However, it is doubly important to consider yet another possible interpretive alternative: the initial phase of the new city might not have been as exclusively political and elite centered as the disembedded state idea implies. For instance, the executions commemorated in the Danzante carvings might not have been politically motivated (Joyce 2000).

> An important goal of the earliest inhabitants [of Monte Albán] was to construct a ceremonial center that symbolized the version of the sacred covenants developed at San José Mogote during the previous century. . . . The sacrifice of captives was one way for nobles to open portals to the underworld . . . and activate the covenant, thereby assuring fertility and prosperity for themselves and their followers. . . . The symbolism of the cosmos and the sacred covenant resonating in the layout of the Main Plaza clearly marked Monte Albán as a mountain of creation, a common concept in Otomanguean world views. . . . The Main Plaza . . . was a public arena where thousands of people participated in rituals that involved the sacred covenant. . . . In such a setting, simultaneously public and symbolic, the new practices involving human sacrifice would have

been dramatic events graphically enacting and renewing the covenant. The effects of ritual drama and mass psychology on participants would have created powerful psychological forces . . . affecting people's dispositions by binding them to rulers, the symbols, and the new social order centered at Monte Albán. (A. Joyce 2000:81–83)

Joyce (2000:84) concludes that human sacrifice "and the close association of elite residences and public politico-religious buildings were the means by which the identity of nobles *came to be* marked as fundamentally separate from that of commoners" (emphasis added). Warring and the execution of enemies, he adds, are not simply explained as elements of an expansionistic state. They were, instead, integral components of the prosecution of religious precepts by Monte Albán leaders. Importantly, this "more sacred form of warfare may have further united people of the Monte Albán polity" (Joyce 2000:84, citing Joyce and Winter 1996:38–39). To put it more directly, warring and enemy sacrifice might not indicate the inherent qualities of a state fully evolved, but the internal weaknesses of administrators engaged in state making. Diverting people's attention to external foes and supernatural forces in order to shore up one's administration at home is a common tactic used by politicians today. In ancient cases (and perhaps not so ancient ones), community formation and identity construction were the driving forces of state making. The state did not evolve first and remake identity and community second. Rather, it was a mutual, negotiated, historical process.

Uruk Period Mesopotamia

This same conclusion has been reached by Gil Stein (2001) and Norman Yoffee (2005) for the earliest states in Mesopotamia (figure 7.8). The state, they might say, was not all it has been cracked up to be. Stein and Yoffee *partially* abandon earlier neoevolutionary frameworks that posited centralized chiefdoms as precursors to the earliest states (Flannery 1999a; Wright 1984). In this same vein, Robert Adams (2003:43) now concludes that "there was a different path to statehood, lacking chiefdoms as a transitional step, in at least the Mesopotamian case."

If we accept this position, we still need to explain Mesopotamia's "seemingly rather abrupt transition to settlements of unambiguously ur-

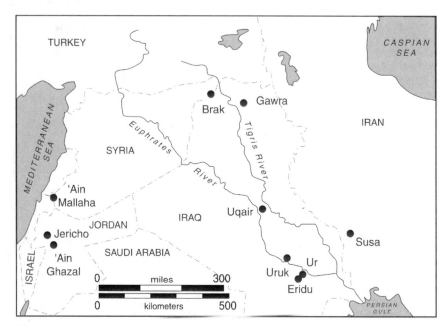

Figure 7.8. Map of Mesopotamia showing select major sites

ban size and complexity" that featured "new forms of social organization with different, more functionally specialized internal structures than those usually associated with chiefdoms" (Adams 2003:43). Those explanations must take into account the histories of places where people gathered, where cultural and economic pluralism was mitigated, and where identities were forged around religious practices, community temples, and divergent or competing social sectors. In short, they must explain the X factor of urbanization.

Although neither Stein, Yoffee, nor Adams (among others) might go so far, their partial abandonment of the standard neoevolutionary line of inquiry and their long-standing concern for the X factor allows us to question the centrality (and by extension the reality) of institutions in our cause-and-effect scenarios. And, perhaps to the chagrin of some, their willingness to redefine Mesopotamian states as heterogeneous, decentered phenomena casts doubt on our ability to strictly segregate states from nonstate societies elsewhere by comparison to Mesopotamia (contra Yoffee's Rule). But Mesopotamianists are open, broad-minded people who are willing to adapt their theories (Pollock and Bernbeck 2005). And in adapting, they will doubtless flesh out, through comparisons of local histories, the relationships of community building, inscription, migration, and warring in this most complex of world historical developments (Emberling 2003; Stein 2005a,b).

The Mesopotamian case begins eight to twelve millennia ago, with Pre-Pottery Neolithic and Pottery Neolithic settlements of food-producing, ancestor-venerating people at places such as Jericho, Çatalhöyük, or 'Ain Mallaha or Ghazal (Emberling 2003; Kuijt and Chesson 2005). By the Ubaid period (5500–4000 B.C.) there are permanent agricultural settlements everywhere, including southern Mesopotamia (Postgate 1992:23). In addition, Henry Wright (1984) and Susan Pollock (1999:86–92) see artifactual, architectural, and regional-settlement evidence of inequality and centralization in the Susiana plain, with the size of some noncommunal buildings and the distribution of clay seal impressions (that marked goods or packages transported from one location to another) indicating control and hence a chiefdom centered on Susa. This settlement, covering about ten hectares by the Late Ubaid period, featured a ten-meter-high platform on which was located

> a temple, a bank of storerooms containing large storage jars and remains of wheat, and a thick-walled building, possibly a residence. . . . The importance of the platform and its buildings . . . lies in the symbolic associations of the sacred—in the form of the temple—with the products of human labor—in the form of stored grain and the platform itself. . . . Even if the people of Susa were convinced that building the platform and the structures upon it was part of their religious obligations that they undertook "voluntarily," this does not mean that these obligations were not a source of material gain or prestige for politico-religious leaders. (Pollock 1999:91)

According to Algaze (1993:120), "Settlement data also point to the Ubaid origins of the Uruk phenomenon. While the overall population densities in the alluvium during Ubaid times were low, a surprising proportion of the total settled area by the Late Ubaid period was represented by settlements that can be categorized as small urban centers on the basis of their size." He mentions Eridu, Tell el'Oueili, Ur, and Uqair as towns of around ten to twelve hectares and notes that public architecture began at such towns and gave "way without interruption to larger versions in the Uruk period" (Algaze 1993:121). Not all of these were temples, with examples of fortified storehouses or other enigmatic buildings indicating "the emerging role of Ubaid towns in the organization of production and in the storage and redistribution of agricultural and other surpluses" (Algaze 1993:121, citing Wright 1986). Others are less convinced of the meaning of the settlement pattern, architectural, and seal arguments, and even interpret the Ubaid period initiation of temple–ziggurat construction at sites such as Eridu, Gawra, and Anu to indicate the religion-based coalescence of community, not polity (Postgate 1992:24; Yoffee 2005:53–54). Splitting the difference, Gil Stein (2003:figure 2) comments concerning the early Ubaid, "Complex societies [were] integrated through ritual."

Many researchers assume that, already at this time, there were cultural exchanges between Ubaid populations, the direction generally being south to north (Pollock 1999; Yoffee 2005:209–210). There were, it seems, Ubaid period leaders, priests, farmers, and traders. People might have made pilgrimages to important temples, and migrations might have occurred. In some areas, seasonally wandering pastoralists may have frequented Ubaid settlements. Some feel that the latter might have come into conflict with the former (Wright 1984). But was there a causal relationship between exchange, migration, warring, and settlement that helps explain what happened next? If we based our answer on southwestern and southeastern North American analogies, it would be yes.

Along the Tigris and Euphrates Rivers in 4000 B.C., "there were few villages of more than about 10 hectares and with more than a few hundreds of people" (Yoffee 2005:210–211). However, later in the Uruk period (4000–3100 B.C.), villages had grown into cities. The largest was Uruk itself, encompassing "about 250 hectares (2.5 square kilometers) . . . [with] a population of about 20,000 people" (Yoffee 2005:211). These cities were "more than just villages writ large" (Pollock 1999:46). Yoffee (2005:54) has described them as urban enclaves with nearly 80 percent of each city-state's population living within the city limits (figure 7.9). For example, the northern Mesopotamian city of Brak was surrounded by "a large 'empty zone' 3-4 kilometers in width . . . with a series of evenly spaced small settlements, none larger than 4 hectares, further away. The 'empty' zone may have been devoted to agriculture in antiquity, as it is in modern times" (Emberling 2003:264).

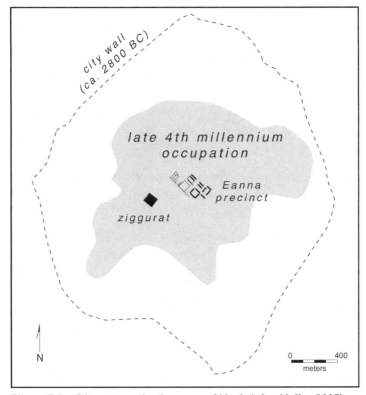

Figure 7.9. Diagrammatic plan map of Uruk (after Yoffee 2005)

Such city–hinterland patterns resulted from the process Norman Yoffee called ruralization (see chapter 6)—where cities redefined cultural landscapes around them—and a demographic implosion:

> This demographic implosion was occasioned by a number of factors: cities became nodal points for military protections from neighbors, for leaders to co-ordinate labor that traveled to a patchwork of fields (which were left fallow every second year), and for the construction of branching canals that irrigated the fields. Emerging city-states were also the locations of regionally important temples . . . that were also centers of exchange. Migrations, from central to southern Mesopotamia and also perhaps from further south, were also stimulated by changing environmental conditions. (Yoffee 2005:54)

The earliest cities were dense, hybrid, urban centers with multiple temples, economic sectors, and residential neighborhoods. They were complex heterarchical entities typified more by their different sectors and various leaders or interest groups than by a unified political hierarchy (Stein 2001). "They were often walled, containing the temple of the city-god on a high platform and a palace and administrative center spatially separated from it" (Emberling 2003:261). Canals, roads, and internal walls divided up their spaces and residential areas, inhabited by people from different homelands who spoke various language dialects. "Mesopotamian city-states are notorious examples of multiethnic communities. . . . Although these city-states provided identifications of citizenship, ethnic relations that transcended city-state boundaries could be mobilized to advantage in the struggle for power within city-states" (Yoffee 1995b:258). City administrations were multivalent in action and authority (Adams 2003:47).

Perhaps for this reason, it is uncertain whether or not one Uruk period city necessarily dominated Mesopotamia. Some feel it likely and point out, as I did in chapter 3, that a fine line might separate incorporation from subjugation (Algaze 1993:9–10; Potts 1999:58ff.). Larger than most ancient cities, Uruk remains the most likely candidate for primate center and the heart of an apparent Uruk expansion (Algaze 1993). Others are less certain about what an Uruk expansion would look like archaeologically (Potts 1999). Was it based on newly formed states? For some, using the word "state" to describe the type of society during the Uruk period introduces undesirable interpretive biases (Emberling 2003:261; Stein 2001:210). And yet the Uruk cities were distinct in that they emerged rapidly and simultaneously. Afterward, much of the individuality of southern Mesopotamian settlements, pottery styles, and daily life that had characterized the Ubaid period seems to have been lost, replaced by more monolithic religious and community identities. Presumably the new identities were based on the discursive meanings propounded by priests and state bureaucrats during state-sponsored construction events in which the masses of laborers ate from crude, plain, and mass-produced bevel-rim bowls (Bernbeck 1999; Pollock 1999).

And it was when such discursive, ideological projections of meaning and identity were subsumed within the everyday realm of social life, following Reinhard Bernbeck (1999), that we can use them to identify Uruk colonists amid the distant villages of Mesopotamia's hinterlands (Stein 2002, 2005b). Indeed, the emergence of Uruk cities seems to have involved "the establishment of the world's earliest-known colonial network, in which a series of outposts was established along trade and communications routes leading to the highland resource zones of Iran and Anatolia" (Stein 2005b:147). Apparently this expansion did not eliminate the household as the basic unit of the Mesopotamian economy (Pollack 1999:117). Southern Mesopotamian households lived, even as colonists, alongside indigenous households in northern communities (Stein 2002). However, the Uruk cities did not conquer and directly control these outlying peoples. Gil Stein (2005b:170) believes that the Uruk trade colonies are indications that the Mesopotamian cities were too weak to have conquered and controlled them, a weakness remedied only later by a conquering ruler from one city-state.

Common Ground

How different is the Ubaid-to-Uruk case, with its heterogeneous gatherings of villagers into cities and colonies, from the case of Chaco Canyon, Casas Grandes, Paso de la Amada, San Lorenzo, San José Mogote, Monte Albán, and Cahokia or any of its Mississippian spin-offs? That is the obvious question that has, some would say, an obvious answer: "Very different."

Indeed, these historical cases were very different from each other in many ways that I have not explained. So, you should feel a little uncomfortable when I compare Uruk city-states to the singular centers of North America and Formative Mesoamerica. Clearly there were differences, contingent on local and regional histories—population densities, long-distance exchange traditions, transportation technologies, surplus production potentialities, and so on—that might seem to preclude a comparative approach. The big error of social evolutionary approaches, after all, is the assumption that whole societies changed uniformly through time.

However, I argued earlier (chapter 1) that recognizing the unique history of each place, people, region, or continent is not the same as rejecting the search for cross-cultural—even universal—processes that might, in their universality, explain those phenomena that were unique in human history (Pauketat 2001b). If you think about it, identifying the unusual happenings in history would be impossible without making cross-cultural comparisons. We all do this, even without thinking about it, as a matter of course.

So the question before us is not about the utility of a comparative approach, but about how we make comparisons and what we compare.

How differs depending on one's theoretical predilections. Scholars with social evolutionary leanings answer that the differences between all of these places were *fundamentally* differences of type or quality (i.e., states versus nonstates, or corporate polities versus network-based ones). They would argue, quite vehemently sometimes, that Mesopotamian cities or Mesoamerican chiefdoms and states are incomparable to, say, southwestern pueblos and Mississippian chiefdoms. Given Yoffee's Rule, we know who wins that argument.

However, scholars with historical-processual tendencies would suggest that the differences are matters of degree, not kind (figures 7.10–7.11). And if they are correct, even just a little, then the parallels that matter (that is, what we compare) are not those that social evolutionists identify. Instead of looking to check off the attributes of institutions or organizations—were there palaces, royal tombs, writing?—we look instead for a series of relationships that played out historically. How were central places built, central orders memorialized, and producer autonomy sacrificed?

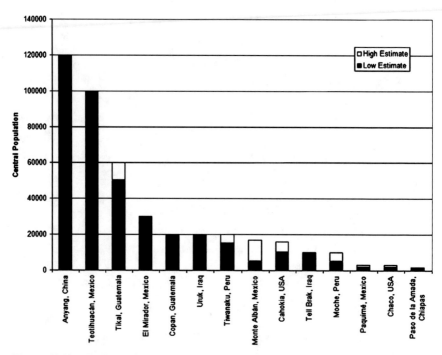

Figure 7.10. Early central populations compared (adapted from Yoffee 2005: table 3.1)

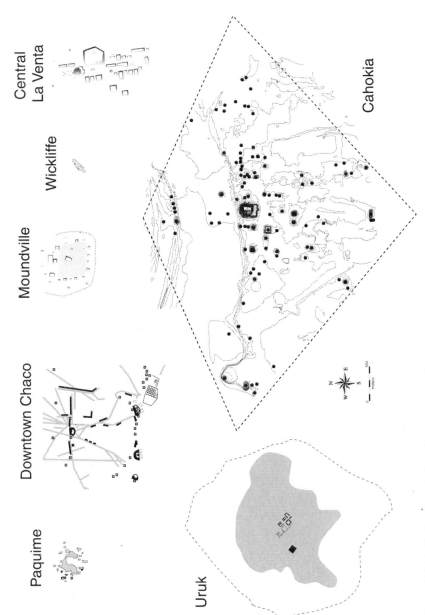

Figure 7.11. Early central site plans compared

Was there evidence of pluralism, widespread participation, or resistance? Not only are such historical patterns intriguing, but archaeologists can see them, find them in the ground, and measure them: they have a material form and occupy space. They are hidden in the building blocks of walls and platform mounds, in the communal yet restricted-access storehouses, and in the design of public space. They demand an explanation.

Returning to the terms used in chapter 3, let's first consider the matter of *organizational variability*. A close examination of the southwestern, Mesoamerican, and Mesopotamian cases reviewed above proves that, despite a persistent belief by some in the inviolate institutions of chiefdoms or states, there is scant evidence of anything but a diversity of hard-to-isolate social or political organizations. There are degrees of centrality, and these are apparent in different media and spatialities at different scales of analysis. Now, depending on how we delineate them regionally, the centrality of Casas Grandes or Monte Albán might seem obvious alongside the extensive transregional Chacoan phenomenon, the nebulous Olmec interaction sphere, or the array of peer Uruk cities (for a good example of such analytical sensitivity to scale and dimensionality, see Nelson 1995). However, much of this depends on arbitrary delineations of regions or interaction spheres, often based in turn on inadequate and incomplete survey data.

In addition, there are hints of heterarchy, negotiation, and resistance within all. And, across the board, there is the indication that ritual and religion were inseparable from polity and governance. No surprise there. But, again, delimiting ritualities (or chiefdoms or states) seems too arbitrary, as the differences are matters of degree, not kind. Why do I say this? In the end, no definitive evidence can be found that governments popped out of the ground fully formed as things distinct from the people who made up communities. In every case, the X factor seems to have been at work, varying in its historical particularities from place to place and time to time. To put it in the words of social evolutionism, governments never stopped evolving. So how can we isolate types?

And communities were (and are), in large part, idealized imagined phenomena recursively related to places, landscapes, and social memories. They are not natural, ever-present building blocks of societies (Pauketat 2000a). People made them, promoted them, and physically constructed them. People promoted some idea of order through the earliest major towns or cities in the Southwest, Formative Mesoamerica, and Mesopotamia. These were monumentalized in Chaco Canyon in oversize architecture, in Paquimé as animal-shaped mounds, at Paso de la Amada and San José Mogote as a balanced central plan, in Mesopotamian cities as temples and ziggurats, and at Monte Albán as a sacred mountaintop space where all people would come to experience, craft, or help construct that communal/political order.

Taking this point to its logical conclusion, we could conclude that the first governments were built into communities. This should not be seen as a devious elite tactic or as a corporate strategy. That would be to confuse cause and effect and strip nonelites of their agency. And if there's one thing we need in the archaeology of chiefdoms and states, it's a little nonelite agency. We would do well to rethink the possibilities: how did people collaborate as a community? How did they give or withhold their labor? The ancient possibilities are probably at least as numerous as the sorts of social, religious, and economic dependencies enumerated by Stephen Silliman (2004:22–25) for colonial California, ranging from seigneurialism to indebted peonage to slavery.

Communities were defined and projected by people in any number of ancient instances that today we call political consolidations, confederations, and expansions (even including conquests). Such words hide the actual histories by which people coalesced or were gathered (see chapter 3). And they obscure the fact that communities were social and religious *movements*, focused on key ideas or individuals and often built on *cultural pluralism* that in turn was as often related to *migration*. For which of the ancient case studies discussed can we not point to some degree of pluralism present at their very foundations? Sure, pluralism would have varied by degree. But it seems increasingly in evidence in the past, once we begin looking for it.

To wit, Sassaman (2005) suspects two or more communities merged to form Poverty Point. Carr (2005c) sees a tripartite alliance in the Scioto valley. Chaco had distant immigrants and periodic visitors from the four corners of the Puebloan world (Lekson 2005). Casas Grandes had arrivals moving in from the Mimbres region, among other places, presaging the expansion of Paquimé (Whalen and Minnis 2001a,b). San Lorenzo appears, by some accounts, to have been an unusually large urbanizing center that, like the smaller and earlier Paso de la Amada, attracted residents from the surrounding regions (Clark 2004). Certainly the Oaxacan centers of San José Mogote and Monte Albán were magnets for outlying people, with demonstrable demographic trends of growth and population loss necessitating movement as a critical dimension of their development (Joyce 2004). Ditto for Mesopotamian cities, with hints that demography and mobility were constantly in flux beginning in the Ubaid period and became more important with the Uruk expansion and colonization of far-off lands (Algaze 1993; Pollock 1999; Stein 2002).

Not long ago, Mesopotamianist Geoff Emberling argued that the incorporation of diversity under one political umbrella was a characteristic of the state. "Unlike prestate societies, states may incorporate culturally differentiated groups within their control. Archaeological theories of states and state formation have neglected this fundamental distinction between states and their precursors" (Emberling 1999:277). However, my review of historical trajectories here (never mind hints from the Kongo, Powhatan, Natchez, Alur, or Kachin provinces) casts doubts on the fundamentality of such a distinction (see chapter 3). Ethnic or linguistic pluralism and nonethnic village-level or corporate diversity, probably often based on the physical movements, migrations, and displacements of people, are common features of many political–cultural complexities and stately simplifications around the world.

If my suspicions regarding migration and identity formation are borne out in future studies, then we will have one more reason to doubt an overly restrictive use of the ideas of the chiefdom and the early state, as well as one more reason to call Cahokia a state, if only to put it in some sort of historical perspective relative to the subsequent transregional Mississippia-nization process. Indeed, using the Emberling criterion, either everything discussed so far has some stately qualities or there is no fundamental break between states and nonstate formations. Maybe Carneiro was right.

This is not to say that various little and big bangs or phase transitions between social formations weren't significant in the ancient past (Yoffee 2005:230). The construction of a new city—say, Monte Albán or New Cahokia—is an obviously rapid and radical discontinuity in the temporal, spatial, and material dimensions of history. Such breaks mark the pervasive restructurings of regional and transregional landscapes: Paquimé's Casas Grandes sphere, Chaco's San Juan network, Uruk's expansion, the spread of Poverty Point's transregional culture, the Mississippianization of the Midwest, and the Olmecification of Mesoamerica. Radically rebuilt places and cities or restructured territories and transregional realms may or may not correspond with the appearance of what some people would label chiefdoms or states.

I suspect that many archaeologists who have identified dramatic shifts as based in the evolution of institutions and societies have been right for entirely wrong reasons. Under the sway of deeply ingrained evolutionary logic, archaeologists have sought to figure out how the various building blocks of society could have been rearranged to explain the institutionalization of inequality *within* natural communities. They have been looking to factors within societies to explain hierarchization and the evolution of government.

But newer historicized theories posit two very different things. First, societies are not the proper units of analysis and, second, the construction of important places, including towns and cities, is part of a thick historical process—the X factor—that was contingent on numbers of people on the landscape, their historical dispositions (degree of centrality and plurality), and the genealogies of localized and long-distance movements, migrations, or displacements. Of these, the rate and amplitude of population movement is clearly more important than most have admitted up to this point. This is especially true of migrations or displacements that, oddly, led to the emplacement (literally) of pluralism at key settlements. The regrouped people of these places would comprise little melting pots, where hybrid identities and diverse cultural practices could produce any number of potential historical trajectories. Their emplacement or centralization would lead to long-term historical change. Their cities, that is, would produce societies (Lefebvre 1991). This is why Yoffee (2005) notes:

> Cities were not simply "containers" for a new scale of social and economic and religious activities but were "generative" (Soja 2000; [A.] Smith 2003) of new offices and ranks, a new environment of buildings, streets, and monumental art of various sorts. The density of social interaction in cities was unprecedented from earlier times in most of the earliest civilizations. (Yoffee 2005:62)

In the end, Yoffee (2005:230) does not carry such historical logic to its logical conclusion—by recognizing the need to examine the histories of collective formations, gatherings, and constructions. Instead, he sees cities as qualitatively distinct evolutionary phenomena that crystallized within interaction spheres—a position not so different from Renfrew's (1987) peer polity interaction construct. Yoffee retreats to an evolutionary position that holds cities as products rather than generative dynamos. This allows him to look for the causes of change outside centers (and in interaction spheres). And it allows him to claim that some large places weren't cities.

> Why did other settlements that were centers of worship, exchange, and favorable locations within interaction spheres—such as Chaco or Cahokia—not become cities? One possible reason is that the evolutionary history of agricultural villages in the American Southwest and Southeast was different from that in trajectories towards states. . . . There was a rapid transition to these sites, which were many times larger and more complex than those of previous periods, but these sites were organized, it seems by traditional leaders whose authority was not the product of thousands of years of cumulative social change.

This is to place undue weight on peer polities and tradition, if not also to forget that one undeniably singular New World metropolis—the great city of Teotihuacán—was also a single hypercentralized oddity (Yoffee 2005:229). To explain Teotihuacán, I submit, or Chaco or Cahokia or Paquimé or any number of other prominent cities or protocities, means actually explaining the X factor. And that, in turn, means doing more than appealing to some generic notion that villages evolved into cities via evolutionary phase transitions (Yoffee 2005). We need, instead, to understand the histories of places vis-à-vis plurality, migration, and centrality. Thus I submit that we need to theorize about the history of the gathering process that emplaces pluralism and diversity in either singular centers or nexuses of early cities (Cobb 2005; A. Smith 2003).

Of course, depending on the rates and amplitudes of such gatherings, central places would not long remain (especially given the apparent organizational thresholds of 2000–3000 people noted in chapters 1 and 6) had such *cultural diversity* not been *mitigated* through the formation of new *identities*. For the most part, it seems that such mitigation—the formation of people from peoples—is a place-based experiential process. Peoples produced societies by establishing places. Places, in turn, lent order to the chaotic worlds of people and nature. They were embodiments of history and the cosmos here on earth, and such powers—perceived as political or not—might have been irresistible (Helms 1999; McAnany 2001; Sassaman 2005; Stanish 2003).

That's why monumentality is an omnipresent element of Formative civilizations. It's all about building collective memories and group identities into landscapes: Chaco's great houses, roads, kivas; Casas Grandes's redesigned agricultural landscape, ball courts, communal pits; Paso de la Amada's and San José Mogote's plaza and mound stages; Monte Albán's theatrical spaces, visual dominance over the valley, and celebrated public enemies; Eridu's, Brak's, or Uruk's temple rebuildings and group labor projects; Watson Brake's, Scioto's, or Poverty Point's central gatherings of diversity; and the wall-trench houses and earthen pyramids of Cahokia writ large across the canvas of pan-eastern North America.

Places, then, define peoples and histories, and so our archaeologies must be about comparing the histories of places and peoples in the making, rather than the evolution of institutions, strategies, and societies, decoupled from those experiential histories, as if their evolution led to places. The truth of such place-making theory is, ultimately, in the pudding (see the so-called landscape archaeology of Ashmore 2004; Pollard 2001; Tilley 2004; and others). It lies scattered about in the charred remains of so many early urbanizing places from tiny Burnt Corn Pueblo in the Galisteo basin to sacked cities—San José Mogote, Uruk, Paquimé, and others—where enemies attacked both people *and* places. Places contain history. They physically link people to the landscape and its past. Eliminate those linkages and you erase history and replace it with an alternate history.

In the end, the *placing and re-placing of history* is the new common ground of an archaeology of civilization. We arrive there by walking through the back door to complexity. Sure, it's a messy place of people being and doing particular things in specific spaces with uncertain ends. It's not the neat and clean—and ultimately deceptive—systemic models of evolving corporate and network or chiefly and state-level societies. But in avoiding the top-heavy tautological models of strategizing elites and their evolving institutions, we also steer clear of the strategery of an analytical approach gone awry. And we can step in and fix the various crises in archaeology today.

TRUTH, JUSTICE,
AND THE ARCHAEOLOGICAL WAY

Truth is something you stumble into when you think you're going some place else.

—Jerry Garcia

S o why bother with the old plan if you're not sure you believe in it?" I ask her, as I hand the steaming cup of brew back to the young server. Just coffee, I'd told him. No foam. But the place is crawling with bleary-eyed archaeologists in shapeless conference khakis and cotton shirts, medicating the effects of last night's debauchery with caffeine. And one of them had taken my Americano.

After I ordered, I saw UGS on her way out of the conference coffee bar. We said hello and started chatting about her latest uncertainty as I awaited my drink replacement. UGS explains that she isn't certain if she should bother testing the Obion site in the way she told the National Science Foundation she would. It's a model, she said, that wasn't really hers to begin with: Had the Mississippians at Obion switched from a corporate mode of organization to a network-based one as part of this simple chiefdom's developmental cycle? I let an "O god" slip, which didn't boost her confidence. And after I asked her "why bother" she admitted to a kind of guilt. She wanted to please both NSF and Dr. Science.

"Look," I say, "the National Science Foundation wants good scientific results, and changing your mind isn't a bad thing if you've come up with a better idea. They'd want you to do that. After all, there's not much science where there's no creative thought. Now, as for Dr. Science . . ." I shrug off the thought.

"Yeah," she says, "I've heard the lecture on that one already." UGS confides that the previous day's conversations were thought provoking. Maybe *too* thought provoking, she reflects, since now she has to confront Dr. Science again. And, UGS worries, she'll have to truly *defend* whatever dissertation she produces from all of this. He could, she fears, take her head off if he doesn't like her conclusions.

That reminds me of another young woman, although her nemesis wasn't a professor, I tell UGS. It was herself. "Well," I add, "and an airplane." A few years after our 1987 field season in Arkansas, I was back with a crew looking for more Mississippian sites. One of our workers was at wits' end. It's easy to see why, what with marijuana-growing, gun-toting redneck locals, swarming mosquitoes, cottonmouths, racial segregation, and the ongoing corporate erasure of millennia of human history all around us. It was enough to shake anyone's faith in truth, justice, and the archaeological way.

Going through a personal identity crisis worsened by a grueling field season, this crew member had told her roommate that she could kill herself from loneliness and despair. But the rest of us didn't realize how serious the crisis had become, at least not until the day of the crop dusting incident. Earlier that day, we had watched as the stressed-out woman walked away from the rest of us and tromped across the flat, muddy rice fields of northeast Arkansas, wondering where she was going. But since there was nowhere for her to go, no farmhouses, no roads, nothing, she walked back to us. But now, as we continued surveying, a crop duster pilot flew his Mustang-like airplane into the area to begin spraying pesticides and herbicides on the rice field through which we were walking.

The plane began its flight path, dropping down low a kilometer or so away and, we soon realized, winging its way straight for us. The plane was flying four feet or so off the ground, releasing a heavy spray of chemicals as it went. So we all darted off into the next field. All of us, that is, except the stressed-out crew member. She ignored our calls to "Come on!" and "Get over here!" It seems that she had decided this would be her last stand: a rice field in the middle of Arkansas. Crop dusting redneck exploiters would not get the better of her. By god, the plane would have to veer off its trajectory, because she wouldn't move. She stopped dead in her tracks, stood tall and erect, and faced down the oncoming crop duster in the ultimate game of chicken.

"You might not want to do that," I tell UGS, "with Dr. Science." I smile.

"What?" UGS asks.

"You know, play a game of chicken with your major professor," I explain.

UGS frowns, shakes her head, and urges me to tell the rest of the story.

"It doesn't matter," I say. "The woman survived the incident. The point is not to be obstinate. Instead, archaeologists need to be creative and look for backdoor solutions to front door problems."

But that moral doesn't satisfy UGS, who asks, "Don't you think that what specific people do matters in the long term?"

"Well of course I do," I say. "I was thinking about agency before you were born."

"Well then, surely it mattered to the woman in the story. Maybe it mattered to the pilot. And it seems like it mattered to you, or else you wouldn't have remembered this story," UGS declares.

How annoying, I think. UGS is beginning to take on the characteristics of her arrogant adviser. But, I have to admit, she is right. Yes, I've told this story to many students, changing it here and there, emphasizing this or that, depending on the audience. The point of the story isn't the outcome or even the agency of the woman or the pilot. UGS is right: the story itself—the *telling* of the story—matters to me. Apparently it also matters to UGS, and perhaps it even mattered to the other students to whom I've told it over the years. Perhaps some of them have retold it to their own students.

There is something profound here that we can use to understand Mississippianization. Perhaps it isn't just about the specific people and the political dynamics in one place or another. Maybe understanding Mississippianization—or any civilization—means understanding storytelling too, the tales of heroic superhuman men and women from, say, Cahokia, being the subject of epics told and retold across the American Midwest and South. Maybe, just maybe, archaeologists needed to think more about the ways and the contexts in which stories are told and the ways that memories of places, peoples, and things are created. Maybe UGS needs to hear the end of this story.

"Well, in the end, the pilot was the one who chickened out."

"Really?" she says. "The suicidal woman stood her ground to the end?"

"Yep," I tell her. We watched in slack-jawed horror just fifty meters away, as the plane—only four feet off the ground—flew straight for our five and half foot tall crew member. The pilot must have seen her and had decided to play with her. When the plane was just a split second from taking off her head, the pilot jerked the nose upward 50 or 60 degrees and then, Peter Pan style, zipped over her. The plane's wheels couldn't have been but a few centimeters from her head. And, as if not to look the loser, the pilot opened the chemical bin door and doused our fellow archaeologist with the contents. "She's not in archaeology anymore," I add.

"No, I expect not," says UGS.

Where We Go from Here

I sometimes think our debates in archaeology are a little like the game of chicken we witnessed that day. All of us bring our own biased suppositions to the research we conduct. Some of them are near and dear to us. Others we make unthinkingly. Both sorts are difficult for us to abandon, even if we are confronted by somebody who might take off our head. These suppositions and styles are often deeply engrained in our being, inculcated and reproduced in life and research experiences in ways that make replacing them with radical alternative theories difficult.

I think that social evolutionism is one of these deeply rooted ways of thinking about the past. It involves a whole host of engrained suppositions, and the Dr. Sciences out there are guarding against the alternatives that might seek to break and enter the theoretical house. Confrontations are inevitable, especially if we try to kick in the front door of the house. Of course, that's the reason a backdoor approach to building a historicized theory of civilization might be best. Not that the Pragmatist agrees. He still wants to kick in the front door. He too would have faced down that crop duster. He would have argued with that gunman.

The Pragmatist has complained to me in the past: "It's not like any of this is new. We've been talking about it for years [Hodder 1986; Kus 1983; Tringham 1991]! Liz Brumfiel told us to 'break and enter' evolutionary theory back in 1992! So why don't we just *do it*?"

Now, doing it doesn't mean abandoning the basic comparative approach to understanding human history. But, like all migrations, it does involve redefining and replacing our theories. Our replaced theories shouldn't be based in the sophisticated delusions of 1960s or 1970s anthropology. They shouldn't be based on the evolution of institutions, organizations or, god forbid, societies that some *imagine* existed in their idealized, organically integrated, and hermetically sealed past. Historicized theories suggest otherwise. People constructed such things, but it was the construction itself—considered in terms of population movements, community identities, political theater, and cultural pluralism—that requires explanation. Even ethnographic or ethnohistoric studies of so-called chiefdoms reveal that pre-Contact, pre-Columbian, or prestate people in one part of the world (or even in one part of the Mississippian Southeast) were structurally dissimilar from peoples elsewhere. Ditto for states.

Comparing the scale and configuration of the early cities and centers of the American Southwest, Formative Mesoamerica, and Uruk Mesopotamia to the Archaic, Woodland, and Mississippian places discussed in this book allows us to better appreciate the reasons why we should distance ourselves from the chiefdom models so happily referenced and refined by Mississippianists today. Even many of the smaller eastern sites are as large as or larger than the average ten-hectare Ubaid center. Not to make too much of size, but it might be more appropriate to compare, say, a Coles Creek site to an Ubaid town or a Formative Mesoamerican center than it is to compare Cahokia or Chaco to an ethnographic chiefdom.

At a minimum, we should rethink Mississippianization. First, the so-called Mississippian peoples and places were preceded by Archaic and Woodland mound builders who founded great ceremonial centers as early as 5,600 years ago. Some such places, say Poverty Point or the Scioto valley, seem to have been based in singular gatherings or confederations of people that Yoffee (2005) would probably call ritualities. Elaborate corporate spaces referenced ancient places and were aligned to celestial phenomena: the setting of a solsticial sun, the rising of the moon on its nine-plus-year cycle, or the appearance of the morning star. The new spaces, in turn, disciplined the movements of people, many of whom possibly resided some distance from the sacred places. Experienced at one of North America's early towns, say at Poverty Point or any number of later

Weeden Island and Coles Creek centers, mass celestial bewonderment loaded communal gatherings with political possibilities.

Whatever we call them, Mississippians clearly were not the first complex societies in eastern North America. However, unlike many places save Mesopotamia, there was a great deal of time between eastern North America's first town, Poverty Point, and its first city, Cahokia. In Meso-america, the span of time between Paso de la Amada and San Lorenzo was a mere four or five centuries: add on seven more centuries and we arrive at Monte Albán. In the Southwest, Chaco's dispersed cityscape developed after little more than seven or eight centuries of sedentism, and the gap between it or other classic Hohokam towns and the later urban pueblo of Paquimé was a mere three centuries. Only in Mesopotamia did the development of Uruk cities from towns happen over a period of more than three millennia, depending on whether you begin the clock during the Late Neolithic or the Ubaid period.

But there was an unusually uniform Mississippianization process that, I believe, cannot be understood adequately using ordinary chiefdom models. To explain Mississippianization, we need to consider a continent's big history. Within eastern North America, there is a strong argument to be made that a political–religious movement was responsible for the founding of a new city, Cahokia. As opposed to Dr. Science's antihistori-cal arguments ("we can never know the reasons why Mississippianization began"), it seems increasingly likely that Cahokia's foundations involved in-migrations, cultural pluralism, mitigations of diversity, and the creative reinvention of community. It involved the X factor. Mississippianization, as the dissemination of Cahokian ideas, was the particular history of po-liticizing crop production and domesticizing ideologies of power. Such a history involved the creation and spread of powerful narratives—sto-ries—that were told and retold over generations.

Owing to the historical conditions at places across the Deep South, the Cahokian narrative spread like wildfire throughout the midconti-nent, down the Mississippi, and across the coastal plain. It morphed as well, being remade locally in every case, becoming the narrative of other places: Moundville, Etowah, Spiro, and so on. The extent of the resulting Mississippianized world is startling to some, covering more area than the American Southwest or Formative Mesoamerica and at least as much as Uruk period Mesopotamia. And it may have been actively directed, even aggressively so, along the Mississippi River by Cahokians in their vainglorious attempts to model the world after themselves. Other contemporary and later Mississippian regional phenomena probably included a variety of political communities, overlordships, composite confederacies, theocratic chieftaincies, kin coalitions, seigneurages, and religious cults. However, like chiefdoms, these names imply a single mode of integration, political strategy, or organizational function. What all such names hide are the histories of governance, resistance, foreign relations, militarization, incorporation, provincialization, colonization, and migration (among other things).

Sometimes I think that many eastern North American archaeologists have been taught not to see pre-Columbian complexity and historicity. The Pragmatist would surely agree. The singularity of early Cahokia, with 10,000-plus people and eight to thirteen square kilometers of public and residential spaces in the center alone, is obscured by the ways social evolutionists talk about Mississippian chiefdoms. And the histories of southern intrusions, Spiro's conversion, Etowah's foundation, Moundville's transformation, and the confluence's emergent feudalism, among many other historical formations, are beyond archaeological approaches that artificially synchronize our chronologies and collapse organizational variability into a single sort of "Mississippian chiefdom."

There is much to be gained by rethinking Mississippianism, even though many researchers in eastern North America, for whatever reason, refuse to think outside the box that the received wisdom of chiefdom thinking has put us in. From inside the box, the best we can do is construct self-fulfilling research designs and collect data insufficient to identify historical variability. Such research is a tacit acceptance of archaeology's fate to remain the lesser of the anthropological subdisciplines. And such research will continue to reify a sophisticated old delusion that ensures the looming crisis in Mississippian archaeology will worsen. The Darth Evaders of the world will continue to practice as they have, writing off chunks of the archaeological record for the price of a lucrative corporate contract.

This is not the way it has to be. There's more than one character out there like our Southern Pragmatist holding open the back doors to understanding human history. Like him, they're committed to doing archaeology in a way and at a scale that will let us ask better questions about the past and will give voice to our indignation over the dark forces working against human history. Like our Southern Pragmatist, they recognize the flaws with social evolutionary models, including both the old primary–secondary or simple–complex models and the more recent corporate network or apical constituent varieties. Each is a house of cards that won't withstand the weight of much data.

The question is, Will an uncertain younger generation do more than make minimal modifications to social evolutionary models while leaving the sophisticated delusions intact? And will the minimalist tendencies of people like Dr. Science—founded on deep-seated building block, social evolutionary biases—keep people from looking for those data? How many will care about the destruction of any one region's archaeological heritage—say the erasure of Mississippian history by corporate America's rice fields in Arkansas—if the simplest explanations are always best and we already know the answers? How many would be willing to argue with the dark forces of corporate America at the point of a gun?

If UGS carries out her modest excavations at Obion as originally proposed, she will be able to generate sufficiently equivocal data to support the simple, corporate network, cycling chiefdom model. Anybody could and many archaeologists do. At this point in their career, it might prove embarrassing for them to call a spade a spade (much less to actually use a spade). And so it seems in the mutual interest of many researchers to let the house of cards stand. In the end we may agree with the Pragmatist: a good, hard bump of the theoretical table might be needed to bring down the various models of chiefdoms and other archaeological delusions.

Remember, there's a clear alternative that holds very different implications for explaining the ancient world of Mississippians and the civilizing process in eastern North America and elsewhere. That alternative involves understanding that people, acting as if such institutions, organizations, or societies matter, produce the perception of static institutions, organizations, or societies. It holds that communities, like other organizations, are active projections of identities. And this theoretical alternative holds that we cannot understand these imagined and invented formations separately from understanding "formation" in an active and historical sense and in its physical dimensions. In various places in this book, I've called it a short-tradition view, an agency or practice-based approach, or a historical–processual concern with place making. They are all aspects of the backdoor approach to complexity.

A New Beginning

The backdoor approach entails rethinking our fieldwork and report-age practices. We'll all need more and better-dated data amenable to historical arguments (Pauketat and Alt 2005). And we'll need to construct a new comparative anthropology of ancient history (Brumfiel 2006). My own few comparisons here are barely a start (chapter 7), but they're bolstered by visiting as many archaeological places and site excavations as possible. Gaining a perspective on the scale and dimensionality of some past historical phenomenon is all-important in appreciating your own case studies. Jimmy Griffin knew this. In his day, Griffin drove his old blue Cadillac across eastern North America to see the excavations of others and to eyeball their potsherds.

So, on my way home from Memphis, I decide to find the Obion site and see what UGS is about to undertake. It is located well off the major highway on an old county road not shown on the Tennessee road map. I find it in the middle of a sea of upland cornfields. Thank god it is still intact after all these years.

Several cars are parked along the road, and seven or eight people are standing out in the field. I spy Obion's impressive flat-topped pyramid off in the distance. There are other small mounds, now bumps covered with rows of young maize plants. Far off to the left of this central complex stand UGS, the Southern Pragmatist, and the others, still dressed in their khaki attire. Of course the shadowy corporate sellout, Darth Evader, was nowhere to be seen. No surprise there. He only showed up at the Mid-South conference to schmooze with government archaeologists who, he thought, might be in a position to approve his reports that wrote off sites on behalf of his corporate clients. Besides, the Southern Pragmatist had given him a piece of his mind outside the hotel entrance that night. "You son of a . . .," he'd began. "You don't deserve to be called an archaeologist." The Pragmatist proceeded to explain his feelings to the beady-eyed corporate sellout in considerable detail.

What's happening can be infuriating, as the Pragmatist had noted, but all is not lost. Even out of the direst of circumstances can come good. "That worker of mine, the one who faced down the crop duster," I'd said to UGS, "now works as a schoolteacher. She teaches history." And what about that angry redneck—the one who confronted David Anderson with a gun outside Marianna, Arkansas, and seemed to embody the worst of the dark, antihistorical forces of the Mid-South? After David Anderson collected himself that day, he and Pat Garrow went back to talk to him. The next day—after Dave had convinced him of our true purpose—the would-be shooter was out helping us screen the dirt from our archaeological test excavations in the sorghum field![1] Dave had argued his way around that peculiarly Arkansas application of Yoffee's Rule.

Out at Obion, the sun shines brightly. UGS is reinvigorated. She had exited the conference later on the day of our chance meeting in the hotel coffee bar. She wanted to get things ready to make a controlled surface collection as soon as possible. And recently she had arranged for a geophysical survey by one of a growing number of high-tech archaeologists in the Mid-South. UGS met him at the conference and he was excited about trying out his new magnetometer later the following week. UGS was equally excited, as she learned it was now possible to identify individual Mississippian houses and other features prior to placing a shovel in the ground.

Plastic red pin flags dot the cornfield, already knee-high (although not yet the Fourth of July). I walk out onto the site and greet the crowd and then listen as UGS explains her excavation approach. It has changed. Now, she says, she is going to open up several large blocks in likely residential areas inside and outside the palisade wall. She'll excavate the blocks where the surface collection and the geophysical survey indicated houses and pits, in an attempt to obtain larger samples of superimposed or stratified domestic debris than she'd originally planned. With such data, UGS will later attempt to evaluate the relationship between the domestic practices of several generations of people, the Obion economy, and the variable means whereby Obion residents had been constructing, through time, their community identity. To get at that last part, she will dig whole houses and associated domestic features, not unlike basic excavation approaches used for years (Flannery 1976). Then, however, she'll do a detailed analysis of artifact technological style and architectural construction techniques to get at the microhistories of cultural practices (Alt 2001; Cameron 1998; Dobres 2000; Pauketat and Alt 2005; Snead 2005).

UGS believes she can satisfy the terms of her original proposal by spotlighting domestic contexts, even if this focus doubles as a sleight of hand to placate Dr. Science. She can also, she states, begin rethinking her own approach to understanding the whats, whos, and hows of Mississippianization and political–cultural change in general. Nodding as she talks, UGS seems to convince herself of the plan as she describes it aloud. Perhaps thinking about the wisdom of standing in the way of a low-flying airplane, she seems resolved to stand firm. Things will work out somehow.

At this point, I can't help but offer some advice: "Keep your eyes open for Cahokian potsherds." UGS responds that she will, as the other archaeologists glance around on the ground where they stand. Then the Uncertain Graduate Student hesitates once more. "I'm not really quite sure what I'll find," she confesses.

Of course she worries about finding anything worth the investment of her time and the NSF funds she has to sustain herself and a couple of other helpers over the upcoming weeks. Deep down, she feels intimidated by the task at hand. Will this little dig of hers change the way we think about Mississippianization? Will she somehow prove that the people who once lived in the houses she was about to excavate made a difference in ancient eastern North America? Is any of this relevant to understanding the bigger problems of world history? Should it be? She still isn't certain about such things.

Several of those standing around mumble in agreement with UGS's confession, recollecting their own uncertainty in similar situations. I see the Pragmatist smile knowingly, turning slightly to gaze at the big mound as he does. "Not really quite sure what you'll find?" he asks. "*That*," he grins, "is why we dig."

Note

1. According to David Anderson (personal communication, 2006): Later that fateful afternoon, "the three locals and Pat Garrow and I agreed to relocate to a country store and continue discussions. . . . We obtained permission from the farmers to continue work on the project sites, and resumed work the very next day. In fact, we went back to the project area later that afternoon, about an hour later, to pick up the two crew members who had run off and hidden along the L'Anguille channel. We knew from the farmers that two of the crew had run away, so getting permission to pick them up was our top priority. The farmers gave it once they realized their mistake" (Anderson 1993).

REFERENCES

Abercrombie, Nicholas, Stephen Hill, and Bryan S. Turner (1980) *The Dominant Ideology Thesis.* George Allen & Unwin, London.

Abrams, Philip (1988) Notes on the Difficulty of Studying the State (1977). *Journal of Historical Sociology* 1:58–89.

Adams, Richard E. W. (1991) *Prehistoric Mesoamerica.* Rev. ed. University of Oklahoma Press, Norman.

Adams, Robert McC. (2003) Reflections on the Early Southern Mesopotamian Economy. In *Archaeological Perspectives on Political Economies*, edited by G. M. Feinman and L. M. Nicholas, pp. 41–59. University of Utah Press, Salt Lake City.

Ahler, Steve A., and P. J. DePuydt (1987) *A Report on the 1931 Powell Mound Excavations, Madison County, Illinois.* Reports of Investigations, no. 43. Illinois State Museum, Springfield.

Akridge, Scott, and Hester A. Davis (1993) Know Your President. *Field Notes of the Arkansas Archeological Society* 250:5–7.

Algaze, Guiermo (1993) *The Uruk World System: The Dynamics of Expansion of Early Mesopotamian Civilization.* University of Chicago Press, Chicago.

Alt, Susan M. (1999) Spindle Whorls and Fiber Production at Early Cahokian Settlements. *Southeastern Archaeology* 18:124–133.

Alt, Susan M. (2001) Cahokian Change and the Authority of Tradition. In *The Archaeology of Traditions: Agency and History Before and After Columbus*, edited by T. R. Pauketat, pp. 141–156. University Press of Florida, Gainesville.

Alt, Susan M. (2002) Identities, Traditions, and Diversity in Cahokia's Uplands. *Midcontinental Journal of Archaeology* 27:217–236.

Alt, Susan M. (2005) Archaeology and Explanation: The Hidden Cost of Science. Paper presented at the 70th Annual Meeting of the Society for American Archaeology, March 28–April 3, Salt Lake City, Utah.

Alt, Susan M. (2006a) Cultural Pluralism and Complexity: Analyzing a Cahokian Ritual Outpost. Ph.D. diss., University of Illinois.

Alt, Susan M. (2006b) The Power of Diversity: The Roles of Migration and Hybridity in Culture Change. In *Leadership and Polity in Mississippian Society*, edited by B. M.

REFERENCES

Butler and P. D. Welch, pp. 289–308. Center for Archaeological Investigations, Occasional Paper no. 33. Southern Illinois University, Carbondale.

Ambrose, Stanley H., Jane Buikstra, and Harold W. Krueger (2003) Status and Gender Differences in Diet at Mound 72, Cahokia, Revealed by Isotopic Analysis of Bone. *Journal of Anthropological Archaeology* 22:217–226.

Anderson, Benedict (1983) *Imagined Communities: Reflections on the Origins and Spread of Nationalism.* Verso, London.

Anderson, David G. (1993) Letter to the editor. *Field Notes of the Arkansas Archeological Society* 251:2.

Anderson, David G. (1994) *The Savannah River Chiefdoms: Political Change in the Late Prehistoric Southeast.* University of Alabama Press, Tuscaloosa.

Anderson, David G. (1996) Fluctuations Between Simple and Complex Chiefdoms: Cycling in the Late Prehistoric Southeast. In *Political Structure and Change in the Prehistoric Southeastern United States,* edited by J. F. Scarry, pp. 231–252. University Press of Florida, Gainesville.

Anderson, David G. (1997) The Role of Cahokia in the Evolution of Southeastern Mississippian Society. In *Cahokia: Domination and Ideology in the Mississippian World,* edited by T. R. Pauketat and T. E. Emerson, pp. 248–268. University of Nebraska Press, Lincoln.

Anderson, David G. (1999a) Archaeology in the L'Anguille River Basin, Northeast Arkansas: Large-Scale Survey in the Southeast. In *Arkansas Archaeology: Essays in Honor of Dan and Phyllis Morse,* edited by R. C. Mainfort Jr., and M. D. Jeter, pp. 65–98. University of Arkansas Press, Fayetteville.

Anderson, David G. (1999b) Examining Chiefdoms in the Southeast: An Application of Multiscalar Analysis. In *Great Towns and Regional Polities in the Prehistoric American Southwest and Southeast,* edited by J. E. Neitzel, pp. 215–241. Amerind Foundation/University of New Mexico Press, Albuquerque.

Anderson, David G., and John E. Cornelison (2002) Excavations at Mound A, Shiloh: The 2002 Season. Paper presented at the 59th Southeastern Archaeological Conference, November 6–9, Biloxi, Mississippi.

Anderson, David G., Hazel R. Delcourt, Paul A. Delcourt, John E. Foss, and Phyllis A. Morse (1989) *Cultural Resource Investigations in the L'Anguille River Basin, Lee, St. Francis, Cross, and Poinsett Counties, Arkansas.* Garrow and Associates, Final Contract DACW66-87-C-0046 Report, Memphis District, U.S. Army Corps of Engineers.

Anderson, David G., and Robert C. Mainfort, eds. (2001) *The Woodland Southeast.* University of Alabama Press, Tuscaloosa.

Appadurai, Arjun (1996) *Modernity at Large: Cultural Dimensions of Globalization.* University of Minnesota Press, Minneapolis.

Ashmore, Wendy (2004) Social Archaeologies of Landscape. In *A Companion to Social Archaeology,* edited by Lynn M. Meskell and Robert W. Preucel, pp. 255–271. Blackwell Press, Oxford.

Baines, John, and Norman Yoffee (2000) Order, Legitimacy, and Wealth: Setting the Terms. In *Order, Legitimacy and Wealth in Ancient States,* edited by J. Richards and M. Van Buren, pp. 13–17. Cambridge University Press, Cambridge.

Bareis, Charles J. (1976) *The Knoebel Site, St. Clair County, Illinois.* Illinois Archaeological Survey, Circular 1. Urbana, Illinois.

Bareis, Charles J., and James W. Porter, eds. (1984) *American Bottom Archaeology: A Summary of the FAI-270 Project Contribution to the Culture History of the Mississippi River Valley*. University of Illinois Press, Urbana.

Barker, Alex W. (1992) Powhatan's Pursestrings: On the Meaning of Surplus in a Seventeenth-Century Algonkian Chiefdom. In *Lords of the Southeast: Social Inequality and the Native Elites of Southeastern North America*, edited by A. W. Barker and T. R. Pauketat, pp. 61–80. Archeological Papers of the American Anthropological Association, no. 3. Washington, D.C.

Barker, Alex W. (1993) Settled on Complexity: Defining and Debating Social Complexity in the Lower Mississippi Valley. Paper presented at the 58th annual meeting of the society for American Archaeology, St. Louis.

Barker, Alex W. (1999) *Chiefdoms and the Economics of Perversity*. Ph.D. diss., University of Michigan.

Barrett, S. A. (1933) *Ancient Aztalan*. Reprint, 1970. Greenwood Press, Westport, Connecticut.

Beck, Robin A., Jr. (2003) Consolidation and Hierarchy: Chiefdom Variability in the Mississippian Southeast. *American Antiquity* 68:641–661.

Beehr, Dana, and Stanley H. Ambrose (2007) Were They What They Cooked? Stable Isotopic Analysis of Mississippian Pottery Residues. In *The Archaeology of Food and Identity*, edited by K. C. Twiss, pp. 171–191. Center for Archaeological Investigations, Occasional Paper No. 34. Southern Illinois University, Carbondale.

Bell, Catherine (1997) *Ritual: Perspectives and Dimensions*. Oxford University Press, Oxford.

Bell, Robert E., ed. (1984) *Prehistory of Oklahoma*. Academic Press, Orlando.

Benchley, Elizabeth D. (2000) Mississippian Mound Orientations and a Solar Calendar. In *Mounds, Modoc, and Mesoamerica: Papers in Honor of Melvin L. Fowler*, pp. 255–264. Illinois State Museum Scientific Papers, vol. 28. Springfield, Illinois.

Benson, Elizabeth P., ed. (1996) *The Olmec World: Ritual and Rulership*. The Art Museum, Princeton University, Princeton, NJ.

Benson, Larry, Linda Cordell, Kirk Vincent, Howard Taylor, John Stein, G. Lang Farmer, and Kiyoto Futa (2003) Ancient Maize from Chacoan Great Houses: Where Was It Grown? *Proceedings of the National Academy of Sciences* 100:13111–13115.

Bernardini, Wesley (2005) *Hopi Oral Tradition and the Archaeology of Identity*. University of Arizona Press, Tucson.

Bernbeck, Reinhard (1999) Structure Strikes Back: Intuitive Meanings of Ceramics from Qale Rostam, Iran. In *Material Symbols: Culture and Economy in Prehistory*, edited by J. E. Robb, pp. 90–111. Occasional Paper no. 26. Southern Illinois University, Carbondale.

Bernbeck, Reinhard (n.d.) An Archaeology of Multi-Sited Communities. Manuscript in possession of the author.

Binford, Lewis R. (1972) *An Archaeological Perspective*. Seminar Press, New York.

Binford, Sally R., and Lewis R. Binford, eds. (1968) *New Perspectives in Archaeology*. University of Chicago Press, Chicago.

Birmingham, Robert A., and Leslie E. Eisenberg (2000) *Indian Mounds of Wisconsin*. University of Wisconsin Press, Madison.

Black, Glenn A. (1967) *Angel Site: An Archaeological, Historical, and Ethnological Study*. Indiana Historical Society, Indianapolis.

REFERENCES

Blanton, Richard E. (1978) *Monte Albán: Settlement Patterns at the Ancient Zapotec Capital.* Academic, New York.

Blanton, Richard E., Gary M. Feinman, Stephan A. Kowalewski, and Peter N. Peregrine (1996) A Dual-Processual Theory for the Evolution of Mesoamerican Civilization. *Current Anthropology* 37:1–31.

Blanton, Richard E., Gary M. Feinman, Stephen A. Kowalewski, and Linda M. Nicholas (1999) *Ancient Oaxaca.* Cambridge University Press, Cambridge.

Blanton, Richard E., Stephen A. Kowalewski, Gary M. Feinman, and Laura M. Finsten (1993) *Ancient Mesoamerica: A Comparison of Change in Three Regions.* 2nd ed. Cambridge University Press, Cambridge.

Blitz, John H. (1993) *Ancient Chiefdoms of the Tombigbee.* University of Alabama Press, Tuscaloosa.

Blitz, John H. (1999) Mississippian Chiefdoms and the Fission–Fusion Process. *American Antiquity* 64:577–592.

Blitz, John H., and Karl G. Lorenz (2002) The Early Mississippian Frontier in the Lower Chattahoochee-Apalachicola River Valley. *Southeastern Archaeology* 21:117–135.

Blitz, John H., and Karl G. Lorenz (2006) *The Chattahoochee Chiefdoms.* University of Alabama Press, Tuscaloosa.

Bondarenko, Dmitri (2004) From Local Communities to Megacommunity: Biniland in the 1st Millennium B.C.—Nineteenth Century A.D. In *The Early State: Its Alternatives and Analogues,* edited by L. E. Grinin, R. L. Carneiro, D. M. Bondarenko, N. N. Kradin, and A. V. Korotayev, pp. 325–363. Uchitel, Volgograd, Russia.

Boszhardt, Robert F. (2004) The Late Woodland and Middle Mississippian Component at the Iva Site, La Crosse County, Wisconsin in the Driftless Area of the Upper Mississippi River Valley. *Minnesota Archaeologist* 63:60–85.

Brackenridge, Henry Marie (1814) *Views of Louisiana Together with a Journal of a Voyage up the Missouri River, in 1811.* 1962 ed. Quadrangle Books, Chicago.

Brain, Jeffrey P. (1989) *Winterville: Late Prehistoric Culture Contact in the Lower Mississippi Valley.* Mississippi Department of Archives and History, Archaeological Report no. 23, Jackson, Mississippi.

Brown, James A. (1996) *The Spiro Ceremonial Center: The Archaeology of Arkansas Valley Caddoan Culture in Eastern Oklahoma.* University of Michigan, Museum of Anthropology, Memoir 29. Ann Arbor.

Brown, James A. (2005a) The Cahokian Expression: Creating Court and Cult. In *Hero, Hawk, and Open Hand: American Indian Art of the Ancient Midwest and South,* edited by R. F. Townsend, pp. 105–123. Art Institute of Chicago/Yale University Press, New Haven, CT.

Brown, James A. (2005b) 6,000 Years of Mound Building. *Cambridge Archaeological Journal* 15:113–115.

Brown, James A., and John E. Kelly (2000) Cahokia and the Southeastern Ceremonial Complex. In *Mounds, Modoc, and Mesoamerica: Papers in Honor of Melvin L. Fowler,* pp. 469–510. Illinois State Museum Scientific Papers, vol. 28. Springfield.

Brown, James A., Richard A. Kerber, and Howard D. Winters (1990) Trade and the Evolution of Exchange Relations at the Beginning of the Mississippian Period. In *The Mississippian Emergence,* edited by B. D. Smith, pp. 251–280. Smithsonian Institution Press, Washington, D.C.

Brumfiel, Elizabeth (1992) Breaking and Entering the Ecosystem: Gender, Class, and Faction Steal the Show. *American Anthropologist* 943:551–567.

Brumfiel, Elizabeth (1995) Heterarchy and the Analysis of Complex Societies: Comments. In *Heterarchy and the Analysis of Complex Societies*, edited by R. M. Ehrenreich, C. L. Crumley, and J. E. Levy, pp. 125–131. Archeological Papers of the American Anthropological Association, no. 6. Washington, D.C.

Brumfiel, Elizabeth (1997) The Quality of Tribute Cloth: The Place of Evidence in Archaeological Argument. *American Antiquity* 61:453–462.

Brumfiel, Elizabeth (2000) On the Archaeology of Choice: Agency Studies as a Research Strategem. In *Agency in Archaeology*, edited by M.-A. Dobres and J. Robb, pp. 249–255. Routledge, London.

Brumfiel, Elizabeth (2006) Cloth, Gender, Continuity, and Change: Fabricating Unity in Anthropology. *American Anthropologist* 108:862–877.

Brumfiel, Elizabeth, and Timothy K. Earle (1987) Specialization, Exchange, and Complex Societies: An Introduction. In *Specialization, Exchange, and Complex Societies*, edited by E. M. Brumfiel and T. K. Earle, pp. 1–9. Cambridge University Press, Cambridge.

Buikstra, Jane E. (1976) Hopewell in the Lower Illinois Valley: A Regional Study of Human Biological Variability and Prehistoric Mortuary Behavior. *Northwestern University Archeological Program Scientific Papers*, no. 2. Evanston, IL.

Butler, Brian M. (1991) Kincaid Revisited: The Mississippian Sequence in the Lower Ohio Valley. In *Cahokia and the Hinterlands: Middle Mississippian Cultures of the Midwest*, edited by T. E. Emerson and R. B. Lewis, pp. 264–273. University of Illinois Press, Urbana.

Cameron, Catherine M. (1998) Course Adobe Architecture, Style, and Social Boundaries in the American Southwest. In *The Archaeology of Social Boundaries*, edited by M. T. Stark, pp. 183–207. Smithsonian Institution Press, Washington, D.C.

Cameron, Catherine M. (2002) Sacred Earthen Architecture in the Northern Southwest: The Bluff Great House Berm. *American Antiquity* 67:677–695.

Carl, Peter (2000) City-Image Versus Topography of *Praxis*. *Cambridge Archaeological Journal* 10:328–335.

Carneiro, Robert L. (1967) On the Relationship Between Size of Population and Complexity of Social Organization. *Southwestern Journal of Anthropology* 23:234–243.

Carneiro, Robert L. (1970) A Theory of the Origin of the State. *Science* 169:733–738.

Carneiro, Robert L. (1972) From Autonomous Village to the State: A Numerical Estimation. In *Population Growth: Anthropological Implications*, edited by B. Spooner, pp. 64–77. MIT Press, Cambridge, Massachusetts.

Carneiro, Robert L. (1981) The Chiefdom: Precursor of the State. In *Transitions to Statehood in the New World*, edited by G. Jones and R. Kantz, pp. 37–79. Cambridge University Press, Cambridge.

Carneiro, Robert L. (1998a) Review of *Mississippian Political Economy*, by J. Muller. *Southeastern Archaeology* 17:182–183.

Carneiro, Robert L. (1998b) What Happened at the Flashpoint? Conjectures on Chiefdom Formation at the Very Moment of Conception. In *Chiefdoms and Chieftaincy in the Americas*, edited by E. M. Redmond, pp. 18–42. University Press of Florida, Gainesville.

Carr, Christopher (2005a) The Question of Ranking in Havana Hopewellian Societies: A Retrospective in Light of Multi-Cemetery Ceremonial Organization. In *Gathering*

REFERENCES

Hopewell: Society, Ritual, and Ritual Interaction, edited by C. Carr and D. T. Case, pp. 238–257. Kluwer Academic/Plenum, New York.

Carr, Christopher (2005b) Rethinking Interregional Hopewellian "Interaction." In *Gathering Hopewell: Society, Ritual, and Ritual Interaction*, edited by C. Carr and D. T. Case, pp. 575–623. Kluwer Academic/Plenum, New York.

Carr, Christopher (2005c) The Tripartite Ceremonial Alliance Among Scioto Hopewellian Communities and the Question of Social Ranking. In *Gathering Hopewell: Society, Ritual, and Ritual Interaction*, edited by C. Carr and D. T. Case, pp. 258–338. Kluwer Academic/Plenum, New York.

Carr, Christopher, and D. Troy Case (2005) The Gathering of Hopewell. In *Gathering Hopewell: Society, Ritual, and Ritual Interaction*, edited by C. Carr and D. Troy Case, pp. 19–50. Kluwer Academic/Plenum, New York.

Carr, Christopher, Beau J. Goldstein, and Jaimin Weets (2005) Estimating the Sizes and Social Compositions of Mortuary-Related Gatherings at Scioto Hopewell Earthwork-Mound Sites. In *Gathering Hopewell: Society, Ritual, and Ritual Interaction*, edited by C. Carr and D. Troy Case, pp. 480–532. Kluwer Academic/Plenum, New York.

Chapman, Robert (2003) *Archaeologies of Complexity.* Routledge, London.

Cherry, John F. (1978) Generalisation and the Archaeology of the State. In *Social Organisation and Settlement: Contributions from Anthropology, Archaeology, and Geography*, edited by D. R. Green, C. Haselgrove, and M. Spriggs, pp. 411–437. BAR Series 47. Oxford.

Childe, V. Gordon (1950) The Urban Revolution. *Town Planning Review* 21:3–17.

Clark, Jeffery J. (2001) *Tracking Prehistoric Migrations: Pueblo Settlers Among the Tonto Basin Hohokam.* Anthropological Papers of the University of Arizona. University of Arizona Press, Tucson.

Clark, John E. (1997) The Arts of Government in Early Mesoamerica. *Annual Review of Anthropology* 26:211–234.

Clark, John E. (2004) Mesoamerica Goes Public: Early Ceremonial Centers, Leaders, and Communities. In *Mesoamerican Archaeology: Theory and Practice*, edited by J. A. Hendon and R. A. Joyce, pp. 42–72. Blackwell, Oxford.

Clark, John E. (2006) Mesoamerica's First State. In *The Political Economy of Ancient Mesoamerica: Transformations during the Formative and Classic Periods*, edited by V. L. Scarborough and J. E. Clark. University of New Mexico Press, Albuquerque (in press).

Clark, John E., and Michael Blake (1994) The Power of Prestige: Competitive Generosity and the Emergence of Rank Societies in Lowland Mesoamerica. In *Factional Competition and Political Development in the New World*, edited by E. M. Brumfiel and J. W. Fox, pp. 17–30. Cambridge University Press, Cambridge.

Clark, John E., Jon L. Gibson, and James A. Zeidler (in press) First Towns in the Americas: Searching for Agriculture and Other Enabling Conditions. In *Social and Economic Dynamics in Intermediate Societies*, edited by I. Kuijt and W. Prentiss. University of Arizona Press, Tucson.

Clayton, Lawrence A., Vernon James Knight Jr., and Edward C. Moore, eds. (1993) *The De Soto Chronicles: The Expedition of Hernando de Soto to North America in 1539–1543.* University of Alabama Press, Tuscaloosa.

Cobb, Charles R. (1993) Archaeological Approaches to the Political Economy of Nonstratified Societies. In *Archaeological Method and Theory*, edited by M. B. Schiffer, 5:43–99. University of Arizona Press, Tucson.

Cobb, Charles R. (2003) Mississippian Chiefdoms: How Complex? *Annual Review of Anthropology* 32:63–84.

Cobb, Charles R. (2005) Archaeology and the "Savage Slot": Displacement and Emplacement in the Premodern World. *American Anthropologist* 107:563–574.

Cobb, Charles R., and Brian M. Butler (2002) The Vacant Quarter Revisited: Late Mississippian Abandonment of the Lower Ohio Valley. *American Antiquity* 67:625–641.

Cobb, Charles R., and Patrick H. Garrow (1996) Woodstock Culture and the Question of Mississippian Emergence. *American Antiquity* 61:21–37.

Cobb, Charles R., and Adam King (2005) Re-Inventing Mississippian Tradition at Etowah, Georgia. *Journal of Archaeological Method and Theory* 12:167–192.

Cobb, Charles R., Jeffrey Maymon, and Randall H. McGuire (1999) Feathered, Horned, and Antlered Serpents: Mesoamerican Connections with the Southwest and Southeast. In *Great Towns and Regional Polities in the Prehistoric American Southwest and Southeast*, edited by J. E. Neitzel, pp. 165–181. University of New Mexico Press, Albuquerque.

Coe, Michael D. (2003) *Angkor and the Khmer Civilization.* Thames & Hudson, London.

Coe, Michael D., and Richard A. Diehl (1980) *In the Land of the Olmec: The Archaeology of San Lorenzo Tenochtitlán.* University of Texas, Austin.

Cole, Fay-Cooper, Robert Bell, John Bennett, Joseph Caldwell, Norman Emerson, Richard MacNeish, Kenneth Orr, and Roger Willis (1951) *Kincaid: A Prehistoric Illinois Metropolis.* University of Chicago Press, Chicago.

Collins, James M. (1997) Cahokia Settlement and Social Structures As Viewed from the ICT-II. In *Cahokia: Domination and Ideology in the Mississippian World*, edited by T. R. Pauketat and T. E. Emerson, pp. 124–140. University of Nebraska Press, Lincoln.

Collins, James M., and Michael L. Chalfant (1993) A Second-Terrace Perspective on Monks Mound. *American Antiquity* 58:319–332.

Connerton, Paul (1989) *How Societies Remember.* Cambridge University Press, Cambridge.

Conrad, Lawrence A. (1991) The Middle Mississippian Cultures of the Central Illinois River Valley. In *Cahokia and the Hinterlands: Middle Mississippian Cultures of the Midwest*, edited by T. E. Emerson and R. B. Lewis, pp. 119–156. University of Illinois Press, Urbana.

Cordy, Ross H. (1981) *A Study of Prehistoric Social Change: The Development of Complex Societies in the Hawaiian Islands.* Academic Press, New York.

Crown, Patricia L., and W. H. Wills (2003) Modifying Pottery and Kivas at Chaco: Pentimento, Restoration, or Renewal? *American Antiquity* 68:511–532.

Crumley, Carole L. (1987) A Dialectical Critique of Hierarchy. In *Power Relations and State Formation*, edited by T. C. Patterson and C. W. Gailey, pp. 155–169. Special of the Archeology Section, American Anthropological Association, Washington, D.C.

Crumley, Carole L. (1995a) Heterarchy and the Analysis of Complex Societies. In *Heterarchy and the Analysis of Complex Societies*, edited by R. M. Ehrenreich, C. L. Crumley, and J. E. Levy, pp. 1–5. Archeological Papers of the American Anthropological Association, no. 6. Washington, D.C.

Crumley, Carole L. (1995b) Building an Historical Ecology of Gaulish Politics. In *Celtic Chiefdom, Celtic State*, edited by B. Arnold and D. B. Gibson, pp. 26–33. Cambridge University Press, Cambridge.

REFERENCES

Culin, Stewart ([1907] 1992) *Games of the North American Indians.* University of Nebraska Press, Lincoln.

Curet, L. Antonio (2003) Issues on the Diversity and Emergence of Middle-Range Societies of the Ancient Caribbean: A Critique. *Journal of Archaeological Research* 11:1–42.

Cyphers, Ann (1996) Reconstructing Olmec Life at San Lorenzo. In *Olmec Art of Ancient Mexico,* edited by E. P. Benson and B. de la Fuente, pp. 61–71. National Gallery of Art, Washington, D.C.

Dalan, Rinita (1997) The Construction of Mississippian Cahokia. In *Cahokia: Domination and Ideology in the Mississippian World,* edited by T. R. Pauketat and T. E. Emerson, pp. 89–102. University of Nebraska Press, Lincoln.

Dalan, Rinita A., George R. Holley, William I. Woods, Harold W. Watters Jr., and John A. Koepke (2003) *Envisioning Cahokia: A Landscape Perspective.* Northern Illinois University Press, DeKalb.

D'Altroy, Terence N., and Timothy K. Earle (1985) Staple Finance, Wealth Finance, and Storage in the Inka Political Economy. *Current Anthropology* 26:187–206.

DeBoer, Warren R., and A. B. Kehoe (1999) Cahokia and the Archaeology of Ambiguity. *Cambridge Archaeological Review* 9:261–267.

De Certeau, Michel (1984) *The Practice of Everyday Life.* University of California Press, Berkeley.

DeJarnette, David L., and Steve B. Wimberly (1941) *The Bessemer Site: Excavation of Three Mounds and Surrounding Village Areas Near Bessemer, Alabama.* Museum Paper 17, Geological Survey of Alabama. University, Alabama.

Dillehay, Thomas D. (1995) Mounds of the Social Death: Araucanian Funerary Rites and Political Succession. In *Tombs for the Living: Andean Mortuary Practices,* edited by T. Dillehay. Dumbarton Oaks, Washington, D.C.

Dincauze, Dena F., and Robert J. Hasenstab (1989) Explaining the Iroquois: Tribalization on a Prehistoric Periphery. In *Centre and Periphery: Comparative Studies in Archaeology,* edited by T. C. Champion, pp. 67–87. Unwin Hyman, London.

Di Peso, Charles C. (1974) *Casas Grandes: A Fallen Trading Center of the Gran Chichimeca.* Vols. 1–3. Amerind Foundation, Dragoon/Northland Press, Flagstaff, AZ.

Di Peso, Charles C., J. B. Rinaldo, and G. J. Fenner (1974) *Casas Grandes: A Fallen Trading Center of the Gran Chichimeca.* Vols. 4–8. Amerind Foundation, Dragoon/Northland Press, Flagstaff, AZ.

Dobres, Marcia-Anne (2000) *Technology and Social Agency.* Blackwell, Oxford.

Dobres, Marcia-Anne, and John Robb (2000) *Agency in Archaeology.* Routledge, London.

Douglas, Mary (1967) Primitive Rationing: A Study in Controlled Exchange. In *Themes in Economic Anthropology,* edited by R. Firth, pp. 119–145. Tavistock, London.

Dunnell, R. C. (1989) Aspects of the Application of Evolutionary Theory in Archaeology. In *Archaeological Thought in America,* edited by C. C. Lamberg-Karlovsky, pp. 35–49. Cambridge University Press, Cambridge.

Du Pratz, Antoine Simon Le Page ([1763] 1975) *The History of Louisiana,* edited by J. G. Tregle. Louisiana State University Press, Baton Rouge.

Dye, David H. (2005) Art, Ritual, and Chiefly Warfare in the Mississippian World. In *Hero, Hawk, and Open Hand: American Indian Art of the Ancient Midwest and South,* edited by R. F. Townsend, pp. 191–205. Art Institute of Chicago/Yale University Press, New Haven, CT.

Earle, Timothy (1977) A Reappraisal of Redistribution: Complex Hawaiian Chiefdoms. In *Exchange Systems in Prehistory,* edited by T. K. Earle and J. E. Ericson, pp. 213–229. Academic, New York.

Earle, Timothy (1978) *Economic and Social Organization of a Complex Chiefdom: The Halelea District, Kaua'I, Hawaii.* Museum of Anthropology, Anthropological Papers no. 63. University of Michigan, Ann Arbor.

Earle, Timothy (1987) Chiefdoms in Archaeological and Ethnohistorical Perspective. *Annual Review of Anthropology* 16:279–308.

Earle, Timothy (1997) *How Chiefs Come to Power: The Political Economy in Prehistory.* Stanford University Press, Stanford.

Earle, Timothy (2001) Economic Support of Chaco Canyon Society. *American Antiquity* 66:26–35.

Ekholm, Kajsa (1972) *Power and Prestige: The Rise and Fall of the Kongo Kingdom.* Skriv Service AB, Uppsala.

Emberling, Geoff (1999) The Value of Tradition: The Development of Social Identities in Early Mesopotamian States. In *Material Symbols: Culture and Economy in Prehistory,* edited by J. E. Robb, pp. 277–301. Occasional Paper no. 26. Southern Illinois University, Carbondale.

Emberling, Geoff (2003) Urban Social Transformations and the Problem of the "First City": New Research from Mesopotamia. In *The Social Construction of Cities,* edited by M. L. Smith, pp. 254–268. Smithsonian Institution Press, Washington, D.C.

Emerson, Thomas E. (1989) Water, Serpents, and the Underworld: An Exploration into Cahokia Symbolism. In *The Southeastern Ceremonial Complex: Artifacts and Analysis,* edited by P. Galloway, pp. 45–92. University of Nebraska Press, Lincoln.

Emerson, Thomas E. (1991) Some Perspectives on Cahokia and the Northern Mississippian Expansion. In *Cahokia and the Hinterlands: Middle Mississippian Cultures of the Midwest,* edited by T. E. Emerson and R. B. Lewis, pp. 221–236. University of Illinois Press, Urbana.

Emerson, Thomas E. (1997a) *Cahokia and the Archaeology of Power.* University of Alabama Press, Tuscaloosa.

Emerson, Thomas E. (1997b) Reflections from the Countryside on Cahokian Hegemony. In *Cahokia: Domination and Ideology in the Mississippian World,* edited by T. R. Pauketat and T. Emerson, pp. 190–228. University of Nebraska Press, Lincoln.

Emerson, Thomas E., and Douglas K. Jackson (1984) *The BBB Motor Site (11-Ms-595).* American Bottom Archaeology, FAI-270 Site Reports, no. 6. University of Illinois Press, Urbana.

Emerson, Thomas E., and Timothy R. Pauketat (2002) Embodying Power and Resistance at Cahokia. In *The Dynamics of Power,* edited by M. O'Donovan, pp. 105–125. Center for Archaeological Investigations, Occasional Paper no. 30. Southern Illinois University, Carbondale.

Evans-Pritchard, E. E. (1948) *The Divine Kingship of the Shilluk of the Nilotic Sudan.* Cambridge University Press, Cambridge.

Fairbanks, Charles H. ([1956] 2003) *Archaeology of the Funeral Mound: Ocmulgee National Monument, Georgia.* Tuscaloosa: University of Alabama Press.

Farmer, James D. (1999) Astronomy and Ritual in Chaco Canyon. In *Pueblo Bonito: Center of the Chacoan World,* edited by J. E. Neitzel, pp. 61–71. Smithsonian Institution Press, Washington, DC.

REFERENCES

Feinman, Gary M. (1995) The Emergence of Inequality: A Focus on Strategies and Processes. In *Foundations of Social Inequality*, edited by T. D. Price and G. M. Feinman, pp. 255–279. Plenum, New York.

Feinman, Gary M. (1999) Scale and Social Organization: Perspectives on the Archaic State. In *Archaic States*, edited by G. M. Feinman and J. Marcus, pp. 95–133. School of American Research Press, Santa Fe, NM.

Feinman, Gary M. (2000) Dual-Processual Theory and Social Formations in the Southwest. In *Alternative Leadership Strategies in the Prehispanic Southwest*, edited by B. J. Mills, pp. 207–224. University of Arizona Press, Tucson.

Feinman, Gary M. (2001) Mesoamerican Political Complexity: The Corporate-Network Dimension. In *From Leaders to Rulers*, edited by J. Haas, pp. 151–175. Kluwer Academic/Plenum, New York.

Feinman, Gary M., and Jill E. Neitzel (1984) Too Many Types: An Overview of Sedentary Prestate Societies in the Americas. In *Advances in Archaeological Method and Theory 7*, edited by M. B. Schiffer, pp. 39–102. Academic, New York.

Firth, Raymond (1965) *Primitive Polynesian Economy*. Routledge, London.

Fish, Paul R., and Suzanne K. Fish (1999) Reflections on the Casas Grandes Regional System from the Northwestern Periphery. In *The Casas Grandes World*, edited by C. F. Schaafsma and C. L. Riley, pp. 27–42. University of Utah Press, Salt Lake City.

Flannery, Kent V. (1972) The Cultural Evolution of Civilization. *Annual Review of Ecology and Systematics* 3:399–426.

Flannery, Kent V. (1982) The Golden Marshalltown: A Parable for the Archaeology of the 1980s. *American Anthropologist* 84:265–278.

Flannery, Kent V. (1999a) The Ground Plans of Archaic States. In *Archaic States*, edited by G. M. Feinman and J. Marcus, pp. 15–57. School of American Research Press, Santa Fe, NM.

Flannery, Kent V. (1999b) Process and Agency in Early State Formation. *Cambridge Archaeological Journal* 9:3–21.

Flannery, Kent V., ed. (1976) *The Early Mesoamerican Village*. Academic Press, New York.

Flannery, Kent V., Andrew K. Balkansky, Gary M. Feinman, David C. Grove, Joyce Marcus, Elsa M. Redmond, Robert G. Reynolds, Robert J. Sharer, Charles S. Spencer, and Jason Yaeger (2005) Implications of New Petrographic Analysis for the Olmec "Mother Culture" Model. *Proceedings of the National Academy of Sciences* 103(32):11219–11223.

Flannery, Kent V., and Joyce Marcus (2000) Formative Mexican Chiefdoms and the Myth of the Mother Culture. *Journal of Anthropological Archaeology* 19:1–37.

Fortier, Andrew C., and Dale L. McElrath (2002) Deconstructing the Emergent Mississippian Concept: The Case for the Terminal Late Woodland in the American Bottom. *Midcontinental Journal of Archaeology* 27:171–215.

Fowler, Melvin L. (1975) A Precolumbian Urban Center on the Mississippi. *Scientific American* 233:92–101.

Fowler, Melvin L. (1987) Preface to *Surveyors of the Ancient Mississippi Valley*, by P. C. Sherrod and M. A. Rolingson, pp. ix–xii. Arkansas Archeological Survey Research Series, no. 28. Fayetteville, Arkansas.

Fowler, Melvin L. (1997) *The Cahokia Atlas: A Historical Atlas of Cahokia Archaeology*. Rev. ed. Studies in Archaeology, no. 2. Illinois Transportation Archaeological Research Program, University of Illinois, Urbana.

Fowler, Melvin L., and Robert L. Hall (1978) Late Prehistory of the Illinois Area. In *Handbook of North American Indians*, edited by B. G. Trigger, 15:560–568. Smithsonian Institution, Washington, D.C.

Fowler, Melvin L., Jerome Rose, Barbara Vander Leest, and Steven A. Ahler (1999) *The Mound 72 Area: Dedicated and Sacred Space in Early Cahokia*. Illinois State Museum, Reports of Investigations, no. 54. Springfield.

Frazer, Sir James G. (1947) *The Golden Bough: A Study in Magic and Religion*. Abridged ed. Macmillan, New York.

Fried, Morton H. (1967) *The Evolution of Political Society*. Random House, New York.

Fried, Morton H. (1978) The State, the Chicken, and the Egg; or, What Came First? In *Origins of the State: The Anthropology of Political Evolution*, edited by R. Cohen and E. R. Service, pp. 35–47. Institute for the Study of Human Issues, Philadelphia.

Friedman, Jonathan A. (1982) Catastrophe and Continuity in Social Evolution. In *Theory and Explanation in Archaeology: The Southampton Conference*, edited by C. Renfrew, M. J. Rowlands, and B. A. Seagraves, pp. 175–196. Academic, New York.

Friedman, Jonathan A., and Michael Rowlands (1978) Notes Toward an Epigenetic Model of the Evolution of "Civilisation." In *The Evolution of Social Systems*, edited by J. Friedman and M. Rowlands, pp. 201–276. University of Pittsburgh Press, Pittsburgh.

Fritz, Gayle J. (1990) Multiple Pathways to Farming in Precontact Eastern North America. *Journal of World Prehistory* 4:387–435.

Gallivan, Martin D. (2003) *James River Chiefdoms: The Rise of Social Inequality in the Chesapeake*. University of Nebraska Press, Lincoln.

Galloway, Patricia (1995) *Choctaw Genesis, 1500–1700*. University of Nebraska Press, Lincoln.

Garland, Elizabeth B. (1992) *The Obion Site: An Early Mississippian Center in Western Tennessee*. Cobb Institute of Archaeology, Report of Investigation 7. Mississippi State University, Mississippi State, MS.

Geertz, Clifford (1980) *Negara: The Theatre State in Nineteenth-Century Bali*. Princeton University Press, Princeton, NJ.

Gibbon, Guy E. (1974) A Model of Mississippian Development and Its Implications for the Red Wing Area. In *Aspects of Upper Great Lakes Anthropology*, edited by E. Johnson, pp. 129–137. Minnesota Prehistoric Archaeology Series, no. 11.

Gibson, D. Blair (1995) Chiefdoms, Confederacies, and Statehood in Early Ireland. In *Celtic Chiefdom, Celtic State: The Evolution of Complex Social Systems in Prehistoric Europe*, edited by B. Arnold and D. B. Gibson, pp. 116–128. Cambridge University Press, Cambridge.

Gibson, Jon L. (1974) Poverty Point: The First North American Chiefdom. *Archaeology* 27:97–105.

Gibson, Jon L. (1996) Poverty Point and Greater Southeastern Prehistory: The Culture That Did Not Fit. In *Archaeology of the Mid-Holocene Southeast*, edited by K. E. Sassaman and D. G. Anderson, pp. 288–305. University Press of Florida, Gainesville.

Gibson, Jon L. (2000) *The Ancient Mounds of Poverty Point: Place of the Rings*. University Press of Florida, Gainesville.

Gillespie, Susan D. (2001) Personhood, Agency, and Mortuary Ritual: A Case Study from the Ancient Maya. *Journal of Anthropological Archaeology* 20:73–112.

Gillespie, Susan D. (2005) The Invention of History at La Venta, Tabasco, Mexico. Manuscript in possession of the author.

REFERENCES

Gledhill, John, Barbara Bender, and Morgan T. Larsen, eds. (1989) *State and Society: The Emergence and Development of Social Hierarchy and Political Centralization.* Unwin Hyman, London.

Gluckman, Max (1940) The Kingdom of the Zulu of South Africa. *African Political Systems,* edited by M. Fortes and E. E. Evans-Pritchard, pp. 25–55. Oxford University Press, London.

Goldman, Irving (1970) *Ancient Polynesian Society.* University of Chicago Press, Chicago.

Goldstein, Lynne G. (1991) The Implications of Aztalan's Location. In *New Perspectives on Cahokia: Views from the Periphery,* edited by James B. Stoltman, pp. 209–228. Prehistory, Madison, Wisconsin.

Goldstein, Lynne G., and John D. Richards (1991) Ancient Aztalan: The Cultural and Ecological Context of a Late Prehistoric Site in the Midwest. In *Cahokia and the Hinterlands: Middle Mississippian Cultures of the Midwest,* edited by T. E. Emerson and R. B. Lewis, pp. 193–206. University of Illinois Press, Urbana.

Gramsci, Antonio (1971) *Selections from the Prison Notebooks of Antonio Gramsci.* Translated by Q. Hoare and G. N. Smith. International, New York.

Green, William, and Roland L. Rodell (1994) The Mississippian Presence and Cahokia Interaction at Trempealeau, Wisconsin. *American Antiquity* 59:334–359.

Gregg, Michael L. (1975) A Population Estimate for Cahokia. In *Perspectives in Cahokia Archaeology,* pp. 126–136. Illinois Archaeological Survey, Bulletin 10. Urbana, Illinois.

Griffin, James B. (1952) Culture Periods in Eastern United States Archeology. In *Archeology of Eastern United States,* edited by J. B. Griffin, pp. 352–364. University of Chicago Press, Chicago.

Griffin, James B. (1960) A Hypothesis for the Prehistory of the Winnebago. In *Culture in History: Essays in Honor of Paul Radin,* edited by S. A. Diamond, pp. 809–865. Columbia University Press, New York.

Griffin, James B. (1966) Mesoamerica and the Eastern United States in Prehistoric Times. In *Handbook of Middle American Indians: Archaeological Frontiers and External Connections,* edited by G. Ekholm and G. Willey, 4:111–131. University of Texas Press, Austin.

Griffin, James B. (1967) Eastern North American Archaeology: A Summary. *Science* 156(3772):175–191.

Griffin, James B. (1992) Fort Ancient Has No Class: The Absence of an Elite Group in Mississippian Societies in the Central Ohio Valley. In *Lords of the Southeast: Social Inequality and the Native Elites of Southeastern North America,* edited by A. W. Barker and T. R. Pauketat, pp. 53–59. Archeological Papers of the American Anthropological Association, no. 3. Washington, D.C.

Griffin, James B. (1994) Early and Later Archaeology of the Ocmulgee National Monument Area. In *Ocmulgee Archaeology 1936–1986,* edited by D. J. Hally, pp. 51–54. University of Georgia Press, Athens.

Haas, Jonathan (1982) *The Evolution of the Prehistoric State.* Columbia University Press, New York.

Haas, Jonathan (2001) Cultural Evolution and Political Centralization. In *From Leaders to Rulers,* edited by J. Haas, pp. 3–18. Kluwer Academic/Plenum, New York.

Haas, Jonathan, and Winifred Creamer (1993) *Stress and Warfare Among the Kayenta Anasazi of the Thirteenth Century A.D.* Fieldiana, Anthropology New Series, no. 21. Field Museum of Natural History, Chicago.

Hall, Robert L. (1989) The Cultural Background of Mississippian Symbolism. In *The Southeastern Ceremonial Complex*, edited by P. Galloway, pp. 239–278. University of Nebraska Press, Lincoln.

Hall, Robert L. (1991) Cahokia Identity and Interaction Models of Cahokia Mississippian. In *Cahokia and the Hinterlands: Middle Mississippian Cultures of the Midwest*, edited by T. E. Emerson and R. B. Lewis, pp. 3–34. University of Illinois Press, Urbana.

Hall, Robert L. (1997) *An Archaeology of the Soul: North American Indian Belief and Ritual.* University of Illinois Press, Urbana.

Hall, Robert L. (2000) Sacrificed Foursomes and Green Corn Ceremonialism. In *Mounds, Modoc, and Mesoamerica: Papers in Honor of Melvin L. Fowler*, edited by S. R. Ahler, pp. 245–253. Illinois State Museum Scientific Papers, vol. 28. Springfield.

Hall, Robert L. (2005) The Cahokia Site and Its People. In *Hero, Hawk, and Open Hand: American Indian Art of the Ancient Midwest and South*, edited by R. F. Townsend, pp. 93–103. Yale University Press, New Haven, Connecticut.

Hally, David J. (1993) The Territorial Size of Mississippian Chiefdoms. In *Archaeology of Eastern North America: Papers in Honor of Stephen Williams*, edited by J. B. Stoltman, pp. 143–168. Archaeological Report no. 25. Mississippi Department of Archives and History, Jackson, Mississippi.

Hally, David J. (1994) Introduction. In *Ocmulgee Archaeology, 1936–1986*, edited by D. J. Hally, pp. 1–7. University of Georgia Press, Athens.

Hally, David J., ed. (1994) *Ocmulgee Archaeology: 1936–1986.* University of Georgia Press, Athens.

Hally, David J. (1996) Platform-Mound Construction and the Instability of Mississippian Chiefdoms. In *Political Structure and Change in the Prehistoric Southeastern United States*, edited by J. F. Scarry, pp. 92–127. University Press of Florida, Gainesville.

Hally, David J., and Hypatia Kelly (1998) The Nature of Mississippian Towns in Georgia: The King Site Example. In *Mississippian Towns and Sacred Spaces: Searching for an Architectural Grammar*, edited by R. B. Lewis and C. Stout, pp. 49–63. University of Alabama Press, Tuscaloosa.

Hally, David J., and Mark Williams (1994) Macon Plateau Site Community Patterns. In *Ocmulgee Archaeology 1936–1986*, edited by D. J. Hally, pp. 84–95. University of Georgia Press, Athens.

Halstead, Paul, and John O'Shea (1982) A Friend in Need Is a Friend Indeed: Social Storage and the Origins of Social Ranking. In *Ranking, Resource, and Exchange*, edited by C. Renfrew, pp. 92–99. Cambridge University Press, Cambridge.

Hamilton, F. E. (1999) Southeastern Archaic Mounds: Examples of Elaboration in a Temporally Fluctuating Environment? *Journal of Anthropological Archaeology* 18:344–355.

Hammerstedt, Scott (2005) Mississippian Status in Western Kentucky: Evidence from the Annis Mound. *Southeastern Archaeology* 24:11–27.

Hann, John H. (1988) *Apalachee: The Land Between the Rivers.* University Press of Florida, Gainesville.

Hann, John H. (1994) Leadership Nomenclature Among Spanish Florida Natives and Its Linguistic and Associational Implications. In *Perspectives on the Southeast: Linguistics, Archaeology, and Ethnohistory*, edited by P. B. Kwachka, pp. 94–105. University of Georgia Press, Athens.

REFERENCES

Harris, Marvin (1968) Comments. In *New Perspectives in Archaeology*, edited by S. R. Binford and L. R. Binford, pp. 359–361. University of Chicago Press, Chicago.

Hassig, Ross (1985) *Trade, Tribute, and Transportation: the Sixteenth-Century Political Economy of the Valley of Mexico*. University of Oklahoma Press, Norman.

Hassig, Ross (1998) Anasazi Violence: A View from Mesoamerica. In *Deciphering Anasazi Violence*, edited by P. Y. Bullock, pp. 53–68. HRM Books, Santa Fe, NM.

Heckenberger, Michael J. (2005) *The Ecology of Power: Culture, Place, and Personhood in the Southern Amazon, A.D. 1000–2000*. Routledge, New York.

Heckenberger, Michael J., James B. Peterson, and Eduardo G. Neves (1999) Village Size and Permanence in Amazonia: Two Archaeological Examples from Brazil. *Latin American Antiquity* 10:353–376.

Heckenberger, M. J., A. Kuikuro, U. T. Kuikuro, J. C. Russell, M. J. Schmidt, C. Fausto, and B. Franchetto (2003) Amazonia 1492: Pristine Forest or Cultural Parkland? *Science* 301:710–714.

Hegmon, Michelle (2005) Beyond the Mold: Questions of Inequality in Southwest Villages. In *North American Archaeology*, edited by T. R. Pauketat and D. D. Loren, pp. 212–234. Blackwell, Oxford.

Heidegger, Martin (1986) *Being and Time*. State University of New York Press, Albany.

Helms, Mary W. (1979) *Ancient Panama: Chiefs in Search of Power*. University of Texas Press, Austin.

Helms, Mary W. (1992) Long-Distance Contacts, Elite Aspirations, and the Age of Discovery in Cosmological Context. In *Resources, Power, and Interregional Interaction*, edited by E. M. Schortman and P. A. Urban, pp. 157–174. Plenum, New York.

Helms, Mary W. (1993) *Craft and the Kingly Ideal: Art, Trade, and Power*. University of Texas Press, Austin.

Helms, Mary W. (1999) Why Maya Lords Sat on Jaguar Thrones. *Material Symbols: Culture and Economy in Prehistory*, edited by J. R. Robb, pp. 56–69. Center for Archaeological Investigations, Occasional Paper No. 26. Southern Illinois University, Carbondale.

Hendon, Julia A., and Rosemary Joyce (2004) *Mesoamerican Archaeology*. Blackwell, Oxford.

Hickey, Gerald C. (1982) *Sons of the Mountains: Ethnohistory of the Vietnamese Central Highlands to 1954*. Yale University Press, New Haven, CT.

Hilgeman, Sherri L. (2000) *Pottery and Chronology at Angel*. University of Alabama Press, Tuscaloosa.

Hobsbawm, Eric (1983) Introduction: Inventing Traditions. In *The Invention of Tradition*, edited by E. Hobsbawm and T. Ranger, pp. 1–14. Cambridge University Press, Cambridge.

Hodder, Ian (1986) *Reading the Past*. Cambridge University Press, Cambridge.

Hodder, Ian (1999) *The Archaeological Process: An Introduction*. Blackwell, Oxford.

Hodder, Ian (2004) The "Social" in Archaeological Theory: An Historical and Contemporary Perspective. In *A Companion to Social Archaeology*, edited by Lynn Meskell and Robert W. Preucel, pp. 23–42. Blackwell, Oxford.

Hoffman, Michael P. (1994) Ethnic Identities and Cultural Change in the Protohistoric Period of Eastern Arkansas. In *Perspectives on the Southeast: Linguistics, Archaeology, and Ethnohistory*, edited by P. B. Kwachka, pp. 61–70. University of Georgia Press, Athens.

Holley, George R. (1999) Late Prehistoric Towns in the Southeast. In *Great Towns and Regional Polities in the Prehistoric American Southwest and Southeast*, edited by J. E. Neitzel, pp. 22–38. Amerind Foundation/University of New Mexico Press, Albuquerque.

REFERENCES

Holley, George R., Rinitia A. Dalan, and Phillip A. Smith (1993) Investigations in the Cahokia Site Grand Plaza. *American Antiquity* 58:306–319.

Holley, George R., Kathryn E. Parker, Harold W. Watters, Jr., Julie N. Harper, Michels Skele, Jennifer E. Ringberg, Alan J. Brown, and Don L. Booth (2001) *The Knoebel Locality, Scott Joint-Use Archaeological Project.* Office of Contract Archaeology, Southern Illinois University, Edwardsville.

Holmes, William H. (1903) Aboriginal Pottery of the Eastern United States. In *Twentieth Annual Report of the Bureau of American Ethnology,* pp. 1–201. Smithsonian Institution, Washington, D.C.

Howland, Henry R. (1877) Recent Archaeological Discoveries in the American Bottom. *Buffalo Society of Natural Sciences, Bulletin* 3 (5):204–211.

Jackson, Douglas K., Andrew C. Fortier, and Joyce A. Williams (1992) *The Sponemann Site 2 (11-Ms-517): The Mississippian and Oneota Occupations.* American Bottom Archaeology, FAI-270 Site Reports, no. 24. University of Illinois Press, Urbana.

Johnson, Gregory A. (1982) Organizational Structure and Scalar Stress. In *Theory and Explanation in Archaeology: The Southampton Conference,* edited by C. Renfrew, M. Rowlands, and B. Segraves, pp. 389–421. Academic, New York.

Johnson, Gregory A. (1989) Dynamics of Southwestern Prehistory: Far Outside—Looking In. In *Dynamics of Southwest Prehistory,* edited by L. S. Cordell and G. J. Gumerman, pp. 371–390. Smithsonian Institution Press, Washington, D.C.

Johnson, Matthew (1996) *An Archaeology of Capitalism.* Blackwell, Oxford.

Jones, B. Calvin (1982) Southern Cult Manifestations at the Lake Jackson Site, Leon County, Florida: Salvage Excavation of Mound 3. *Midcontinental Journal of Archaeology* 7:3–44.

Joyce, Arthur A. (2000) The Founding of Monte Albán: Sacred Propositions and Social Practices. In *Agency in Archaeology,* edited by M.-A. Dobres and J. R. Robb, pp. 72–91. Routledge, London.

Joyce, Arthur A. (2004) Sacred Space and Social Relations in the Valley of Oaxaca. *Mesoamerican Archaeology: Theory and* Practice, edited by J. A. Hendon and R. A. Joyce, pp. 192–216. Blackwell, Oxford.

Joyce, Arthur A., and Marcus Winter (1996) Ideology, Power, and Urban Society in Prehispanic Oaxaca. *Current Anthropology* 37:33–86.

Joyce, Arthur A., Andrew G. Workinger, Byron Hamann, Peter Kroefges, Maxine Oland, and Stacie M. King (2004) Lord 8 Deer "Jaguar Claw" and the Land of the Sky: The Archaeology and History of Tututepec. *Latin American Antiquity* 15:273–297.

Joyce, Rosemary A. (2004) Unintended Consequences? Monumentality as a Novel Experience in Formative Mesoamerica. *Journal of Archaeological Method and Theory* 11:5–29.

Joyce, Rosemary A. (2005) Archaeology of the Body. *Annual Review of Anthropology* 34:139–158.

Judge, W. James (2004) Chaco's Golden Century. In *In Search of Chaco: New Approaches to an Archaeological Enigma,* edited by D. G. Noble, pp. 1–6. School of American Research Press, Santa Fe, NM.

Junker, Laura Lee (2004) Political Economy in the Historic Period Chiefdoms and States of Southeast Asia. In *Archaeological Perspectives on Political Economies,* edited by G. M. Feinman and L. M. Nicholas, pp. 223–251. University of Utah Press, Salt Lake City.

REFERENCES

Keeley, Lawrence H. (1996) *War Before Civilization: The Myth of the Peaceful Savage*. Oxford University Press, Oxford.

Kehoe, Alice B. (1998) *The Land of Prehistory: A Critical History of American Archaeology*. Routledge, London.

Kehoe, Alice B. (2005) Wind Jewels and Paddling Gods: The Mississippian Southeast in the Postclassic Mesoamerican World. In *Gulf Coast Archaeology: The Southeastern United States and Mexico*, edited by N. M. White, pp. 260–280. University Press of Florida, Gainesville.

Kelly, John E. (1990) The Emergence of Mississippian Culture in the American Bottom Region. In *The Mississippian Emergence*, edited by B. D. Smith, pp. 113–152. Smithsonian Institution Press, Washington, D.C.

Kelly, John E. (1991) The Evidence for Prehistoric Exchange and Its Implications for the Development of Cahokia. In *New Perspectives on Cahokia: Views from the Periphery*, edited by J. B. Stoltman, pp. 65–92. Monographs in World Archaeology, no. 2. Prehistory, Madison, Wisconsin.

Kelly, John E. (1994) The Archaeology of the East St. Louis Mound Center: Past and Present. *Illinois Archaeology* 6:1–57.

Kelly, John E. (1997) Stirling-Phase Sociopolitical Activity at East St. Louis and Cahokia. In *Cahokia: Domination and Ideology in the Mississippian World*, edited by T. R. Pauketat and T. E. Emerson, pp. 141–166. University of Nebraska Press, Lincoln.

Kelly, John E. (2000) Introduction. In *The Cahokia Mounds*, by W. K. Moorehead, pp. 1–35. University of Alabama Press, Tuscaloosa.

Kelly, John E. (2002) The Pulcher Tradition and the Ritualization of Cahokia: A Perspective from Cahokia's Southern Neighbor. *Southeastern Archaeology* 21:136–148.

Kelly, John E., Steven J. Ozuk, and Joyce A. Williams (1990) *The Range Site 2: The Emergent Mississippian Dohack and Range Phase Occupations*. American Bottom Archaeology, FAI-270 Reports, vol. 20. University of Illinois Press, Urbana.

Kertzer, David I. (1988) *Ritual, Politics, and Power*. Yale University Press, New Haven, CT.

Kidder, Tristram R. (1991) New Directions in Poverty Point Settlement Archaeology: An Example from Northeast Louisiana. In *The Poverty Point Culture: Local Manifestations, Subsistence Practices, and Trade Networks, Geoscience and Man*, edited by K. M. Byrd, 29:27–53. Louisiana State University, Baton Rouge.

Kidder, Tristram R. (1998) Mississippi Period Mound Groups and Communities in the Lower Mississippi Valley. In *Mississippian Towns and Sacred Spaces: Searching for an Architectural Grammar*, edited by R. B. Lewis and C. Stout, pp. 123–150. University of Alabama Press, Tuscaloosa.

Kidder, Tristram R. (2002a) Mapping Poverty Point. *American Antiquity* 67:89–101.

Kidder, Tristram R. (2002b) Woodland Period Archaeology of the Lower Mississippi Valley. In *The Woodland Southeast*, edited by D. G. Anderson and R. C. Mainfort, pp. 66–90. University of Alabama Press, Tuscaloosa.

Kidder, Tristram R. (2004) Plazas as Architecture: An Example from the Raffman Site, Northeast Louisiana. *American Antiquity* 69:514–532.

Kidder, Tristram R., and Gayle J. Fritz (1993) Subsistence and Social Change in the Lower Mississippi Valley: Excavations at the Reno Brake and Osceola Sites, Louisiana. *Journal of Field Archaeology* 20:281–297.

King, Adam (2003) *Etowah: The Political History of a Chiefdom Capital*. University of Alabama Press, Tuscaloosa.

King, Adam (2005) Power and the Sacred: Mound C and the Etowah Chiefdom. In *Hero, Hawk, and Open Hand: American Indian Art of the Ancient Midwest and South,* edited by R. F. Townsend, pp. 151–166. Art Institute of Chicago/Yale University Press, New Haven, CT.

King, Adam, and Jennifer A. Freer (1995) The Mississippian Southeast: A World-Systems Perspective. In *Native American Interactions: Multiscalar Analyses and Interpretations in the Eastern Woodlands,* edited by M. S. Nassaney and K. E. Sassaman, pp. 266–288. University of Tennessee Press, Knoxville.

King, Adam, and Maureen S. Meyers (2002) Exploring the Edges of the Mississippian World. *Southeastern Archaeology* 21:113–116.

Kintigh, Keith W., Donna M. Glowacki, and Deborah L. Huntley (2004) Long-Term Settlement History and the Emergence of Towns in the Zuni Area. *American Antiquity* 69:432–456.

Kirchoff, Paul (1955) The Principles of Clanship in Human Society. *Davidson Journal of Anthropology* 1:1–10.

Knight, Vernon James, Jr. (1986) The Institutional Organization of Mississippian Religion. *American Antiquity* 51:675–687.

Knight, Vernon James, Jr. (1997) Some Developmental Parallels Between Cahokia and Moundville. In *Cahokia: Domination and Ideology in the Mississippian World,* edited by T. R. Pauketat and T. E. Emerson pp. 227–249. University of Nebraska Press, Lincoln.

Knight, Vernon James, Jr. (2001) Feasting and the Emergence of Platform Mound Ceremonialism in Eastern North America. In *Feasts: Archaeological and Ethnographic Perspectives on Food, Politics, and Power,* edited by M. Dietler and B. Hayden, pp. 311–333. Smithsonian Institution Press, Washington, D.C.

Knight, Vernon James, Jr., and Vincas P. Steponaitis (1998) *Archaeology of the Moundville Chiefdom.* Smithsonian Institution Press, Washington, D.C.

Knight, Vernon James, Jr., James A. Brown, and George E. Lankford (2001) On the Subject Matter of Southeastern Ceremonial Complex Art. *Southeastern Archaeology* 20:129–153.

Knight, Vernon James, Jr., Lyle Konigsberg, and Susan Frankenberg (n.d.) A Gibbs Sampler Approach to the Dating of Phases in the Moundville Sequence. Manuscript in possession of the author.

Koldehoff, Brad, Charles O. Witty, and Mike Kolb (2000) Recent Investigations in the Vicinity of Mounds 27 and 28 at Cahokia: The Yale Avenue Borrow Pit. *Illinois Archaeology* 12:199–217.

Kosse, K. (1990) Group Size and Societal Complexity: Thresholds in the Long-Term Memory. *Journal of Anthropological Archaeology* 9:275–303.

Kowalewski, Stephen A., Gary M. Feinman, Laura Finsten, Richard E. Blanton, and Linda M. Nicholas (1989) *Monte Alban's Hinterland: Prehispanic Settlement Patterns in Tlacolula, Etla, and Ocatlán, the Valley of Oaxaca, Mexico.* University of Michigan Museum of Anthropology, Memoir 23. Ann Arbor.

Kristiansen, Kristian (1991) Chiefdoms, States, and Systems of Social Evolution. In *Chiefdoms: Power, Economy, and Ideology,* edited by T. Earle, pp. 16–43. Cambridge University Press, Cambridge.

Kuijt, Ian, and Meredith S. Chesson (2005) Lumps of Clay and Pieces of Stone: Ambiguity, Bodies, and Identity As Portrayed in Neolithic Figurines. In *Archaeologies of the*

REFERENCES

Middle East: Critical Perspectives, edited by S. Pollock and R. Bernbeck, pp. 152–183. Blackwell, Oxford.

Kuper, Hilda (1965) *An African Aristocracy: Rank Among the Swazi*. Oxford University Press, Oxford.

Kus, Susan M. (1979) Archaeology and Ideology: The Symbolic Organization of Space. Ph.D. diss., University of Michigan.

Kus, Susan M. (1983) The Social Representation of Space: Dimensioning the Cosmological and the Quotidian. In *Archaeological Hammers and Theories*, edited by J. A. Moore and A. S. Keene, pp. 277–298. Academic, New York.

Kus, Susan M. (1989) Sensuous Human Activity and the State: Towards an Archaeology of Bread and Circuses. In *Domination and Resistance*, edited by D. Miller, M. Rowlands, and C. Tilley, pp. 140–154. Routledge, London.

Kus, Susan M., and Victor Raharigaona (2001) To Dare to Wear the Cloak of Another Before Their Very Eyes: State Co-optation and Local Re-Appropriation in Mortuary Rituals of Central Madagascar. In *Social Memory, Identity, and Death: Anthropological Perspectives on Mortuary Rituals*, edited by M. Chesson, pp. 114–131. Archeological Papers of the American Anthropological Association, no. 10. Washington, D.C.

Larson, Lewis H., Jr. (1971) Archaeological Implications of Social Stratification at the Etowah Site, Georgia. In *Approaches to the Social Dimensions of Mortuary Practices*, edited by J. A. Brown, pp. 58–67. Society for American Archaeology, Memoir 25. Washington, D.C.

LaVere, David (1998) *The Caddo Chiefdoms: Caddo Economics and Politics, 700–1835*. University of Nebraska Press, Lincoln.

Leach, Edmund R. (1965) *Political Systems of Highland Burma: A Study of Kachin Social Structure*. Beacon, Boston.

LeBlanc, Steven A. (1983) *The Mimbres People: Ancient Pueblo Painters of the American Southwest*. Thames & Hudson, London.

LeBlanc, Steven A. (1989) Cultural Dynamics in the Southern Mogollon Area. In *Dynamics of Southwest Prehistory*, edited by L. S. Cordell and G. J. Gumerman, pp. 179–207. Smithsonian Institution Press, Washington, D.C.

LeBlanc, Steven A. (1999) *Prehistoric Warfare in the American Southwest*. University of Utah Press, Salt Lake City.

Lefebvre, Henri (1991) *The Production of Space*. Translated by D. Nicholson-Smith. Blackwell, Oxford.

Lekson, Stephen H. (1999a) *The Chaco Meridian: Centers of Political Power in the Ancient Southwest*. AltaMira, Walnut Canyon, CA.

Lekson, Stephen H. (1999b) Was Casas a Pueblo? In *The Casas Grandes World*, edited by C. F. Schaafsma and C. L. Riley, pp. 84–92. University of Utah Press, Salt Lake City.

Lekson, Stephen H. (2002) War in the Southwest, War in the World. *American Antiquity* 67:607–624.

Lekson, Stephen H. (2005) Chaco and Paquime: Complexity, History, Landscape. In *North American Archaeology*, edited by T. R. Pauketat and D. D. Loren, pp. 235–272. Blackwell, Oxford.

Lekson, Stephen H., and Catherine M. Cameron (1995) The Abandonment of Chaco Canyon, the Mesa Verde Migrations, and the Reorganization of the Pueblo World. *Journal of Anthropological Archaeology* 14:184–202.

Lekson, Stephen H., and Peter N. Peregrine (2004) A Continental Perspective for North American Archaeology. *SAA Archaeological Record* 4:15–19.

Lepper, Bradley T. (1998) The Archaeology of the Newark Earthworks. In *Ancient Earthen Enclosures of the Eastern Woodlands*, edited by R. C. Mainfort, Jr. and L. P. Sullivan, pp. 114-134. University Press of Florida, Gainesville.

Lepper, Bradley T. (2005) The Newark Earthworks: Monumental Geometry and Astronomy at a Hopewellian Pilgrimage Center. In *Hero, Hawk, and Open Hand: American Indian Art of the Ancient Midwest and South,* edited by R. F. Townsend, pp. 73–81. Art Institute of Chicago/Yale University Press, New Haven, CT.

Lewis, R. Barry (1991) The Early Mississippi Period in the Confluence Region and Its Northern Relationships. In *Cahokia and the Hinterlands: Middle Mississippian Cultures of the Midwest*, edited by T. E. Emerson and R. B. Lewis, pp. 274–294. University of Illinois Press, Urbana.

Lewis, R. Barry, Charles Stout, and Cameron B. Wesson (1998) The Design of Mississippian Towns. In *Mississippian Towns and Sacred Spaces: Searching for an Architectural Grammar,* edited by R. B. Lewis and C. Stout, pp. 1–21. University of Alabama Press, Tuscaloosa.

Lewis, R. Barry, and Charles Stout, eds. (1998) *Mississippian Towns and Sacred Spaces: Searching for an Architectural Grammar.* University of Alabama Press, Tuscaloosa.

Lightfoot, Kent G. (2005) The Archaeology of Colonization: California in Cross-Cultural Perspective. In *The Archaeology of Colonial Encounters: Comparative Perspectives,* edited by G. J. Stein, pp. 207–235. School of American Research Press, Santa Fe, NM.

Lindauer, Owen, and John H. Blitz (1997) Higher Ground: The Archaeology of North American Platform Mounds. *Journal of Archaeological Research* 5:169–207.

Little, Keith J. (1999) The Role of Late Woodland Interactions in the Emergence of Etowah. *Southeastern Archaeology* 18:45–56.

Loren, Diana D. (2005) Creolization in the French and Spanish Colonies. In *North American Archaeology,* edited by T. R. Pauketat and D. D. Loren, pp. 297–318. Blackwell, Oxford.

Loughridge, R. H. (1888) *Report on the Geological and Economic Features of the Jackson Purchase Region.* Kentucky Geological Survey, Frankfort.

Low, Setha M. (1996) The Anthropology of Cities: Imagining and Theorizing the City. *Annual Review of Anthropology* 25:383–409.

Mainfort, Robert C., Jr. (1996) The Reelfoot Lake Basin, Kentucky and Tennessee. In *Prehistory of the Central Mississippi Valley,* edited by C. H. McNutt, pp. 77–96. University of Alabama Press, Tuscaloosa.

Malville, Nancy J., William C. Byrnes, H. Allen Lim, and Ramesh Basnyat (2001) Commercial Porters of Eastern Nepal: Health Status, Physical Work Capacity, and Energy Expenditure. *American Journal of Human Biology* 13:44-56.

Marcus, Joyce (1983) The Conquest Slabs of Building J, Monte Alban. In *The Cloud People: Divergent Evolution of the Zapotec and Mixtec Civilizations,* edited by K. V. Flannery and J. Marcus, pp. 106–108. Academic, New York.

Marcus, Joyce (1999) The Peaks and Valleys of Ancient States: An Extension of the Dynamic Model. In *Archaic States,* edited by Gary M. Feinman and Joyce Marcus, pp. 59–94. School of American Research, Santa Fe, NM.

Marcus, Joyce, and Gary M. Feinman (1998) Introduction. In *Archaic States,* edited by Gary M. Feinman and Joyce Marcus, pp. 3–13. School of American Research, Santa Fe, NM.

REFERENCES

Marcus, Joyce, and Kent V. Flannery (1996) *Zapotec Civilization: How Urban Society Evolved in Mexico's Oaxaca Valley.* Thames & Hudson, London.

Maschner, Herbert D. G., ed. (1996) *Darwinian Archaeologies.* Plenum, New York.

Mathews, Roger (2005) Factoids for the Mythoclast. *Cambridge Archaeological Journal* 15:254–256.

Maxham, Mintcy D. (2004) Native Constructions of Landscapes in the Black Warrior Valley, Alabama, AD 1020–1520. Ph.D. diss., University of North Carolina.

McAnany, Patricia A. (2001) Cosmology and the Institutionalization of Hierarchy in the Maya Region. In *From Leaders to Rulers,* edited by J. Haas, pp. 125–148. Kluwer Academic/Plenum, New York.

McGuire, Randall (1983) Breaking Down Cultural Complexity: Inequality and Heterogeneity. *Advances in Archaeological Methods and Theory* 6:91–142.

McGuire, Randall (1992) *A Marxist Archaeology.* Academic, New York.

McIntosh, Susan, ed. (1999) *Beyond Chiefdoms: Pathways to Complexity in Africa.* Cambridge University Press, Cambridge.

Mehrer, Mark W. (1995) *Cahokia's Countryside: Household Archaeology, Settlement Patterns, and Social Power.* Northern Illinois University Press, DeKalb.

Mehrer, Mark W., and James M. Collins (1995) Household Archaeology at Cahokia and in Its Hinterlands. In *Mississippian Communities and Households*, edited by J. D. Rogers and B. D. Smith, pp. 32–57. University of Alabama Press, Tuscaloosa.

Meskell, Lynn (2004) *Object Worlds in Ancient Egypt: Material Biographies Past and Present.* Berg, Oxford.

Meskell, Lynn, and Robert W. Preucel, eds. (2004) *A Companion to Social Archaeology.* Blackwell, Oxford.

Milanich, Jerald T., Ann S. Cordell, Vernon J. Knight Jr., Timothy A. Kohler, and Brenda J. Sigler-Lavelle (1984) *McKeithen Weeden Island: The Culture of Northern Florida AD 200–900.* Academic Press, Orlando, Florida.

Mills, Barbara J. (2000) Alternative Models, Alternative Strategies: Leadership in the Prehispanic Southwest. In *Alternative Leadership Strategies in the Prehispanic Southwest*, edited by B. J. Mills, pp. 3–18. University of Arizona Press, Tucson.

Mills, Barbara J. (2002) Recent Research on Chaco: Changing Views on Economy, Ritual, and Society. *Journal of Archaeological Research* 10:65–117.

Milner, George R. (1984) *The Robinson's Lake Site.* American Bottom Archaeology FAI-270 Site Reports, vol. 10. University of Illinois Press, Urbana.

Milner, George R. (1986) Mississippian Period Population Density in a Segment of the Central Mississippi Valley. *American Antiquity* 51:227–238.

Milner, George R. (1996) Development and Dissolution of a Mississippian Society in the American Bottom, Illinois. In *Political Structure and Change in the Prehistoric Southeastern United States,* edited by J. F. Scarry, pp. 27–52. University Press of Florida, Gainesville.

Milner, George R. (1998) *The Cahokia Chiefdom: The Archaeology of a Mississippian Society.* Smithsonian Institution Press, Washington, D.C.

Milner, George R. (1999) Warfare in Prehistoric and Early Historic Eastern North America. *Journal of Archaeological Research* 7:105–151.

Milner, George R. (2004) Old Mounds, Ancient Hunter-Gatherers, and Modern Archaeologists. In *Signs of Power: The Rise of Cultural Complexity in the Southeast,* edited by J. L. Gibson and P. J. Carr, pp. 300–315. University of Alabama Press, Tuscaloosa.

Milner, George R. (2005) *The Moundbuilders: Ancient Peoples of Eastern North America.* Thames and Hudson, London.

Milner, George R., Thomas E. Emerson, Mark W. Mehrer, Joyce A. Williams, and Duane Esarey (1984) Mississippian and Oneota Period. In *American Bottom Archaeology,* edited by C. J. Bareis and J. W. Porter, pp. 158–186. University of Illinois Press, Urbana.

Milner, George R., and Sissel Schroeder (1999) Mississippian Sociopolitical Systems. In *Great Towns and Regional Polities in the Prehistoric American Southwest and Southeast,* edited by J. E. Neitzel, pp. 95–107. University of New Mexico Press, Albuquerque.

Moore, John H. (1994) Ethnoarchaeology of the Lamar People. In *Perspectives on the Southeast: Linguistics, Archaeology, and Ethnohistory,* edited by P. B. Kwachka, pp. 126–141. University of Georgia Press, Athens.

Morse, Dan F. (1977) The Penetration of Northeast Arkansas by Mississippian Culture. In *For the Director: Research Essays in Honor of James B. Griffin,* edited by C. E. Cleland, pp. 186–211. University of Michigan, Museum of Anthropology, Anthropological Papers, no. 61. Ann Arbor.

Morse, Dan F., and Phyllis A. Morse (1983) *The Archaeology of the Central Mississippi Valley.* Academic, New York.

Muller, Jon (1984) Mississippian Specialization and Salt. *American Antiquity* 49:489–507.

Muller, Jon (1986) *Archaeology of the Lower Ohio River Valley.* Academic, Orlando, Florida.

Muller, Jon (1987) Salt, Chert, and Shell: Mississippian Exchange and Economy. In *Specialization, Exchange, and Complex Societies,* edited by E. Brumfiel and T. Earle. Cambridge University Press, Cambridge, pp. 10–21.

Muller, Jon (1989) The Southern Cult. In *The Southeastern Ceremonial Complex: Artifacts and Analysis,* edited by P. Galloway, pp. 11–26. University of Nebraska Press, Lincoln.

Muller, Jon (1997) *Mississippian Political Economy.* Plenum, New York.

Muller, Jon (1999) Southeastern Interaction and Integration. In *Great Towns and Regional Polities in the Prehistoric American Southwest and Southeast,* edited by J. E. Neitzel, pp. 143–158. Amerind Foundation/University of New Mexico Press, Albuquerque.

Muller, Jon, and Jeanette E. Stephens (1991) Mississippian Sociocultural Adaptation. In *Cahokia and the Hinterlands: Middle Mississippian Cultures of the Midwest,* edited by T. E. Emerson and R. B. Lewis, pp. 297–310. University of Illinois Press, Urbana.

Muller, Jon, and David R. Wilcox (1999) Powhatan's Mantle as Metaphor: Comparing Macroregional Integration in the Southwest and Southeast. In *Great Towns and Regional Polities in the Prehistoric American Southwest and Southeast,* edited by J. E. Neitzel, pp. 159–164. Amerind Foundation/University of New Mexico Press, Albuquerque.

Nassaney, Michael S. (1991) Spatial-Temporal Dimensions of Social Integration During the Coles Creek Period in Central Arkansas. In *Stability, Transformation, and Variation: The Late Woodland Southeast,* edited by M. S. Nassaney and C. R. Cobb, pp. 177–220. Plenum, New York.

Nassaney, Michael S. (1992) Communal Societies and the Emergence of Elites in the Prehistoric American Southeast. In *Lords of the Southeast: Social Inequality and the Native Elites of Southeastern North America,* edited by A. W. Barker and T. R. Pauketat, pp. 111–143. Archeological Papers of the American Anthropological Association, no. 3. Washington, D.C.

REFERENCES

Nassaney, Michael S. (1994) The Historical and Archaeological Context of Plum Bayou Culture in Central Arkansas. *Southeastern Archaeology* 13:36–55.

Nassaney, Michael S. (2001) The Historical–Processual Development of Late Woodland Societies. In *The Archaeology of Traditions: History and Agency Before and After Columbus*, edited by T. R. Pauketat, pp. 157–173. University Press of Florida, Gainesville.

Neitzel, Jill E. (1999) Examining Societal Organization in the Southwest: An Application of Multiscalar Analysis. In *Great Towns and Regional Polities in the Prehistoric American Southwest and Southeast*, edited by J. E. Neitzel, pp. 183–205. Amerind Foundation/University of New Mexico Press, Albuquerque.

Neitzel, Jill E., ed. (1999) *Great Towns and Regional Polities in the Prehistoric American Southwest and Southeast*. Amerind Foundation/University of New Mexico Press, Albuquerque.

Nelson, Ben A. (1995) Complexity, Hierarchy, and Scale: A Controlled Comparison Between Chaco Canyon, New Mexico, and La Quemada, Zacatecas. *American Antiquity* 60:597–618.

Nelson, Margaret C., and Michelle Hegmon (2001) Abandonment Is Not As It Seems: An Approach to the Relationship Between Site and Regional Abandonment. *American Antiquity* 66:213–236.

Nelson, Margaret C., and Gregson Schachner (2002) Understanding Abandonments in the North American Southwest. *Journal of Archaeological Research* 10:167–206.

Nichols, Deborah L., and Thomas H. Charlton, eds. (1997) *The Archaeology of City-States: Cross-Cultural Approaches*. Smithsonian Institution Press, Washington, D.C.

Oberg, Kalervo (1955) Types of Social Structure Among the Lowland Tribes of South and Central America. *American Anthropologist* 57:472–487.

O'Brien, Michael J. (2001) *Mississippian Community Organization: The Powers Phase in Southeastern Missouri.* Kluwer Academic/Plenum, New York.

O'Brien, Patricia J. (1989) Cahokia: The Political Capital of the "Ramey" State? *North American Archaeologist* 10 :275–292.

O'Brien, Patricia J. (1991) Early State Economics: Cahokia, Capital of the Ramey State. In *Early State Economics*, edited by H. J. M. Claessen and P. van de Velde, pp. 143–175. Transaction, London.

O'Brien, Patricia J. (1993) Cultural Taxonomy, Cross-Cultural Types, and Cahokia. *Illinois Archaeology* 5:481–497.

O'Brien, Patricia J. (1994) Prehistoric Politics: Petroglyphs and the Political Boundaries of Cahokia. *Gateway Heritage: Quarterly Magazine of the Missouri Historical Society,* Summer, pp. 30–47.

Overstreet, David F. (2000) Cultural Dynamics of the Late Prehistoric Period in Southern Wisconsin. In *Mounds, Modoc, and Mesoamerica: Papers in Honor of Melvin L. Fowler,* edited by S. R. Ahler, pp. 405–438. Illinois State Museum Scientific Papers, vol. 28. Springfield.

Patterson, Thomas C. (1987) Tribes, Chiefdoms, and Kingdoms in the Inca Empire. In *Power Relations and State Formation,* edited by T. C. Patterson and C. W. Gailey, pp. 117–127. Special of the Archeology Section. American Anthropological Association, Washington, D.C.

Patterson, Thomas C. (1995) *Toward a Social History of Archaeology in the United States.* Harcourt Brace, Fort Worth, Texas.

Pauketat, Timothy R. (1983) A Long-Stemmed Spud from the American Bottom. *Midcontinental Journal of Archaeology* 8:1–12.

Pauketat, Timothy R. (1987) Mississippian Domestic Economy and Formation Processes: A Response to Prentice. *Midcontinental Journal of Archaeology* 12:77–88.

Pauketat, Timothy R. (1989) Monitoring Mississippian Homestead Occupation Span and Economy Using Ceramic Refuse. *American Antiquity* 54:288–310.

Pauketat, Timothy R. (1992) The Reign and Ruin of the Lords of Cahokia: A Dialectic of Dominance. In *Lords of the Southeast: Social Inequality and the Native Elites of Southeastern North America*, edited by Alex W. Barker and Timothy R. Pauketat, pp. 31–51. Archeological Papers of the American Anthropological Association, no. 3. Washington, D.C.

Pauketat, Timothy R. (1993) *Temples for Cahokia Lords: Preston Holder's 1955–1956 Excavations of Kunnemann Mound*. Museum of Anthropology, University of Michigan Memoir no. 26. Ann Arbor.

Pauketat, Timothy R. (1994) *The Ascent of Chiefs: Cahokia and Mississippian Politics in Native North America*. University of Alabama Press, Tuscaloosa.

Pauketat, Timothy R. (1997) Cahokian Political Economy. In *Cahokia: Domination and Ideology in the Mississippian World*, edited by T. R. Pauketat and T. E. Emerson, pp. 30–51. University of Nebraska Press, Lincoln.

Pauketat, Timothy R. (1998) Refiguring the Archaeology of Greater Cahokia. *Journal of Archaeological Research* 6:45–89.

Pauketat, Timothy R. (2000a) Politicization and Community in the Pre-Columbian Mississippi Valley. In *The Archaeology of Communities: A New World Perspective*, edited by M. A. Canuto and J. Yaeger, pp. 16–43. Routledge, London.

Pauketat, Timothy R. (2000b) The Tragedy of the Commoners. In *Agency in Archaeology*, edited by M.-A. Dobres and J. Robb, pp. 113–129. Routledge, London.

Pauketat, Timothy R. (2001a) A New Tradition in Archaeology. In *The Archaeology of Traditions: Agency and History Before and After Columbus*, edited by T. R. Pauketat, pp. 1–16. University Press of Florida, Gainesville.

Pauketat, Timothy R. (2001b) Practice and History in Archaeology: An Emerging Paradigm. *Anthropological Theory* 1:73–98.

Pauketat, Timothy R. (2002) A Fourth-Generation Synthesis of Cahokia and Mississippianization. *Midcontinental Journal of Archaeology* 27:149–170.

Pauketat, Timothy R. (2003a) Materiality and the Immaterial in Historical–Processual Archaeology. In *Essential Tensions in Archaeological Method and Theory*, edited by T. L. VanPool and C. S. VanPool, pp. 41–53. University of Utah Press, Salt Lake City.

Pauketat, Timothy R. (2003b) Resettled Farmers and the Making of a Mississippian Polity. *American Antiquity* 68:39–66.

Pauketat, Timothy R. (2004) *Ancient Cahokia and the Mississippians*. Cambridge University Press, Cambridge.

Pauketat, Timothy R. (2005) The Forgotten History of the Mississippians. In *North American Archaeology*, edited by T. R. Pauketat and D. D. Loren, pp. 187–212. Blackwell, Oxford.

Pauketat, Timothy R., ed. (2005) *The Archaeology of the East St. Louis Mound Center: Southside Excavations*. Illinois Transportation Archaeological Research Program, Report of Investigations (in press).

REFERENCES

Pauketat, Timothy R. (2007) War, Rumors of War, and the Production of Violence. In *The Archaeology of War in Practice*, edited by A. Nielsen and W. Walker. Amerind Foundation, Dragoon, AZ (in press).

Pauketat, Timothy R., and Susan M. Alt (2003) Mounds, Memory, and Contested Mississippian History. In *Archaeologies of Memory*, edited by R. M. Van Dyke and S. E. Alcock, pp. 151–179. Blackwell, Oxford.

Pauketat, Timothy R., and Susan M. Alt (2004) Compounds and Keeps for Cahokians (and Their Political–Historical Implications). Paper presented at the joint Midwest and Southeastern Archaeological Conference, October 21–23, 2004, St. Louis, Missouri.

Pauketat, Timothy R., and Susan M. Alt (2005) Agency in a Postmold? Physicality and the Archaeology of Culture-Making. *Journal of Archaeological Method and Theory* 12:213–236.

Pauketat, Timothy R., Susan M. Alt, and Jeffrey D. Kruchten (2005) Final Report of the Cahokia Extension Waterline and Grand Plaza Test Unit Projects. Report submitted to the Illinois Historic Preservation Agency, Springfield, Illinois.

Pauketat, Timothy R., and Thomas E. Emerson (1997) Introduction: Domination and Ideology in the Mississippian World. In *Cahokia: Domination and Ideology in the Mississippian World*, edited by T. R. Pauketat and T. E. Emerson, pp. 30–51. University of Nebraska Press, Lincoln.

Pauketat, Timothy R., and Thomas E. Emerson (1999) The Representation of Hegemony as Community at Cahokia. In *Material Symbols: Culture and Economy in Prehistory*, edited by J. Robb, pp. 302–317. Occasional Paper no. 26. Southern Illinois University, Carbondale.

Pauketat, Timothy R., and Thomas E. Emerson, eds. (1997) *Cahokia: Domination and Ideology in the Mississippian World.* University of Nebraska Press, Lincoln.

Pauketat, Timothy R., Lucretia S. Kelly, Gayle J. Fritz, Neal H. Lopinot, Scott Elias, and Eve Hargrave (2002) The Residues of Feasting and Public Ritual at Early Cahokia. *American Antiquity* 67:257–279.

Pauketat, Timothy R., and Neal H. Lopinot (1997) Cahokian Population Dynamics. In *Cahokia: Domination and Ideology in the Mississippian World*, edited by T. R. Pauketat and T. E. Emerson, pp. 103–123. University of Nebraska Press, Lincoln.

Pauketat, Timothy R., and Diana D. Loren (2005) Alternative Histories and North American Archaeology. In *North American Archaeology*, edited by T. R. Pauketat and D. D. Loren, pp. 1–29. Blackwell, Oxford.

Pauketat, Timothy R., and Mark A. Rees (1996) Early Cahokia Project 1994 Excavations at Mound 49, Cahokia (11-S-34-2). Report submitted to the Illinois Historic Preservation Agency, Springfield.

Pauketat, Timothy R., Mark A. Rees, and Stephanie L. Pauketat (1998) *An Archaeological Survey of the Horseshoe Lake State Park, Madison County, Illinois.* Illinois State Museum Reports of Investigations, no. 55. Springfield.

Paynter, Robert, and Randall H. McGuire (1991) The Archaeology of Inequality: Material Culture, Domination, and Resistance. In *The Archaeology of Inequality*, edited by R. H. McGuire and R. Paynter, pp. 1–27. Blackwell, Oxford.

Peebles, Christopher S., and Susan M. Kus (1977) Some Archaeological Correlates of Ranked Societies. *American Antiquity* 42:421–448.

Peregrine, Peter N. (1992) *Mississippian Evolution: A World-System Perspective.* Prehistory, Madison, Wisconsin.

Peregrine, Peter N. (2001) Matrilocality, Corporate Strategy, and the Organization of Production in the Chacoan World. *American Antiquity* 66:36–46.

Peregrine, Peter N., and Stephen H. Lekson (2006) Southeast, Southwest, Mexico: Continental Perspectives on Mississippian Polities. In *Leadership and Polity in Mississippian Society*, edited by B. M. Butler and P. D. Welch, pp. 351–364. Center for Archaeological Investigations, Occasional Paper no. 33. Southern Illinois University, Carbondale, Illinois.

Phillips, Philip (1970) *Archaeological Survey in the Lower Yazoo Basin, Mississippi, 1949–1955*. Papers of the Peabody Museum of Archaeology and Ethnology No. 60. Harvard University, Cambridge.

Phillips, Philip, and James A. Brown (1978) *Pre-Columbian Shell Engravings from the Craig Mound at Spiro, Oklahoma*. Peabody Museum Press, Harvard University, Cambridge, Massachusetts.

Phillips, Phillip, James A. Ford, and James B. Griffin (1951) *Archaeological Survey in the Lower Mississippi Alluvial Valley, 1940–1947*. Papers of the Peabody Museum of Archaeology and Ethnology, vol. 25. Harvard University, Cambridge, MA.

Plog, Fred, and Steadman Upham (1983) The Analysis of Prehistoric Political Organization. In *The Development of Political Organization in Native North America*, edited by E. Tooker, pp. 199–213. American Ethnological Society, Washington, D.C.

Pluckhahn, Thomas J. (2003) *Kolomoki: Settlement, Ceremony, and Status in the Deep South, A.D. 350–750*. University of Alabama Press, Tuscaloosa.

Pollack, David (2004) *Caborn-Welborn: Constructing a New Society After the Angel Chiefdom Collapse*. University of Alabama Press, Tuscaloosa.

Pollard, Joshua (2001) The Aesthetics of Depositional Practice. *World Archaeology* 33:315–333.

Pollock, Susan (1999) *Ancient Mesopotamia: The Eden That Never Was*. Cambridge University Press, Cambridge.

Pollock, Susan, and Reinhard Bernbeck, eds. (2005) *Archaeologies of the Middle East: Critical Perspectives*. Blackwell, Oxford.

Postgate, J. N. (1992) *Early Mesopotamia: Society and Economy at the Dawn of History*. Routledge, London.

Potts, D. T. (1999) *The Archaeology of Elam: Formation and Transformation of an Ancient Iranian State*. Cambridge University Press, Cambridge.

Powell, Mary Lucas (1992) *Status and Health in Prehistory*. Smithsonian Institution Press, Washington, D.C.

Powell, Mary Lucas (1994) Human Skeletal Remains from Ocmulgee National Monument. In *Ocmulgee Archaeology 1936–1986*, edited by D. J. Hally, pp. 116–129. University of Georgia Press, Athens.

Powell, Mary Lucas (1998) Of Time and the River: Perspectives on Health During the Moundville Chiefdom. In *Archaeology of the Moundville Chiefdom*, edited by V. J. Knight and V. P. Steponaitis, pp. 102–119. Smithsonian Institution Press, Washington, D.C.

Prentice, Guy (1983) Cottage Industries: Concepts and Implications. *Midcontinental Journal of Archaeology* 8:1–16.

Price, Barbara J. (1978) Secondary State Formation: An Explanatory Model. In *Origins of the State: The Anthropology of Political Evolution*, edited by R. Cohen and E. R. Service, pp. 161–186. Institute for the Study of Human Issues, Philadelphia.

REFERENCES

Price, James E. (1978) The Settlement Pattern of the Powers Phase. In *Mississippian Settlement Patterns*, edited by B. D. Smith, pp. 201–231. Academic Press, New York.

Price, James E., and James B. Griffin (1979) *The Snodgrass Site of the Powers Phase of Southeast Missouri*. Museum of Anthropology, University of Michigan, Anthropological Papers, no. 66. Ann Arbor.

Radin, Paul (1948) *Winnebago Hero Cycles: A Study in Aboriginal Literature*. Waverly, Baltimore.

Radin, Paul (1990) *The Winnebago Tribe*. University of Nebraska Press, Lincoln.

Read, Margaret (1970) *The Ngoni of Nyasaland*. Frank Cass, London.

Redmond, Elsa M. (1998) The Dynamics of Chieftaincy and the Development of Chiefdoms. In *Chiefdoms and Chieftaincy in the Americas*, edited by E. M. Redmond, pp. 1–17. University Press of Florida, Gainesville.

Reed, Nelson A. (1977) Monks and Other Mississippian Mounds. In *Explorations in Cahokia Archaeology*, edited by M. L. Fowler, pp. 31–42. Illinois Archaeological Survey Bulletin, no. 7. Urbana, Illinois.

Reed, Nelson A., John W. Bennett, and James W. Porter (1968) Solid Core Drilling of Monks Mound: Technique and Findings. *American Antiquity* 33:137–148.

Renfrew, Colin (1973) *Before Civilization*. Jonathan Cape, London.

Renfrew, Colin (1987) Introduction: Peer Polity Interaction and Socio-Political Change. In *Peer Polity Interaction and Socio-Political Change*, edited by C. Renfrew and J. F. Cherry, pp. 1–18. Cambridge University Press, Cambridge.

Renfrew, Colin (2001) Production and Consumption in a Sacred Economy: The Material Correlates of High Devotional Expression at Chaco Canyon. *American Antiquity* 66:14–25.

Richards, John D. (1992) *Ceramics and Culture at Aztalan: A Late Prehistoric Village in Southeast Wisconsin*. Ph.D. diss., University of Wisconsin.

Rogers, J. Daniel (1996) Markers of Social Integration: The Development of Centralized Authority in the Spiro Region. In *Political Structure and Change in the Prehistoric Southeastern United States*, edited by J. F. Scarry, pp. 53–68. University Press of Florida, Gainesville.

Rogers, J. Daniel, and Bruce D. Smith (1995) *Mississippian Communities and Households*. University of Alabama Press, Tuscaloosa.

Rolingson, Martha Ann (1990) The Toltec Mounds Site: A Ceremonial Center in the Arkansas River Lowland. In *The Mississippian Emergence*, edited by B. D. Smith, pp. 27–49. Smithsonian Institution Press, Washington, DC.

Rolingson, Martha A. (1998) *Toltec Mounds and Plum Bayou Culture: Mound D Excavations*. Arkansas Archeological Survey Research Series, no. 54. Fayetteville.

Rolingson, Martha A. (2002) Plum Bayou Culture of the Arkansas-White River Basin. In *The Woodland Southeast*, edited by D. G. Anderson and R. C. Mainfort, pp. 44–65. University of Alabama Press, Tuscaloosa.

Rose, Jerome C. (1999) Mortuary Data and Analysis. In *The Mound 72 Area: Dedicated and Sacred Space in Early Cahokia*, edited by M. L. Fowler, J. Rose, B. Vander Leest, and S. A. Ahler, pp. 63–82. Illinois State Museum, Reports of Investigations, no. 54. Springfield.

Rountree, Helen C. (1989) *The Powhatan Indians of Virginia: Their Traditional Culture*. University of Oklahoma Press, Norman.

Rountree, Helen C., and E. Randolph Turner III (1998) The Evolution of the Powhatan Paramount Chiefdom in Virginia. In *Chiefdoms and Chieftaincy in the Americas*, edited by E. M. Redmond, pp. 265–296. University Press of Florida, Gainesville.

Rowlands, Michael (1987) Centre and Periphery: A Review of a Concept. In *Centre and Periphery in the Ancient World*, edited by M. Rowlands, M. Larsen, and K. Kristiansen, pp. 1–11. Cambridge University Press, Cambridge.

Russo, M. (1994) Why We Don't Believe in Archaic Ceremonial Mounds and Why We Should: The Case from Florida. *Southeastern Archaeology* 13:93–108.

Russo, M. (1996) Southeastern Archaic Mounds. In *Archaeology of the Mid-Holocene Southeast*, edited by K. E. Sassaman and D. G. Anderson, pp. 259–287. University Press of Florida, Gainesville.

Russo, M. (2002) Architectural Features at Fig Island. In *The Fig Island Ring Complex (38CH42): Coastal Adaptation and the Question of Ring Function in the Late Archaic*, edited by R. Saunders, pp. 85–97. Report submitted to South Carolina Department of Archives and History Under Grant no. 45-01-16441, Columbia, South Carolina.

Sahlins, Marshall D. (1958) *Social Stratification in Polynesia*. University of Washington Press, Seattle.

Sahlins, Marshall D. (1972) *Stone Age Economics*. Aldine, Chicago.

Sahlins, Marshall D. (1985) *Islands of History*. University of Chicago Press, Chicago.

Sahlins, Marshall D., and Elman R. Service (1960) *Evolution of Culture*. University of Michigan Press, Ann Arbor.

Saitta, Dean J. (1994) Agency, Class, and Archaeological Interpretation. *Journal of Anthropological Archaeology* 13:201–227.

Salzer, Robert J., and Grace Rajnovich (2000) *The Gottschall Rockshelter: An Archaeological Mystery*. Prairie Smoke Press, St. Paul, Minnesota.

Sanders, William T., and Barbara J. Price (1968) *Mesoamerica: The Evolution of a Civilization*. Random House, New York.

Sassaman, Kenneth E. (2001) Hunter–gatherers and Traditions of Resistance. In *The Archaeology of Tradition: Agency and History Before and After Columbus*, edited by T. Pauketat, pp. 218–236. University Press of Florida, Gainesville.

Sassaman, Kenneth E. (2004) Complex Hunter-Gatherers in Evolution and History: A North American Perspective. *Journal of Archaeological Research* 12:227–280.

Sassaman, Kenneth E. (2005) Poverty Point as Structure, Event, Process. *Journal of Archaeological Method and Theory* 12:335–364.

Saunders, J. W., R. D. Mandel, R. T. Saucier, E. Thurman Allen, C. T. Hallmark, J. K. Johnson, E. H. Jackson, C. M. Allen, G. L. Stringer, D. S. Frink, J. K. Feathers, S. Williams, K. J. Gremillion, M. F. Vidrine, and R. Jones (1997) A Mound Complex in Louisiana at 5400–5000 Years Before the Present. *Science* 277:1796–1799.

Saunders, Rebecca (1994) The Case for Archaic Mounds in Southeastern Louisiana. *Southeastern Archaeology* 13:118–134.

Saunders, Rebecca (2001) Negotiated Tradition? Native American Pottery in the Mission Period in La Florida. In *The Archaeology of Traditions: Agency and History Before and After Columbus*, edited by T. R. Pauketat, pp. 77–93. University Press of Florida, Gainesville.

Saunders, Rebecca (2002) Summary and Conclusions. In *The Fig Island Ring Complex (38CH42): Coastal Adaptation and the Question of Ring Function in the Late Archaic*, edited by R. Saunders, pp. 154–159. Report submitted to South Carolina Department of Archives and History Under Grant no. 45-01-16441. Columbia.

Scarry, C. Margaret (1998) Domestic Life on the Northwest Riverbank at Moundville. In *Archaeology of the Moundville Chiefdom*, edited by V. J. Knight and V. P. Steponaitis, pp. 63–101. Smithsonian Institution Press, Washington, D.C.

REFERENCES

Scarry, John R. (1996) The Nature of Mississippian Societies. In *Political Structure and Change in the Prehistoric Southeastern United States*, edited by J. R. Scarry, pp. 12–24. University Press of Florida, Gainesville.

Scarry, John R. (1999) How Great Were the Southeastern Polities? In *Great Towns and Regional Polities in the Prehistoric American Southwest and Southeast*, edited by Jill E. Neitzel, pp. 59–74. University of New Mexico Press, Albuquerque, NM.

Schaafsma, Curtis F., and Carroll L. Riley (1999) The Casas Grandes World: Analysis and Conclusions. In *The Casas Grandes World*, edited by C. F. Schaafsma and C. L. Riley, pp. 237–249. University of Utah Press, Salt Lake City.

Schaafsma, Polly (1999) Tlalocs, Kachinas, Sacred Bundles, and Related Symbolism in the Southwest and Mesoamerica. In *The Casas Grandes World*, edited by C. F. Schaafsma and C. L. Riley, pp. 164–192. University of Utah Press, Salt Lake City.

Schambach, Frank (2002) Fourche Maline: A Woodland Period Culture of the Trans-Mississippi South. In The *Woodland Southeast*, edited by D. G. Anderson and R. C. Mainfort Jr., pp. 91–112. University of Alabama Press, Tuscaloosa.

Schnell, Frank T., Vernon J. Knight Jr., and Gail S. Schnell (1981) *Cemochechobee: Archaeology of a Mississippian Ceremonial Center on the Chattahoochee River.* University Press of Florida, Gainesville.

Schroeder, Sissel (2004) Power and Place: Agency, Ecology, and History in the American Bottom, Illinois. *Antiquity* 78:821–827.

Schroedl, Gerald F. (1994) A Comparison of the Origins of Macon Plateau and Hiwassee Island Cultures. In *Ocmulgee Archaeology 1936–1986*, edited by D. J. Hally, pp. 138–143. University of Georgia Press, Athens.

Schroedl, Gerald F. (1998). Mississippian Towns in the Eastern Tennessee Valley. In *Mississippian Towns and Sacred Spaces: Searching for an Architectural Grammar*, edited by R. B. Lewis and C. Stout, pp. 64–92. University of Alabama Press, Tuscaloosa.

Schroedl, Gerald F., C. Clifford Boyd Jr., and R. P. Stephen Davis Jr. (1990) Explaining Mississippian Origins in East Tennessee. In *The Mississippian Emergence*, edited by B. D. Smith, pp. 175–196. Smithsonian Institution Press, Washington, D.C.

Scott, James C. (1990) *Domination and the Arts of Resistance: Hidden Transcripts.* Yale University Press, New Haven, CT.

Sears, William H. (1992) Mea Culpa. *Southeastern Archaeology* 11:66–71.

Seeman, Mark F. (2004) Hopewell Art in Hopewell Places. In *Hero, Hawk, and Open Hand: American Indian Art of the Ancient Midwest and South*, edited by R. F. Townsend, pp. 57–71. Art Institute of Chicago/Yale University Press, New Haven, CT.

Service, Elman R. (1962) *Primitive Social Organization.* Random House, New York.

Service, Elman R. (1975) *Origins of the State and Civilization: The Process of Cultural Evolution.* Norton, New York.

Service, Elman R. (1978) Classical and Modern Theories of the Origins of Government. In *Origins of the State: The Anthropology of Political Evolution*, edited by R. Cohen and E. R. Service, pp. 21–34. Institute for the Study of Human Issues, Philadelphia.

Shafer, Harry J. (1999) The Mimbres Classic and Postclassic: A Case for Discontinuity. In *The Casas Grandes World*, edited by C. F. Schaafsma and C. L. Riley, pp. 121–133. University of Utah Press, Salt Lake City.

Shanks, Michael, and Christopher Tilley (1987) *Social Theory and Archaeology.* Polity Press, Cambridge, England.

Sherrod, P. Clay, and Martha A. Rolinson (1987) *Surveyors of the Ancient Mississippi Valley.* Arkansas Archeological Survey Research Series, no. 28. Fayetteville, Arkansas.

Silliman, Stephen W. (2004) *Lost Laborers in Colonial California: Native Americans and the Archaeology of Rancho Petaluma.* University of Arizona Press, Tucson.

Silliman, Stephen W. (2005) Social and Physical Landscapes of Contact. In *North American Archaeology,* edited by T. R. Pauketat and D. D. Loren, pp. 273–296. Blackwell, Oxford.

Silverberg, R. (1968) *Mound Builders of Ancient America: The Archaeology of a Myth.* New York Graphic Society, Greenwich, CT.

Simon, Mary L. (2002) Red Cedar, White Oak, and Bluestem Grass: The Colors of Mississippian Construction. *Midcontinental Journal of Archaeology* 27:273–308.

Smith, Adam T. (2003) *The Political Landscape: Constellations of Authority in Early Complex Polities.* University of California Press, Berkeley.

Smith, Bruce D. (1978) Variation in Mississippian Settlement Patterns. In *Mississippian Settlement Patterns,* edited by B. D. Smith, pp. 479–503. Academic, New York.

Smith, Bruce D. (1986) The Archaeology of the Southeastern United States: From Dalton to de Soto, 10,500–500 B.P. *Advances in World Archaeology* 5:1–92.

Smith, Bruce D. (1990) Introduction: Research on the Origins of Mississippian Chiefdoms in Eastern North America. In *The Mississippian Emergence,* edited by B. D. Smith, pp. 1–8. Smithsonian Institution Press, Washington, D.C.

Smith, Marvin T. (2003) *Coosa: The Rise and Fall of a Southeastern Mississippian Chiefdom.* University Press of Florida, Gainesville.

Smith, Marvin T., and David J. Hally (1992) Chiefly Behavior: Evidence from Sixteenth-Century Spanish Accounts. In *Lords of the Southeast: Social Inequality and the Native Elites of Southeastern North America,* edited by A. W. Barker and T. R. Pauketat, pp. 99–109. Archeological Papers of the American Anthropological Association, no. 3. Washington, D.C.

Smith, Monica A. (2003) Introduction: The Social Construction of Ancient Cities. In *The Social Construction of Ancient Cities,* edited by M. L. Smith, pp. 1–36. Smithsonian Institution Press, Washington, D.C.

Snead, James E. (2004) Ancestral Pueblo Settlement Dynamics: Landscape, Scale, and Context in the Burnt Corn Community. *Kiva* 69:243–269.

Snead, James E. (2005) History, Place, and Social Power in the Galisteo Basin, AD 1250–1325. Paper presented at the 70th Annual Meeting of the Society for American Archaeology. Salt Lake City, Utah.

Sofaer, Anna (1997) The Primary Architecture of the Chacoan Culture: A Cosmological Expression. In *Anasazi Architecture and American Design,* edited by B. H. Morrow and V. B. Price, pp. 88–132. University of New Mexico Press, Albuquerque.

Soja, Edward (2000) *Postmetropolis: Critical Studies of Cities and Regions.* Blackwell, Oxford.

Southall, Aidan (1956) *Alur Society: A Study in Process and Types of Domination.* W. Heffer, Cambridge, United Kingdom.

Spencer, Charles S. (1982) *Cuicatlán Cañada and Monte Albán: A Study in Primary State Formation.* Academic, New York.

Squier, Ephraim G., and Edwin H. Davis ([1848] 1998) *Ancient Monuments of the Mississippi Valley,* edited by D. J. Meltzer. Smithsonian Institution Press, Washington D.C.

Stahl, Ann Brower (2001) *Making History in Banda: Anthropological Visions of Africa's Past.* Cambridge University Press, Cambridge.

REFERENCES

Stahl, Ann Brower (2004) Comparative Insights into the Ancient Political Economies of West Africa. In *Archaeological Perspectives on Political Economies*, edited by G. M. Feinman and L. M. Nicholas, pp. 253–270. University of Utah Press, Salt Lake City.

Stanish, Charles (2003) The Evolution of Chiefdoms: An Economic Anthropological Model. In *Archaeological Perspectives on Political Economies*, edited by G. M. Feinman and L. M. Nicholas, pp. 7–24. University of Utah Press, Salt Lake City.

Stein, Gil J. (1998) Heterogeneity, Power, and Political Economy: Some Current Research Issues in the Archaeology of Old World Complex Societies. *Journal of Archaeological Research* 6:1–44.

Stein, Gil J. (2001) "Who Was King? Who Was Not King?": Social Group Composition and Competition in Early Mesopotamian State Societies. In *From Leaders to Rulers*, edited by J. Haas, pp. 205–231. Kluwer Academic/Plenum, New York.

Stein, Gil J. (2002) Colonies Without Colonialism: A Trade Diaspora Model of Fourth Millennium B.C. Mesopotamian Enclaves in Anatolia. In *The Archaeology of Colonialism*, edited by C. L. Lyons and J. K. Papadopoulos, pp. 26–64. Getty Research Institute, Los Angeles, California.

Stein, Gil J. (2005a) Introduction: The Comparative Archaeology of Colonial Encounters. In *The Archaeology of Colonial Encounters: Comparative Perspectives*, edited by G. J. Stein, pp. 3–31. School of American Research Press, Santa Fe, NM.

Stein, Gil J. (2005b) The Political Economy of Mesopotamian Colonial Encounters. In *The Archaeology of Colonial Encounters: Comparative Perspectives*, edited by G. J. Stein, pp. 143–171. School of American Research Press, Santa Fe, NM.

Steponaitis, Vincas P. (1978) Location Theory and Complex Chiefdoms: A Mississippian Example. In *Mississippian Settlement Patterns*, edited by B. D. Smith, pp. 417–453. Academic Press, New York.

Steponaitis, Vincas P. (1986) Prehistoric Archaeology in the Southeastern United States, 1970–1985. *Annual Review of Anthropology* 15:363–404.

Steponaitis, Vincas P. (1991) Contrasting Patterns of Mississippian Development. In *Chiefdoms: Power, Economy, and Ideology*, edited by T. Earle, pp. 193–228. Cambridge University Press, Cambridge.

Steward, Julian H., and Louis C. Faron (1959) *Native Peoples of South America.* McGraw-Hill, New York.

Stocking, George W., Jr. (1982) *Race, Culture, and Evolution: Essays in the History of Anthropology.* University of Chicago Press, Chicago.

Stoltman, James B. (1991) Cahokia As Seen from the Peripheries. In *New Perspectives on Cahokia: Views from the Periphery*, edited by J. B. Stoltman, pp. 349–354. Prehistory, Madison, Wisconsin.

Stoltman, James B. (2000) A Reconsideration of the Cultural Processes Linking Cahokia to Its Northern Hinterlands During the Period A.D. 1000–1200. In *Mounds, Modoc, and Mesoamerica: Papers in Honor of Melvin L. Fowler*, edited by S. R. Ahler, pp. 439–467. Illinois State Museum Scientific Papers, vol. 28. Springfield.

Stoltman, James B., and George W. Christiansen (2000) The Late Woodland Stage in the Driftless Area of the Upper Mississippi Valley. In *Late Woodland Societies: Tradition and Transformation Across the Midcontinent*, edited by T. E. Emerson, D. L. McElrath, and A. C. Fortier, pp. 497–524. University of Nebraska Press, Lincoln.

Stout, Charles, and R. Barry Lewis (1998) Mississippian Towns in Kentucky. In *Mississippian Towns and Sacred Spaces: Searching for an Architectural Grammar,* edited by R. B. Lewis and C. Stout, pp. 151–178. University of Alabama Press, Tuscaloosa.

Sullivan, Lynne P., ed. (1995) *The Prehistory of the Chickmauga Basin in Tennessee,* 2 vols. University of Tennessee Press, Knoxville.

Swanson, Steve (2003) Documenting Prehistoric Communication Networks: A Case Study in the Paquimé Polity. *American Antiquity* 68:753–767.

Swanton, John R. (1998) *Indian Tribes of the Lower Mississippi Valley and Adjacent Coast of the Gulf of Mexico.* Dover Publications, Mineola, New York.

Tambiah, Stanley (1976) *World Conqueror and World Renouncer: A Study in Religion and Polity in Thailand Against an Historical Background.* Cambridge University Press, Cambridge.

Taylor, Donna (1975) Some Locational Aspects of Middle-Range Hierarchical Societies. Ph.D. diss., City University of New York.

Taylor, Walter W. (1983) *A Study of Archeology.* Center for Archaeological Investigations, Southern Illinois University, Carbondale.

Theler, James L., and Robert F. Boszhardt (2000) The End of the Effigy Mound Culture: The Late Woodland to Oneota Transition in Southwestern Wisconsin. *Midcontinental Journal of Archaeology* 25:289–312.

Thomas, Cyrus (1907) Cahokia or Monk's Mound. *American Anthropologist* 9:362–365.

Thomas, Cyrus ([1894] 1985) *Report on the Mound Explorations of the Bureau of Ethnology.* Smithsonian Institution Press, Washington, D.C.

Tilley, Christopher (2004) *The Materiality of Stone: Explorations in Landscape Phenomenology.* Berg, Oxford.

Titterington, Paul F. (1938) *The Cahokia Mound Group and Its Village Site Materials.* Privately published, St. Louis, Missouri.

Toll, H. Wolcott (2001) Making and Breaking Pots in the Chaco World. *American Antiquity* 66:47–55.

Toll, H. Wolcott (2004) Artifacts in Chaco: Where They Came From and What They Mean. In *In Search of Chaco: New Approaches to an Archaeological Enigma,* edited by D. G. Noble, pp. 33–40. School of American Research Press, Santa Fe, NM.

Trigger, Bruce G. (1990) Monumental Architecture: A Thermodynamic Explanation of Symbolic Behaviour. *World Archaeology* 22(2):119–132.

Tringham, Ruth E. (1991) Households with Faces: The Challenge of Gender in Prehistoric Architectural Remains. In *Engendering Archaeology: Women and Prehistory,* edited by J. M. Gero and M. W. Conkey, pp. 93–131. Blackwell, Oxford.

Trouillot, Michel-Rolph (1985) *Silencing the Past: Power and the Production of History.* Beacon, Boston.

Trubitt, Mary Beth D. (2000) Mound Building and Prestige Goods Exchange: Changing Strategies in the Cahokia Chiefdom. *American Antiquity* 675:669–690.

Upham, Steadman (1987) A Theoretical Consideration of Middle Range Societies. In *Chiefdoms in the Americas,* edited by R. D. Drennan and C. A. Uribe, pp. 345–368. University Press of America, Lanham, MD.

Upham, Steadman (1990) Decoupling the Processes of Political Evolution. In *The Evolution of Political Systems: Sociopolitics in Small-Scale Sedentary Societies,* edited by S. Upham, pp. 1–17. School of American Research Press, Santa Fe, NM.

Van Dyke, Ruth M. (2003) Memory and the Construction of Chacoan Society. In *Archaeologies of Memory,* edited by R. M. Van Dyke and S. E. Alcock, pp. 180–200. Blackwell, Oxford.

REFERENCES

Van Dyke, Ruth M. (2004) Memory, Meaning, and Masonry: The Late Bonito Chacoan Landscape. *American Antiquity* 69:413–431.

Vansina, J. (1962) A Comparison of African Kingdoms. *Africa* 32:324–335.

Vincent, Joan (1990) *Anthropology and Politics: Visions, Traditions, and Trends.* University of Arizona Press, Tucson.

Vivian, R. Gwinn (2004) Puebloan Farmers of the Chacoan World. In *In Search of Chaco: New Approaches to an Archaeological Enigma,* edited by D. G. Noble, pp. 7–13. School of American Research Press, Santa Fe, NM.

Vogel, Joseph O., and Jean Allan (1985) Mississippian Fortifications at Moundville. *Archaeology* 38(5):62–63.

Walker, Winslow M. (1936) *The Troyville Mounds, Catahoula Parish, Louisiana.* Bureau of American Ethnology, Bulletin 113. Smithsonian Institution, Washington, D.C.

Wallerstein, Immanuel (1974) *The Modern World System I: Capitalist Agriculture and the Origins of the European World-Economy in the Sixteenth Century.* Academic, San Diego, CA.

Waring, Antonio J. (1968) The Southern Cult and Muskogean Ceremonial. In *The Waring Papers: The Collected Works of Antonio J. Waring, Jr.,* edited by S. Williams, pp. 30–69. Papers of the Peabody Museum of Archaeology and Ethnology, Volume 58. Harvard University, Cambridge Massachusetts.

Weets, Jaimin, Christopher Carr, David Penney, and Gary Carriveau (2005) Smoking Pipe Compositions and Styles as Evidence of the Social Affiliations of Mortuary Ritual Participants at the Tremper Site, Ohio. In *Gathering Hopewell: Society, Ritual, and Ritual Interaction,* edited by C. Carr and T. D. Case, pp. 533–552. Kluwer Academic/ Plenum, New York.

Welch, Paul D. (1990) The Occupational History of the Bessemer Site. *Southeastern Archaeology* 13:1–26.

Welch, Paul D. (1991) *Moundville's Economy.* University of Alabama Press, Tuscaloosa.

Welch, Paul D. (1998a) Middle Woodland and Mississippian Occupations of the Savannah Site in Tennessee. *Southeastern Archaeology* 17:79–91.

Welch, Paul D. (1998b) Outlying Sites Within the Moundville Chiefdom. In *Archaeology of the Moundville Chiefdom,* edited by V. J. Knight Jr., and V. P. Steponaitis, pp. 133–166. Smithsonian Institution Press, Washington, D.C.

Welch, Paul D. (2006) *Archaeology at Shiloh Indian Mounds, 1899–1999.* University of Alabama Press, Tuscaloosa.

Wesler, Kit W. (2001) *Excavations at Wickliffe Mounds.* University of Alabama Press, Tuscaloosa.

Whalen, Michael E., and Paul E. Minnis (1996) Ball Courts and Political Centralization in the Casas Grandes Region. *American Antiquity* 61:732–746.

Whalen, Michael E., and Paul E. Minnis (1999) Leadership at Casas Grandes, Chihuahua, Mexico. In *Alternative Leadership Strategies in the Prehistoric Southwest,* edited by B. J. Mills, pp. 168–179. University of Arizona Press, Tucson.

Whalen, Michael E., and Paul E. Minnis (2001a) *Casas Grandes and Its Hinterland: Prehistoric Political Organization in Northwest Mexico.* University of Arizona Press, Tucson.

Whalen, Michael E., and Paul E. Minnis (2001b) The Casas Grandes Regional System: A Late Prehistoric Polity of Northwestern Mexico. *Journal of World Prehistory* 15:313–364.

Wheatley, Paul (1971) *Pivot of the Four Quarters: a Preliminary Enquiry into the Origins and Character of the Ancient Chinese City.* Edinburgh: Edinburgh University Press.

White, Nancy Marie (2005) Prehistoric Connections Around the Gulf Coast. In *Gulf Coast Archaeology: The Southeastern United States and Mexico,* edited by N. M. White, pp. 1–55. University Press of Florida, Gainesville.

Wilcox, David R. (1993) The Evolution of the Chacoan Polity. In *The Chimney Rock Archaeological Symposium,* edited by J. McKim Malville and G. Matlock, pp. 76–90. USDA Forest Service Rocky Mountain Forest and Range Experiment Station General Technical Report RM-227. Fort Collins, CO.

Willey, Gordon R., and Jeremy A. Sabloff (1993) *A History of American Archaeology.* 3rd ed. W. H. Freeman, San Francisco.

Willey, Gordon R., Charles C. Di Peso, William A. Ritchie, Irving Rouse, John H. Rowe, and Donald W. Lathrap (1956) An Archaeological Classification of Culture Contact Situations. In *Seminars in Archaeology: 1955,* edited by R. Wauchope, pp. 1–30. Society for American Archaeology, Memoir 11. Salt Lake City, Utah.

Williams, Mark (1994) The Origins of the Macon Plateau Site. In *Ocmulee Archaeology 1936–1986,* edited by D. J. Hally, pp. 130–137. University of Georgia Press, Athens.

Williams, Mark, and Gary Shapiro (1990) Paired Towns. In *Lamar Archaeology: Mississippian Chiefdoms in the Deep South,* edited by M. Williams and G. Shapiro, pp. 163–174. University of Alabama Press, Tuscaloosa.

Williams, Mark, and Gary Shapiro (1996) Mississippian Political Dynamics in the Oconee Valley, Georgia. In *Political Structure and Change in the Prehistoric Southeastern United States,* edited by J. F. Scarry, pp. 128–149. University Press of Florida, Gainesville.

Williams, Samuel Cole, ed. (1930) *Adair's History of the American Indians.* Promontory, New York.

Williams, Stephen (1990) The Vacant Quarter and Other Late Events in the Lower Valley. In *Towns and Temples Along the Mississippi,* edited by D. H. Dye, pp. 170–180. University of Alabama Press, Tuscaloosa.

Williams, Stephen, and Jeffrey P. Brain (1983) *Excavations at the Lake George Site, Yazoo County, Mississippi, 1958–1960.* Papers of the Peabody Museum of Archaeology and Ethnology, vol. 74. Harvard University, Cambridge, MA.

Willoughby, Charles C. (1897) An Analysis of Decorations upon Pottery from the Mississippi Valley. *Journal of American Folklore* 10:9–20.

Wills, W. H. (2000) Political Leadership and the Construction of Chacoan Great Houses, A.D. 1020–1140. In *Alternative Leadership Strategies in the Prehispanic Southwest,* edited by B. J. Mills, pp. 19–44. University of Arizona Press, Tucson.

Wilson, Gregory D. (2005) *Between Plaza and Palisade: Household and Community Organization at Early Moundville.* Ph.D. diss., University of North Carolina.

Wilson, Gregory D., Jon Marcoux, and Brad Koldehoff (2006) Square Pegs in Round Holes: Organizational Diversity Between Early Moundville and Cahokia. In *Leadership and Polity in Mississippian Society,* edited by B. M. Butler and P. D. Welch, pp. 43-72. Center for Archaeological Investigations, Occasional Paper no. 33. Southern Illinois University, Carbondale.

Windes, Thomas C. (2004) The Rise of Early Chacoan Great Houses. In *In Search of Chaco: New Approaches to an Archaeological Enigma,* edited by D. G. Noble, pp. 15–21. School of American Research, Santa Fe, New Mexico.

Windes, Thomas C., and Peter J. McKenna (2001) Going Against the Grain: Wood Production in Chacoan Society. *American Antiquity* 66:119–140.

Wolf, Eric (1982) *Europe and the People Without History.* University of California Press, Berkeley.

REFERENCES

Worth, John E. (1998) *Timucuan Chiefdoms of Spanish Florida.* 2 vols. University Press of Florida, Gainesville.

Wright, Henry T. (1977) Recent Research on the Origin of the State. *Annual Review of Anthropology* 6:379–397.

Wright, Henry T. (1984) Prestate Political Formations. In *On the Evolution of Complex Societies: Essays in Honor of Harry Hoijer 1982*, edited by T. K. Earle, pp. 41–77. Undena, Malibu, CA.

Wright, Henry T. (1986) The Evolution of Civilizations. In *American Archaeology Past and Future: A Celebration of the Society for American Archaeology 1935–1985*, edited by D. J. Meltzer, D. D. Fowler, and J. A. Sabloff, pp. 323–365. Smithsonian Institution Press, Washington, DC.

Wright, Henry T., and Gregory Johnson (1975) Population, Exchange, and Early State Formation in Southwestern Iran. *American Anthropologist* 77:267–289.

Yerkes, Richard W. (1983) Microwear, Microdrills, and Mississippian Craft Specialization. *American Antiquity* 48:499–518.

Yerkes, Richard W. (1991) Specialization in Shell Artifact Production at Cahokia. In *New Perspectives on Cahokia: Views from the Periphery*, edited by J. B. Stoltman, pp. 49–64. Prehistory, Madison, Wisconsin.

Yoffee, Norman (1993) Too Many Chiefs? (or Safe Texts for the '90s). In *Archaeological Theory: Who Sets the Agenda?* edited by N. Yoffee and A. Sherratt, pp. 60–78. Cambridge University Press, Cambridge.

Yoffee, Norman (1995a) A Mass in Celebration of the Conference. In *The Archaeology of Society in the Holy Land*, edited by Thomas E. Levy, pp. 242–248. Leicester University Press, London.

Yoffee, Norman (1995b) The Obvious and the Chimerical: City-States in Archaeological Perspective. In *The Archaeology of City-States: Cross-Cultural Approaches*, edited by D. L. Nichols and T. H. Charlton, pp. 255–263. Smithsonian Institution Press, Washington, D.C.

Yoffee, Norman (1995c) Political Economy in Early Mesopotamian States. *Annual Review of Anthropology* 24:281–311.

Yoffee, Norman (1997) The Obvious and the Chimerical: City-States in Archaeological Perspective. In *The Archaeology of City-States: Cross-Cultural Approaches*, edited by D. L. Nichols and T. H. Charlton, pp. 255–263. Smithsonian Institution Press, Washington, DC.

Yoffee, Norman (2005) *Myths of the Archaic State: Evolution of the Earliest Cities, States, and Civilizations.* Cambridge University Press, Cambridge.

Yoffee, Norman, Suzanne K. Fish, and George R. Milner (1999) Comunidades, Ritualities, Chiefdoms: Social Evolution in the American Southwest and Southeast. In *Great Towns and Regional Polities in the Prehistoric American Southwest and Southeast*, edited by J. A. Neitzel, pp. 261–271. University of New Mexico Press, Albuquerque.

Yoffee, Norman, and Andrew Sherratt, eds. (1993) *Archaeological Theory: Who Sets the Agenda?* Cambridge University Press, Cambridge.

Young, Bilone W. and Melvin L. Fowler (2000) *Cahokia: The Great Native American Metropolis.* University of Illinois Press, Urbana.

Zeder, Melinda A. (2003) Food Provisioning in Urban Societies: A View from Northern Mesopotamia. In *The Social Construction of Ancient Cities*, edited by M. L. Smith, pp. 156–183. Smithsonian Institution Press, Washington, D.C.

INDEX

Note: Page numbers in *italics* indicate illustrations.

ABOUT THE AUTHOR

Timothy R. Pauketat is professor of anthropology at the University of Illinois, Urbana-Champaign, having taught previously at the State University of New York and the University of Oklahoma. With over twenty-five years of archaeological experience in eastern North America, he seeks to understand the relationships between politics, religion, violence, materiality, and history. He specializes in the archaeology of the Mississippian period and has authored or edited eight books and numerous articles, including *Ancient Cahokia* (2004), *North American Archaeology* (with D. Loren, 2005), *The Archaeology of Traditions* (2001), and *Cahokia's Big Bang and the Story of Ancient North America* (forthcoming).